THE HUNTER'S GUIDE TO
BUTCHERING, SMOKING & CURING
WILD GAME & FISH

Philip Hasheider

Voyageur Press

Dedication

This book is dedicated to my late nephew, David Hasheider, who was an avid hunter and held a deep reverence and respect for the land and the creatures that inhabit it.

First published in 2013 by Voyageur Press, an imprint of Quarto Publishing Group USA Inc., 400 First Avenue North, Suite 400, Minneapolis, MN 55401 USA

Voyageur Press titles are also available at discounts in bulk quantity for industrial or sales-promotional use. For details write to Special Sales Manager at Quarto Publishing Group USA Inc., 400 First Avenue North, Suite 400, Minneapolis, MN 55401 USA.

To find out more about our books, visit us online at www.voyageurpress.com.

ISBN-13: 978-0-7603-4375-3

Library of Congress Cataloging-in-Publication Data
  Hasheider, Philip, 1951-
  The hunter's guide to butchering, smoking, and curing wild game and fish / by Philip Hasheider.
      pages cm
  Includes index.
  ISBN 978-0-7603-4375-3 (pbk.)
  1. Game and game-birds, Dressing of. 2. Slaughtering and slaughter-houses. 3. Meat--Preservation. I. Title.
  SK283.8.H37 2013
  799.2'5--dc23
                              2012051137

Editor: Elizabeth Noll
Design Manager: James Kegley
Layout by: Mandy Kimlinger
Illustrations by: Trevor Burks

Printed in China

Photo credits: Shutterstock.com: 28, 27, 46, 64, 65, 84, 100, 106, 134, 146, 172

Contents

INTRODUCTION

Hunting wild game has been a human activity since the beginning of our existence. The pursuit, capture, and consumption of wild animals, fish, and fowl provided protein for our early hunter-gatherer ancestors. In many countries, the long arc of history has seen a transformation of hunter-gatherers into consumers who routinely purchase their daily meals at supermarkets, restaurants, and convenience stores. Most people no longer hunt for their food. This means that expertise in handling wild game, which was once commonplace, has declined.

Hunting Defined

Hunting, in its most widely accepted meaning, involves the search for wild game animals that will provide meat protein to the diet. This term today refers to lawful hunting (where specific rules are obeyed) and not to poaching, which is the killing, trapping, or capture of an animal contrary to established law.

The ethics of today's hunting culture require hunters to use as much of the carcass meat as possible. To hunt, shoot, and kill an animal simply for sport should be discouraged and is, in many ways, illegal. The exception to this involves the elimination of vermin to prevent the spread of diseases or overpopulation. Vermin, such as rats, are not typically a part of the North American diet and are not held to the same ethical treatment.

Societal Evolution

For our hunter-gatherer ancestors, a successful hunt, in which prey were killed and subsequently eaten, was a matter of survival; with no success, there was little or nothing to eat. The development of small tribes or clans into cohesive units may have been as much for hunting purposes as it was for group protection and socializing—the more hunters, the greater their chances for success. To keep all members satisfied, distribution of the captured prey was determined by the group in a manner that was fair and equitable. Food had to be shared in sufficient quantities to ensure adequate nutrition for the hunters, who needed to maintain their strength for future hunts.

As human civilization evolved, community participation was an integral part of its

Hunting can occur in many different locales, such as in grassy fields, which often contain small-game animals like rabbits. Each habitat provides unique experiences and challenges for hunters.

Wild game found in hilly or mountainous terrain may make the hunting experience more challenging. A successful hunt with a trophy to take home can provide a lifetime of memories and stories.

development. Shared concerns helped bind people together, as did marriages within groups. This cohesiveness encouraged the sharing of difficult tasks such as planting, harvesting, and butchering, among others.

A major shift occurred in food-gathering methods during the Industrial Revolution. As people left rural areas for urban employment, there was no longer ready access to wild game or the opportunity to hunt. Urban areas with dense populations restricted animal husbandry due to potential human health problems.

With the rise of meat markets and local butchers, people gradually shifted away from hunting as a necessary method for obtaining meat to hunting as a pastime or sport.

Diet Evolution

There are two types of meat protein presently available to consumers: wild game and domestically raised. There is an ongoing debate about the health benefits of each.

Our distant ancestors hunted wild game that was available, which typically included small game such as birds and fowl, rodents, turtles, rabbits, and anything else that might have wandered across their paths. Large animals that were hunted often included bison, deer, bear, moose, and elk.

Over time, as populations changed and migrated to urban areas, diets subsequently changed as well. As less effort was required to secure a meal, physical activity decreased and associated health problems increased.

This change in diet also paralleled a decrease in the use of some animals as food sources and an increase in the use of others. Today, the typical diet in the United States draws from four groups of animals for most of its meat: cattle, sheep, pigs, and domestic fowl. The vast majority of consumers rarely eat any other kind of animal, especially those we now label as exotics but that may have been normal fare for our ancestors. Exotics include squirrels, rabbits, frogs, snakes, turtles, or other small animals.

As a result of these changes, most people no longer know where their food comes from and, rather than observing or participating in its processing, they purchase meats that may have been processed great distances from where the animals were raised. This situation in turn now seems to be a driving force for those seeking locally grown foods.

Another attitude shift has recently surfaced regarding wild game meat. Television shows, food networks, magazines, blogs, chefs, restaurant reviews, and a vast array of other media outlets now promote wild game as a food source. This increased attention to the uniqueness and value of wild game has made people aware of its potential benefits.

A Healthy Choice

Are there health benefits to including wild game in our diets? The answer to this question

Some Typical Large Wild Game Animals Available for Hunting in the United States

Bear: American Black, American Brown, Grizzly, Polar

Caribou: Alaska Yukon Barren Ground, Mountain, Quebec-Labrador, Woodland

Deer: Gray Brown Brocket, Mule, Sitka Blacktail, Whitetail

Elk: American, Rocky Mountain, Roosevelt

Moose: Alaska Yukon, Canada, Shiras

Sheep: California Bighorn, Dall, Desert Bighorn, Rocky Mountain Bighorn, Stone

Other: American Alligator, American Bison, Bobcat, Canada Lynx, Musk Ox, Pronghorn Antelope

has many facets. The simple answer is that wild game such as deer, elk, and antelope tend to have very lean meat due to their active lifestyle and natural diet. Their meat is typically lower in total and saturated fat than red meat found in beef. In comparison to lean cuts of beef and pork, game meat has about one-third fewer calories, and game birds about one-half the calories. Fish, with high omega-3 fatty acids, appear to offer more health benefits then either wild or domestic game animals.

There are, however, health-related concerns outside of simple nutrition to consider in any discussion of wild game. Among these are chronic wasting disease (CWD), which can be found in deer and elk, and the potentially harmful lead levels found in some hunted animals.

Benefits of Hunting

Nature continually selects the best breeding stock to ensure that the species will survive.

All game animals, except perhaps those at the highest level of the food chain such as the bear or wolf, face threats from predators. Other factors, such as weather, disease, and competition, influence any given population. All game animals have the potential to produce many more young than the habitat can support.

Reproductive rates are usually high among small game and upland birds. Nature keeps game populations in check by maintaining high mortality rates, because when too many animals survive, a population explodes, creating a tremendous demand on the habitat. This often causes disease, stunted growth, and eventual starvation.

Sixty to 80 percent of upland birds, waterfowl, and small game die each year. Often, only 20 to 40 percent of the fall population is comprised of individuals over one year of age.

Big-game populations, however, have a relatively low reproductive potential and the average animal lives longer; typically 65 to 85 percent of the fall populations are made up of older individuals. Despite this, big-game populations can reach high levels because predators take only an occasional young animal. Herds may grow so large that food shortages result in areas with few hunting pressures. Game populations tend to remain stable if the habitat is not disturbed and hunting pressure is regulated.

It can be argued that programs that promote sustained-yield harvests produce the healthiest wildlife populations, because they are continually renewing them with young offspring. An aging population does not reproduce as well and is prone to health problems. The welfare of the entire population seems more important than the fate of surplus individuals.

Hunter safety is the foremost concern when heading into the wild. You should have weather-appropriate clothing that also adheres to state regulations, and suitable gear and equipment to make field dressing more efficient.

Millions of Americans have developed their appreciation and understanding of the land and its wildlife through hunting. A hunter enters into the natural habitat of the animals or fowl they are pursuing, whether it is a wooded area, marsh, open prairie, or stream. Coming into contact with nature can be a satisfying experience. It has inspired many to join conservation clubs, hunting organizations, and wildlife and wetland preservation groups to become intimately involved with the propagation, maintenance, and sustainability of species they are interested in hunting.

Hunting can be an important part of wildlife management. It gives resource managers a valuable tool to control animal populations that might otherwise exceed the carrying capacity of their habitat and threaten the well-being of other wildlife. In the case of chronic wasting disease, hunting helps ensure human health and safety.

Hunting Realities

Animals may be hunted in the wild or sourced from licensed commercial production facilities that specialize in raising big game. Regulations apply to both commercially produced and hunted game, and if you choose to secure animals through either route, you are obligated to know, understand, and follow the rules and regulations governing them.

Because it is considered a privilege to hunt and receive licenses to secure game, you are also obligated to minimize the suffering of the animal and to make a quick and efficient harvest to achieve optimal meat quality. You'll also want to prevent or minimize waste of the carcass.

There are differences in size between big-game animals, and these differences may influence your choice or your ability to handle a carcass in the field. It is much easier to harvest, clean, and cut up a 150-pound deer than a 500-pound elk, or an even larger moose.

You should plan ahead before embarking on a big-game harvest to ensure that you can safely and efficiently dress and transport the carcass, sometimes over large distances. Plan for as many variables as possible, to reduce the risk to yourself and the possible contamination of the carcass if you have a successful hunt. These variables may include transport, weather conditions, distance from shelter, and equipment.

A wide variety of small-game species can be harvested for home use, including rabbits, raccoons, fish, squirrels, turtles, and snakes. Except for feral pigs and domestic rabbits, all of these animals are controlled by designated hunting seasons and licensing programs. Learn which apply to any particular area and abide by the established rules and regulations.

Take Precautions

While wild game and fowl have a very low risk of contamination from antibiotics or other chemicals used in promoting growth in domestically raised animals, they are susceptible to diseases and parasites. Wild game can also be exposed to potentially hazardous water sources resulting from chemical spills or other environmental disasters, though this is unlikely for the majority of species across the United States.

There is a potential health risk in consuming any kind of meat. One of the most viable reasons for hunting and fishing is that it allows you to observe, harvest, and process your own wild game and know where it came from. You will determine the manner in which it is handled from field to table, and how it is processed.

Being diligent in your observations about the outward health of the animal or fowl you procure will alleviate most fears about potentially tainted meat. Knowing the correct processing steps will minimize or eliminate any potential contamination and result in better meat quality.

Regulations

Hunting regulations exist to protect wild game animals and birds from excessive population depletion. Without them, some species could be harvested to the point where their populations could not maintain sufficient numbers to ensure their long-term existence.

Each state has primary responsibility and authority over the hunting of wildlife within their state boundaries. The exception is any species that has been placed on a national registry of endangered species, which is then under federal jurisdiction.

The best source of information regarding hunting seasons, areas that are either open or closed to hunting, bag limits, and other questions are the state wildlife agencies that sell hunting licenses. Licenses are required for hunting, fishing, and trapping, except in the case of special permits, which may be required in some cases due to physical limitations or age. Monies collected from these licenses are used for research, replenishing populations, and other aspects of wildlife program administration.

If applicable, hunters should also familiarize themselves with the restrictions and regulations regarding the number and species of migratory game birds or wild game legally harvested in other countries.

How to Use This Book

The purpose of this book is to provide hunters with accurate information on all aspects of the butchering process, from slaughtering to processing, and on the preservation of the meat. A detailed, step-by-step process for deconstructing wild game allows you to safely and successfully transform a carcass into a family meal. The principles

Whether from birds, waterfowl, or big-game animals, wild game meat can be served in a variety of savory meals. There are many ways to enjoy your successful hunt.

of curing and preserving the meat are also explained. Different meat cuts are discussed in each section, and other products, such as sausages, receive attention too. The recipes for similar animals and fowl are included as examples and represent only a fraction of what you can do with each of them.

Regardless of the reasons for hunting, fishing, or trapping, hunters must know how to properly handle animal carcasses to ensure food safety from field to table. Eliminating steps that can lead to spoilage is an important part of hunting. This book focuses on wild game and the deconstruction and safe processing of the harvested meat. For those wanting more information about butchering and processing domestically raised animals, *The Complete Book of Butchering, Smoking, Curing, and Sausage Making* is also available from Voyageur Press.

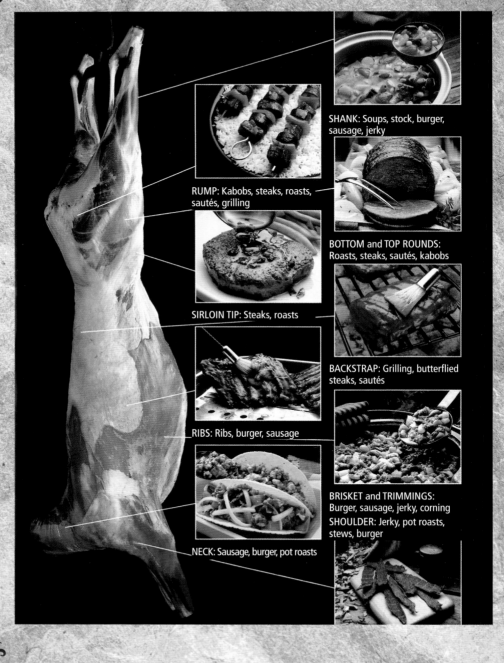

RUMP: Kabobs, steaks, roasts, sautés, grilling

SHANK: Soups, stock, burger, sausage, jerky

SIRLOIN TIP: Steaks, roasts

BOTTOM and TOP ROUNDS: Roasts, steaks, sautés, kabobs

BACKSTRAP: Grilling, butterflied steaks, sautés

RIBS: Ribs, burger, sausage

BRISKET and TRIMMINGS: Burger, sausage, jerky, corning
SHOULDER: Jerky, pot roasts, stews, burger

NECK: Sausage, burger, pot roasts

Chapter 1

MUSCLES ARE MEAT

The history of utilizing meat for nutrition has an interesting evolution. For our distant ancestors, meat was anything that moved and could be hunted, such as birds, reptiles, turtles, and wild game of all kinds. As animals became domesticated, they were included in the human diet.

This idea of anything that moves being a possible meal has evolved; today, the term *meat*, as used in American society, generally refers to the muscles derived from an animal carcass, specifically those in one of four groups: cattle, pigs, sheep, and poultry. In the past, the internal organs of animals were highly prized parts of the carcass. Although many are still used today in a variety of food, pharmaceutical, and health care applications, their value has become secondary to that of the muscles.

The decrease in selection choices has resulted from three major changes in our society: cultural conditioning, industrial urbanization, and the difficulty in domesticating some wild species and/or their supply. Cultural conditioning resulted from a lack of variation in available food choices, particularly away from wild game. What was familiar and more readily available became the new norm. The movement of rural residents to urban centers during America's industrialization period resulted in the need to purchase meat from a local market rather than butchering animals you'd raised yourself. Some wild species such as bison, elk, and antelope were difficult, if not impossible, to domesticate or procure, resulting in fewer being used for meat purposes.

This change in eating preferences and choices has not gone unnoticed. In 1997, the World Health Organization (WHO) issued a report stating that affluent populations habitually consume a diet that was unknown to humans a mere ten generations ago.

Muscle Structure and Function

In its basic sense, the term *muscle* refers to numerous bundles of cells and fibers that contract and expand to produce bodily movements, whether horizontal on land or vertical in flight. There are three major types: skeletal, cardiac, and smooth muscles.

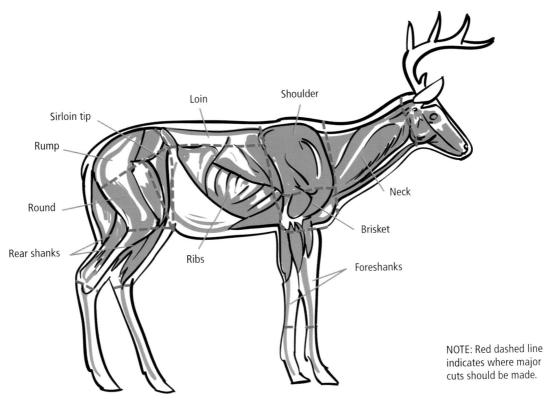

Loin

Shoulder

Sirloin tip

Rump

Neck

Round

Brisket

Rear shanks

Ribs

Foreshanks

NOTE: Red dashed line indicates where major cuts should be made.

The muscles and skeletal structures of cervids (deer, moose, elk, and antelope) are very similar. Some big-game cervids are larger than others, but this does not alter the location of the muscles, only the size and volume.

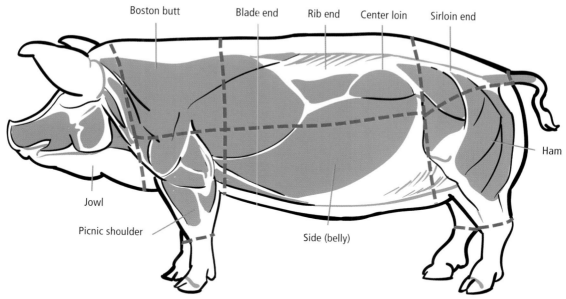

Boston butt   Blade end   Rib end   Center loin   Sirloin end

Ham

Jowl

Picnic shoulder

Side (belly)

Wild pigs are difficult to hunt, but can provide a large volume of meat if successfully harvested. Studying a pig's anatomy prior to hunting will help you minimize waste when you field dress it.

Most animal muscle is about 75 percent water, 20 percent protein, and 5 percent fat, carbohydrates, and assorted minerals.

Skeletal muscles are linked to bone by bundles of collagen fibers known as tendons. These muscles have several components known as muscle fibers that bundle together in various configurations to give them a striated appearance. These fibers form the basic mechanism that controls muscle contraction.

Smooth muscles are commonly found in organs or internal systems, such as the digestive tract, reproductive organs, circulatory system, and urinary tract. The cardiac muscle is found in the heart.

In meat, skeletal muscles are the most important of the three types because of quantity as well as economic and nutritional value. These muscles support the body and initiate movement.

Skeletal muscles are the only voluntary muscles in the body, meaning they are actively controlled by the animal's intentions. The smooth and cardiac muscles are involuntary, meaning their movements are controlled by their own imprinted genetic nature rather than intentions.

A dense connective tissue sheath called the epimysium covers the skeletal muscles. Each of these muscles is divided into sections, called bundles, by a thick connective tissue layer called the perimysium. Clusters of fat cells, small blood vessels, and nerve bundles are found in this layer. The fat cells appear white; this is referred to as marbling. These fat deposits give the muscle flavor and moisture when cooked.

The purpose and reflex action of different muscle groups ultimately determine their texture. Knowing their location will give you a better understanding of why some meat cuts are easier to cook or have more flavor than others.

Muscle Fiber Differences

Not all muscles are the same. Even their basic makeup—the muscle fibers—are different. There are two types of muscle fibers: slow-twitch, which contract slowly but can keep going for a long time, and fast-twitch, which contact rapidly but get tired more quickly.

One example of how both kinds of muscle fibers work in an animal is the wild turkey. Although they can fly short distances, such as from the ground to a perch, turkeys are not known for their sustained flying abilities. They rely on their legs for rapid movement. Their most active muscles—legs and thighs—are considered slow-twitch muscles. These are full of blood vessels that contain muscle hemoglobin (sometimes referred to as myoglobin), which delivers oxygen to the muscles. The more myoglobin a muscle contains, the darker the muscle will be.

The "white" meat of the wild turkey is the result of well-rested muscles. In fowl, the breast muscles are most often used for flying, but because wild turkeys do little sustained flying, there is no need for a rich supply of oxygen to these muscles. The wings, which are fast-twitch muscles, are designed for quick bursts of energy, but they quickly fatigue. They are fueled by glycogen, which gives them an immediate explosion of energy for moving quickly.

In a general sense, however, game birds are usually considered "white" meat even though their breast meat may be darker than domestic chicken and turkey because they are birds of flight. Similarly, all game mammals are considered "red" meat, and would be comparable in that sense to domestically raised beef.

Proteins

Within the muscle cells are pigment proteins. The differences in these proteins are responsible for variations in color between beef and pork (where beef is darker), or between a chicken or wild turkey leg and breast.

Wild game animals typically yield meat cuts that are less tender than domestically raised animals. Also, cuts from older animals are referred to as being "tough," meaning they will not be cut or chewed as easily as meat from younger animals. One major factor affecting this condition is collagen, the single most abundant protein found in mammals. It is present in all tissues, but the highest concentrations are found in bone, skin, tendons, cartilage, and muscle.

Collagen is an insoluble fibrous protein that primarily functions as a source of strength and support for muscles and, in the case of skin, as a barrier for keeping out foreign materials. It is the chief component of connective tissue filaments. Muscles whose primary purpose is to support structures such as front and rear legs typically have high connective tissue content, while the loin and back areas have less, making these cuts more desirable and higher in economic value. Collagen changes with age, leading to less tender cuts in older animals. The best way to break down collagen is with moist-heat cooking methods.

Carcasses also have a yellow connective tissue called backstrap. This is a large strip of elastin, which is also found in arterial walls, that gives elasticity to muscle tissues. Strips of elastin or backstrap cannot be broken apart or altered in form with moist-heat cooking, and are usually discarded. Muscle tissue contains only very small amounts of elastin, making it highly consumable.

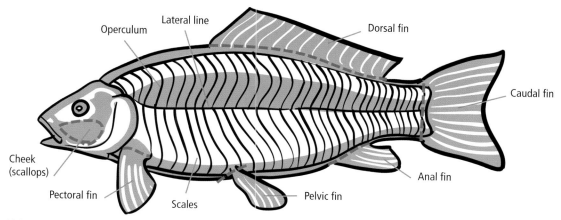

Fish have smooth, cardiac, and striated muscles. Fish muscles are very delicate and can bruise easily; take extra precaution in handling caught fish to minimize damage to their muscles.

Fish Muscles

In almost all fish, the large muscles of the body and tail comprise the majority of the body mass. There are many other smaller muscles associated with the head and fins, but these are more difficult to excise from the fish when cleaning it. Fish muscles are often divided into red muscle and white muscle.

Red muscle is identified by its many capillaries. It appears red from the high concentration of red oxygen-binding pigments in the hemoglobin and muscle tissues. This is necessary for high levels of continuous swimming activity.

Fish with different activity levels usually have different configurations of red fibers scattered in the white muscle that makes up most of their body mass. This is thought to have an effect on some fish, in that those that carry their red muscle bands deeper toward the body core permit a conservation of metabolic heat, which allows for faster muscle contraction and higher swimming velocity.

The white muscle fibers are thicker than the red, have a poorer blood supply, and have no oxygen-carrying pigment. This means muscle contraction is not dependent on the fish's oxygen supply. White muscle usually converts glycogen to lactic acid via anaerobic pathways. This makes white muscles most useful in short bursts of swimming.

Like mammals, fish have three major types of muscles: cardiac, smooth, and striated. Cardiac muscles are simply muscles of the heart. The smooth muscles are in the reproductive and excretory ducts, the eyes, and other organs. The striated muscles run in irregular vertical bands, and various patterns are found in different types of fish. These muscles compose the bulk of the body and function by producing body undulations that propel the fish forward.

Fish muscle segments, called myomeres, are divided into an upper and a lower half by a groove running along the middle of the fish's body. These broad muscles are the part of the fish that we eat.

Bird Muscles

Most birds have about 175 different muscles, which control the movements of wings, legs, feet, tongue, eyes, ears, neck, lungs, body wall,

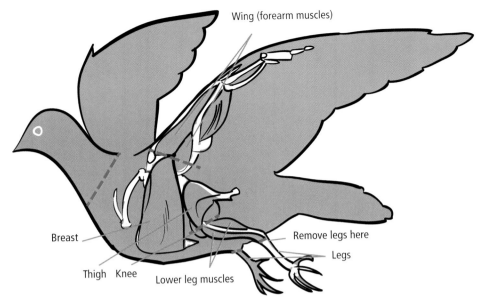

Wild upland game birds and waterfowl are similar in skeletal construction, although their size may vary. Avian muscle structures are also similar and can be butchered in much the same manner, whether they are quail, wild turkey, or ducks. The cooking method will determine how you use them for your meals.

and skin. These muscles are concentrated near the bird's center of gravity.

The largest of these muscles are the pectorals, or breast muscles. They form the bulk of the fleshy mass in the breast and make up about 15 to 20 percent of the bird's total body weight. They also provide the powerful downstroke of the wings, and are the major support for a bird in flight. The muscle that raises the wing then acts against the pectorals. This is the supracoracoideus, which is located below and in front of the pectoral muscles. It is necessarily smaller because the bird's downward stroke, enabled by the pectorals, needs more energy and power to propel the body upward against gravity.

Skin muscles play a critical role in flight, and may or may not become part of a meal after being roasted or cooked.

Converting Muscle to Meat

Changes happen within the muscles of an animal after it is harvested. Some life processes stop almost immediately, such as brain activity, heart action, lung function, blood transport, digestive action, and mobility. Other life processes gradually cease over a slightly longer time period. The changes that occur within the muscles can ultimately affect the eating quality of the meat.

Initially, upon an animal's death, the muscle pH begins to gradually drop. This happens because the glycogen reserves within the animal's muscles are depleted and then converted to lactic acid. Oxygen is no longer available to the muscle cells after the animal is bled, causing lactic acid to build up and pH to drop.

With the loss of certain muscle reserves, such as creatine phosphates, which aid muscle movements, the muscle filaments can no longer slide over one another and the muscle becomes still and rigid, resulting in a condition known as rigor mortis.

Several factors influence the amount of time it takes an animal's muscles to reach their final pH levels. These include the species, cooling rate, and the extent of the animal's struggle at the time of death. Deer and wild sheep muscles take longer to reach their final pH than those of a wild pig. Cooling affects the time because metabolism is slowed when the carcass is subjected to lower temperatures. Finally, the animals' activity level immediately prior to the killing will affect the pH; less activity will prolong the period of pH decline.

During the period after the slaughter or harvest, changes also occur in the muscle proteins as they begin to break down. This process, referred to as "aging," generally occurs during the cool-storage period and results in increased meat tenderness. Protein fracturing will continue for one to two weeks, after which there is little appreciable increase in tenderness.

Meat Quality Challenges

For generations, people butchering animals have known the importance of harvesting healthy animals that are not excited or stressed immediately prior to slaughter. If an animal undergoes vigorous stress or exercise before harvest, the glycogen content within the muscles may drop dramatically. This can result in a higher pH remaining in the muscles, causing the meat to become dark, firm, and dry, and effectively reducing the tenderness and quality.

High-pH meat is typically dark in color, believed to be the result of a greater water-holding capacity, which causes muscle fibers to swell. The meat from such animals generally has a reduced shelf life because a higher pH is more likely to accommodate bacterial growth.

A second quality problem can result from the rate of pH decline. If the muscle pH drops too rapidly after killing, due to the muscle temperature being too high, the muscle can become pale and soft. A rapid drop in pH often results in a soft, mushy texture; pale color; and a lack of ability to hold moisture. This condition is typically caused by high-stress situations—if a "fright or flight" response is initiated, stimulating nervousness and sweating, the animal's muscle temperature can be affected.

There are meat quality issues associated with harvest and postharvest handling of carcasses, and there are also quality and food safety issues that can affect animals before harvest. These issues include animal health, pregnancy, injury and bruising, and genetic influences. Recognizing unhealthy or unthrifty animals can help avoid subsequent meat quality problems. Common ailments can affect the quality and wholesomeness of a carcass.

Bruising is another condition that can affect meat quality. A bruise results from the hemorrhaging of a blood vessel under the hide of the animal. Although you can do little to prevent bruising in wild game, you should not use any bruised meat for food.

Other Factors Affecting Meat Quality

Other factors that can affect meat quality include toxins, bacteria, and viruses; and temperature, time, and moisture. For many years it was thought that the muscle of an animal was sterile if it had not been injured, cut into, or bruised. In recent years, however, researchers have found viable bacteria within otherwise undamaged muscle tissue. This means that when you harvest an animal, whether domestic or wild, extreme care must be taken to prevent the introduction of foreign bodies into the carcass. This care begins with the knives you use to sever the jugular vein at the beginning of the

Quick Tips for Aging Meat

- Aging is not recommended for carcasses with little or no fat covering, as the meat may dry out.
- Leave the hide on to maintain proper temperature and protect carcass muscles.
- Use proper cooling temperatures.
- If aged, age only 2 to 3 days before processing.
- No aging needed if grinding meat.

slaughtering process and continues until the cuts have been packaged, sealed, and stored, or the meat is immediately cooked for use. Sanitation is extremely important and is discussed in greater detail elsewhere.

Preventing and retarding the development of harmful microorganisms should be your primary objective in harvesting your animal or in home processing any meat products. Consuming microorganisms that have grown and propagated in meat can cause illness or even death. This concern should not be taken lightly. When health problems arise related to eating meat, it is generally a result of intoxication or infection. Intoxication occurs when the microbe produces a toxin that is subsequently eaten by a human and causes sickness. Infection occurs when an organism such as salmonella or listeria is eaten by a human, then grows and disrupts the normal functions of the body.

There are several types of toxins, including exotoxins and endotoxins. Exotoxins are located outside the bacterial cell and are composed of proteins that can be destroyed by heat through cooking. Exotoxins are among the most poisonous substances known

to humans. One very harmful exotoxin is *Clostridium botulinum*, which causes tetanus and botulism poisoning.

Endotoxins attach to the outer membranes of cells but are not released unless the cell is disrupted. These are complex fat and carbohydrate molecules, such as *Staphylococcus aureus*, that are not destroyed by heat.

Bacteria are the most common microorganisms that can grow on meat. Not all bacteria are dangerous, however; human skin may carry as many as one thousand different kinds of bacteria.

Molds and yeasts are fungi that can affect meat quality, although their effect is far less significant than toxins or bacteria. Molds typically cause spoilage in grains, cereals, flour, and nuts that have low moisture content and in fruits that have a low pH. Yeasts are generally involved when a food product contains high amounts of sugar. Yeasts that affect meat are usually not a problem because of the low sugar or carbohydrate content of muscle.

While viruses have the potential to cause foodborne diseases, they generally only affect raw or uncooked shellfish. Viruses are inert and unable to multiply outside a host cell. However, avian influenza (or bird flu as it is commonly known) is of some concern to hunters. Avian influenza is an illness caused by several different strains of influenza viruses that have adapted to a specific host. All known viruses that cause influenza in birds belong to the influenza A virus. If humans contract bird flu, it is usually a result of either handling infected dead birds or from contact with infected fluids. Although it is easy for humans to become infected by birds, it is much more difficult for humans to pass the virus to each other without close and lasting contact. The last recorded incident of bird flu affecting humans in the United States occurred in New York in 2003.

A parasite infection will occur in the live animal before it occurs in a human. There are three parasites that are of major concern to humans: *Trichinella spiralis*, or trichinosis; *Toxoplasma gondii*, or toxoplasma; and *Anisakis marina*, or anisakis. Trichinosis has long been identified as a parasite that can live in swine muscle and be transferred to humans through raw or uncooked pork. Toxoplasma is a small protozoan that exists throughout the world and has been observed in a wide range of birds and mammals. Anisakis is a roundworm parasite found only in fish. Using adequate or recommended cooking temperatures and times will destroy parasites.

One parasite that affects cervids such as deer and moose, but fortunately not humans, is *Parelaphostrongylus tenuis*, or brainworm. This parasite can be passed from deer to moose via a secondary host such as a land snail. The deer pass the larvae of the parasite in their feces. A land snail feeds on these feces, absorbing the larvae. A moose consumes the land snail, allowing the larvae to enter its digestive tract, from where they migrate into the vascular system and make their way to the central nervous system. The moose's immune system tries to eliminate this invader. Swelling often occurs, causing neurological symptoms such as blindness, deafness, circle walking, awkward head and body carriage, paralysis, and eventually death. Brainworm does not affect noncervid species, and humans cannot get it from eating moose meat.

Chronic wasting disease (CWD) is a progressive fatal illness of deer, elk, and moose. It has gained national attention after being discovered in animals from fifteen states and two Canadian provinces.

CWD damages portions of the brain and causes progressive loss of body condition, behavioral changes, excessive salivation, and ultimately death. It is believed to be caused by a prion protein that has been found in the brains of similarly affected animals.

Although the mode of transmission is not fully understood, it is thought that the disease is spread through direct animal-to-animal contact or exposure to contaminated feed and water. To date, no strong evidence of CWD transmission to humans has been reported.

Precautions can be taken against CWD, such as not shooting, handling, or eating any deer, elk, or moose that appears sick or decimated, or tests positive for CWD. Hunters harvesting animals in a known CWD-positive area may wish to have their animal tested for CWD before consuming any of the meat. Information about testing is available from most state wildlife agencies.

If you field dress any deer, elk, or moose, it is a good precaution to wear gloves, bone-out the meat from the animal, and minimize handling of the brain and spinal cord tissues. Also, avoid eating the brain, spinal cord, eyes, spleen, and lymph nodes.

Temperature and Time Effects on Meat Quality

Mismanagement of temperature is one of the most common reasons for outbreaks of foodborne diseases, as is the amount of time food spends at a critical temperature—for example, the correct temperature is either used too late or for too short a period.

Meat can generally be kept safe from harmful bacteria if stored under 40 degrees Fahrenheit. Cooking prevents most microorganisms from growing, but does not kill them.

Some parasites can be killed if kept in a frozen state for various lengths of time, but most microorganisms merely go dormant and can revive when thawed. If meat is thawed from a frozen state it should be used as soon as possible and not refrozen.

To kill microorganisms with heat, you must maintain a recommended temperature for a minimum period of time. You will damage or kill microorganisms more effectively by reaching a given temperature and holding it for a period of time rather

Microbes Affecting Meat Quality

Microbe	Typical Cause	Effect	Control
Salmonella	Grows best in nonacid foods, transferred from farm animals and animal products to humans.	Insulation from 3 to 36 hours. Digestive upsets. Symptoms may last 1 to 7 days.	Killed by pasteurization. Avoid cross contamination from raw meat to cooked food or food eaten raw.
Escherichia coli (E. coli)	Improper harvest methods, unsanitary handling of meat, improper cooking, fecal contamination.	Severe abdominal illness; watery, bloody diarrhea; vomiting. Can affect kidney function and central nervous system.	Destroyed by internal temperatures of 160°F.
C. jejuni	Typically found in raw chicken because of high body temperature and pH.	Diarrhea, abdominal cramps, nausea symptoms last 2 to 3 days.	Avoid cross contamination between raw and cooked meat. Use good hygiene. Destroyed by pasteurization.
Listeria	Grows in damp areas, sewage, sludge; can survive freezing.	Most vulnerable are infants, chronically ill, elderly, and pregnant women. Can cause meningitis, encephalitis, or abscession.	Avoid raw milk products in meat recipes. Use good sanitation while processing meat. Avoid cross contamination of raw and cooked foods. Avoid postcooking contamination.

than reaching a higher temperature but holding it for a shorter period.

Meat can be kept safe when it is hot or cold, but not in between. If meat is being cooked, it should pass between 40 to 140 degrees Fahrenheit in four hours or less. If it is being cooled, it should pass from 140 to 40 degrees Fahrenheit within the same amount of time.

Most microorganisms are killed at 140 degrees Fahrenheit, but not all. The outside of a piece of meat may have become contaminated during your processing, but the interior can be considered sterile, or nearly so, unless it has been cut into. When a piece of meat is cooked by conventional methods (except with a microwave oven), the outside cooks first and reaches a higher end temperature than the inside. Recent recommendations state that meat should be cooked to 160 degrees Fahrenheit, since some microorganisms can survive a 140 degrees Fahrenheit temperature. Poultry meat is more alkaline and should be cooked to 180 degrees Fahrenheit; if red meat is to be reheated it should reach 165 degrees Fahrenheit for optimum safety. If you are grinding meat, be aware that it can become contaminated more easily than whole cuts because more of the meat particle surface areas are exposed and more processing and handling steps are involved.

Moisture in meat is essential for palatability but is also a medium for microbial growth. The level of moisture in fresh meat is high enough to provide spoilage organisms with an ideal environment for growth. Researchers have found that moisture levels of at least 18 percent will allow molds to grow in meat. Drying meat through a smoking process will typically eliminate any moisture concerns.

Oxygen is necessary for any living animal to survive, but it is not a welcome agent when processing meat. Aerobic microbes need oxygen to grow. These include yeasts, molds, and many bacteria. Microbes that cannot grow when oxygen is present are called anaerobic. This group of microbes can be deadly because they include clostridium, which produces a toxin, and a group called putrifiers, which degrade proteins and produce foul-smelling gases. Preventing the growth of anaerobic microbes is essential if your food preservation plan includes canning.

Soon after an animal is harvested, the muscle undergoes a gradual change in pH, declining from about 7.0 to 5.5. This decline results from the loss of glycogen held within the muscle and its conversion to lactic acid. The degree of acidity or alkalinity (pH) will influence the growth of microorganisms. More will thrive at a point that is nearly neutral—a pH of 7.0—than at any other level above or below. Although meat pH ranges from about 4.8 to 6.8, microorganisms generally grow more slowly at a pH of 5.0 or below. This acidity level helps preserve many sausages and acts as a flavor enhancer. Acidity levels are not a concern unless there is a long delay in processing the carcass at room temperatures.

A whole carcass has the minimum amount of exposed surface area. As large cuts are made, more area is exposed. When it is cut into smaller pieces, still more area is exposed. If the meat is ground, this exposes the most area for possible contamination. Simply put, the more the meat is processed, the more it may be exposed to microorganisms. To help reduce microbial activity, use clean, sanitary equipment and table surfaces and keep work area temperatures low while working as quickly as possible.

Primal Cuts

The term *primal cuts* refers to the first cuts, which separate the carcass into a few large portions before it is broken down into smaller, more manageable pieces. This breaking down of large portions into smaller ones allows you to separate the more desirable cuts from the rest of the carcass meat. This process will transform a heavy, unwieldy, oddly shaped carcass into pieces that can be packaged and neatly stacked in freezers. Although the term typically refers to the slaughtering of domestic animals, it can also be applied to the butchering of wild game.

Primal cuts separate the carcass into three general divisions: the legs, which contain the large muscles used for locomotion; the back and loin, which are composed of large support muscle systems; and the thinner body walls.

From these sections, the subprimal cuts or subdivisions are made. These cuts produce pieces that can be further broken down into even smaller pieces or used for grinding.

Seven Main Cuts

In domestic animal carcasses, if part of the bone is included in the cut, it is called a bone-in cut and can be classified into one of seven types based on the muscle or bone shape and the size of the bone relative to it. Although you will not often include the bone in your meat processing of wild game, the divisions are still relevant. These seven primary retail cuts include the shoulder (arm), loin, rib, leg, hip, blade, and belly or plate. Familiarizing yourself with them and understanding their location on the animal will help you do a better job of cutting up the carcass.

Loin and rib: Two of the seven cuts, the loin and rib, have an eye muscle that makes up part of the back's muscle structure. The loin lies in a lengthwise direction on both sides of the spinal column and is a major muscle component. Although it is used in support and movement, its location makes it less used than other major muscle groups. Less use translates into a more tender muscle texture.

The tenderloin is a small muscle connected to the underside of the backbone just in front of the pelvic area. Along with the loin, it is one of the most tender pieces of meat and most suitable for steaks or roasting whole.

The ribs are designed for the protection of the internal organs and to provide sufficient room to allow them to expand and contract as the animal eats or fasts. Ribs are connected by small amounts of muscle and connective tissue. Their high ratio of bone to meat makes ribs less valuable as cuts, but the meat can be very useful either ground into sausages or used fresh in cooking.

Ribs can be sawed into 5- to 7-inch pieces for barbecuing. They can be cut into widths, usually two to four ribs wide, depending on the size of the animal. Ribs can also be cut into shorter pieces and used in stews.

Legs and shoulder (arm): The legs and shoulder cuts have a similar cross-section because of the round bones involved. However, there is a difference in the leg muscle configuration at the top, bottom, eye, and sirloin tip when compared to the shoulder cuts. Shoulder cuts are located in the front legs and contain more small muscles arranged in a different pattern.

The shank of the hind leg, like that of the foreleg, contains considerable connective tissue and is best for ground or stew meat. The sirloin tip is the football-shaped muscle at the front of the hind leg. It makes an excellent roast. It can also be cooked whole as a roast or cut into steaks.

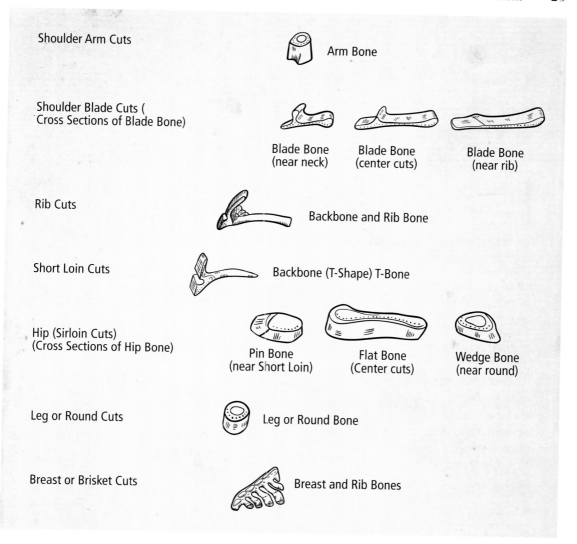

Shoulder Arm Cuts

Arm Bone

Shoulder Blade Cuts (
Cross Sections of Blade Bone)

Blade Bone
(near neck)

Blade Bone
(center cuts)

Blade Bone
(near rib)

Rib Cuts

Backbone and Rib Bone

Short Loin Cuts

Backbone (T-Shape) T-Bone

Hip (Sirloin Cuts)
(Cross Sections of Hip Bone)

Pin Bone
(near Short Loin)

Flat Bone
(Center cuts)

Wedge Bone
(near round)

Leg or Round Cuts

Leg or Round Bone

Breast or Brisket Cuts

Breast and Rib Bones

Hip and blade: The hip and blade are two different cuts that both have flat or irregularly shaped bones. The cuts from the hip are composed of a small number of fairly large, parallel muscles, while the blade cuts have numerous small, nonparallel muscles, much like those found in the foreleg. These portions can be stewed or ground into meat patties or sausages.

Belly or plate: The seventh type of cut is the belly or plate. This is easily recognized by the alternating layers of fat, lean, and rib bones that make up the body wall and complete the enclosure of the internal organs. The meat taken from this cut includes the brisket.

Bones: From a butchering standpoint, bones have little market value. Bones from home processing are often discarded or

Cut	Carcass Location	Use
Shank	Lower shoulder and hind legs	Soups, stock, burger, sausage, jerky
Shoulder (arm)	Behind neck and above shank	Jerky, pot roasts, stews, burger, sausage
Neck	Neck	Sausage, burger, pot roasts
Brisket and Belly	Between and behind front legs	Burger, sausage, jerky, corning
Ribs	Ribs	Ribs, burger, sausage, stews
Loin (Backstrap)	Along both sides of spinal column	Grilling, butterflied, steaks, sautés
Bottom and Top Round	Lower hindquarters	Roasts, steaks, sautés, kabobs
Rump	Upper hindquarters	Kabobs, steaks, roasts, sautés, grilling

used as pet treats. However, bones can be used to make soup stocks. The center part of the larger round bones is hollow and filled with the marrow, which is either red or yellow. Yellow bone marrow is mostly fat, while red bone marrow is partly fat but is interlaced with a network of blood vessels, connective tissue, and blood-forming cells. The proteins found in these cells can add to the nutritional value of sauces, soups, and other dishes. However, avoid using any bones along the spinal column or from the head area.

Carcass Size and Yield

In general, the larger the animal, the larger the cuts and total meat volume. The size of the cuts and volume will decrease relative to the decreasing size of the animal. There are cuts available in squirrels, rabbits, and other small-game animals, but there will only be small pieces that can be used. However, the carcass yield percentages tend to remain fairly constant within each species, regardless of the size of the animal. By using good cutting techniques, you can increase the amount of meat available and minimize wastage of carcass parts.

Carcass yield is the term used to identify the amount of meat processed from the whole animal. Different percentages are involved as the carcass is broken down from its original weight to the specific cuts. There is a loss of total carcass weight as the viscera, hide, blood, and other portions are discarded.

Live weight is the amount the animal weighs prior to harvest. This is often difficult to determine because live game animals tend not to be captured for weighing. Studies are available that estimate the live weight of an animal retroactively. By using its dressed carcass weight, with considerations made for the amount of fat and other body conditions, an estimate can be made for the possible live weight.

Carcass weight refers to the total weight of the carcass after all the dressing procedures have been completed and the insides of the animal removed. It is most often measured without the hide still attached and is sometimes referred to as *dressing percentage*.

Cutting yield is the proportion of the weight left after trimming and subdivision of the carcass into various cuts. For example, a mature white-tailed deer can be heavy, but much of its weight, perhaps 60 percent, may be distributed among nonmeat areas such as the hide, blood, and bones. This leaves about 40 percent total meat product.

Increased Awareness for Food Safety

Understanding the factors affecting meat quality shouldn't discourage those who want to process their own meat. Rather, it should increase your awareness of potential problems resulting from mishandling or inadequate processing of food products. By understanding where problems can occur, you can take the necessary precautions to avoid them.

Humans have safely processed meat for generations because they understood the basic principles of meat preservation. You can learn those principles by studying this book.

Chapter 2

PREPARATION & TOOLS

❖

This chapter will discuss some of the general concepts and equipment you'll need regardless of whether you are hunting big-game animals such as deer, elk, or moose, or small-game animals like squirrels or rabbits. These basic considerations also apply to wild fowl and domestic poultry.

More detail about the field dressing of each type of animal will be covered in later chapters. However, there are general techniques that apply to all game animals, which will be discussed here.

The purpose of this book is to explain the breaking down of the carcass (butchering) and the preservation of the meat (smoking, curing), and to provide recipes for home use. But first,

Equipment for field dressing includes (1) a folding lock-back knife and a spare, (2) a small whetstone or sharpening steel, (3) several foot-long pieces of strong kitchen string, (4) two clean sponges, (5) plastic bags, (6) rubber gloves, (7) a block and tackle, and (8) 20 feet of 1/4-inch nylon rope. If hunting moose or elk, also bring (9) cloth bags for carrying out the quarters if skinned, and (10) a belt axe or folding game saw for quartering. Hooks (11) can be slipped over the edges of the split ribcage and tied to trees to hold the body open while gutting. Take along a first-aid kit, which can be stowed in your pack.

you need to have a successful hunt and be able to retrieve a properly handled carcass.

Licenses and Tagging

All hunting of wild game, waterfowl, and fish requires a license or permit from either a state or federal wildlife agency. These agencies develop season lengths, bag limits, and other considerations as they attempt to monitor and enhance stable wild game populations. You'll need to apply for these licenses, most often in person at a registered outlet where you plan to do your hunting.

These agencies provide all the information you'll need to stay within their laws or guidelines. In some instances, a lottery system is used to select those who will be granted a license or permit to hunt a particular species, such as black bear or bighorn sheep. These types of lotteries require that you apply far in advance of the season start. If you're interested in hunting a particular species in a state, familiarize yourself with their game hunting laws and fully obey them. You'll also need to know of any relevant federal laws.

Most licenses can be purchased at local outlets authorized by the state or federal wildlife agencies. Most licenses, except for fish, come with a tag that must be applied to the carcass for proper identification. Instructions for placement come with the license and tag. These tags will have a number corresponding to your license, so the dead animal can be claimed by you and not by someone else. The licenses and tags are also a way for the state agency to survey and monitor how many animals are harvested in a given area during the season. This provides information that can be used to estimate wildlife populations and help develop management programs.

The best hunting information about seasons and game laws will come from the state agency in question. It is your responsibility to learn, understand, and abide by those state game hunting or fishing laws.

Attitude and Health

The hard work of hunting often begins after your animal is down, particularly with big-game animals. Small-game wildlife, waterfowl, turkeys, or fish require effort to retrieve them but not the physical stamina needed for larger animals.

The true hunter will celebrate his or her success by doing whatever it takes to preserve the best-quality meat possible. An ethical hunt requires that an honest effort be made to utilize the animal in the best possible way—otherwise that hunter has no right to waste an animal's life for what may turn out to be inedible or inferior meat.

Achieving a successful hunt may put a strain upon a person's physical stamina. Hunting can be a particularly physical activity, especially if you have to drag a large carcass for some distance. Be sure you have assistance during your hunt if you are unsure of your physical capabilities. Hunting areas are likely to be some distance—in some cases, great distances—from medical help. This will not be an urban area where assistance is just around the corner.

This is not to discourage you from hunting, but to encourage you to be aware that you may want to hunt with others. Hunting partners can also provide camaraderie; you'll have a shared experience that can be relived many times in the future.

Hunter Safety

Hunting is one of the safest sports in the United States. According to a National Safety Council study, the fatality rate for hunting is less than half that for boating or swimming. The use of fluorescent orange clothing and improved hunter education are cited as the main reasons for this. Every state and Canadian province sponsors some type of firearm safety or hunter education program. Many states require beginning hunters to pass such a course before they can purchase a license. As with hunting laws and guidelines, you are responsible for understanding the safety rules for handling firearms and for proper conduct in the field.

A second dynamic of hunter safety relates to the hunted animal. Always approach any downed animal with caution. Approach it from the rear and ensure that it is dead. Supposedly dead animals have been known to rise, attack, and injure hunters. Even small-game animals may become very aggressive if they're wounded but not fatally shot. Be cautious until you know for certain your hunted animal is truly dead, then unload your gun and place it out of the way.

Equipment Requirements

Before you take to the woods, you'll need to assemble the minimal equipment necessary for field dressing the wild game you plan to hunt. This may also include the means to transport a carcass.

The amount and kind of equipment needed may be determined by whether or not you haul your game out the same day. If you're hunting in a more remote area, you may be forced to leave all or part of the meat in the wild overnight.

Once you've decided on your hunting area and plan, you can begin assembling your gear. For a same-day hunt and retrieval, you can get by with several sharp knives, a whetstone, plastic storage bags, rubber or plastic gloves, a clean cloth or paper towels, a quantity of heavy string, and a few yards of rope.

In the case of an overnight hunt, where you need to leave the meat behind, you should also have a cheesecloth game bag to keep flies and insects out of the carcass and prevent them from laying eggs in it. A meat saw will be useful for quartering the carcass for packing or hauling out in smaller units.

Rain or snow gear may be necessary as well, depending on the time of year and anticipated weather conditions. A comfortable pair of waterproof hunting boots or shoes is also a good investment.

Anticipating your equipment needs without overburdening yourself is a learning experience. Your goal is to pack light but cover the essentials.

Field Dressing

Field dressing is the removal of the internal body cavity parts in preparation for further deconstruction of an animal carcass. This most often occurs in the area where the animal was killed.

Field dressing wild game is an essential part of a successful hunt. Done properly, it helps preserve the unique qualities that wild game meat brings to your table. Done improperly or haphazardly, it can leave you with a tainted or contaminated carcass, resulting in wasted meat. By not using proper techniques, you can lose more than you gain

and the result will be off flavors that may be too strong for your liking.

The flavor of harvested wild game meat is greatly influenced by how quickly and carefully the carcass is field dressed. You can prevent spoiled or wasted meat by paying attention to some simple and easy-to-apply techniques.

Plan Your Actions

Once you are certain an animal is dead and that it is safe to proceed, be sure to tag your carcass as soon as possible, if the state mandates immediate tagging. This single step is sometimes overlooked in the rush of excitement. After tagging the animal, your first priority is to cool down the carcass as quickly as possible. Move the animal to an area that allows adequate working room. You may have to pull it from underbrush or dense overgrowth, or reposition it, to give yourself space to work on the carcass.

Once you have found a space to work, take a moment to listen for any companion animals that may have become interested in the noise and commotion, especially if you are alone. Being attacked by a protective animal could place you in a dangerous position. This may be unlikely, but caution is its own reward.

Next, proceed with the most important steps in dressing the animal. Work efficiently but pace yourself so that you're not over-worked or exhausted by the time you finish. You'll still need strength to move the animal out of the woods, if that's where you are working. Take time to do a good job to ensure your meat will be clean and usable.

Temperature Threats

Temperature is one of the main factors affecting game meat quality. Atmospheric and internal body temperature will both affect and influence how you handle the carcass of a downed animal or bird.

Hunting seasons were established in the fall for several reasons. Hunting in fall allows young to be born in spring and raised to self-sufficiency by fall, so that the adults can be harvested while maintaining a viable population. It also allows for the harvest of game animals in cooler temperatures.

There are more dimensions to this discussion, but these two dynamics have worked to keep hunting a viable option. The challenge every hunter encounters is how to cool the carcass of a downed animal or bird quickly enough to keep the meat from spoiling, often with limited resources.

A big-game animal's normal internal temperature can range from 97 to 103 degrees Fahrenheit. Smaller animals may have slightly higher temperatures because of their faster heart rates. Most birds will have normal temperatures between 100 and 107 degrees Fahrenheit. These temperatures will increase with activity, such as flight while being hunted and fright from an adrenaline rush.

It is important to bring these temperatures down to 40 degrees Fahrenheit within a few hours to prevent growth of spoilage microorganisms that lie deep within the carcass tissues. Following a few simple steps can go a long way in accomplishing this. First, try to dress the carcass as soon as possible. Opening the carcass and removing the organs and intestines helps release a large amount of internal heat that would otherwise be captured inside. Also, when the animal is no longer moving, it is not creating any heat in its muscles.

The process of field dressing will be discussed in greater detail in each chapter, but know that you can help avoid spoilage problems by not leaving your birds, deer,

You can hang field-dressed big game in a tree to speed its cooling. Hanging also helps protect it from scavenging animals if you must leave to get help carrying it out. Use a block and tackle for easier lifting.

squirrels or other game intact for an extended period of time.

The atmospheric (outside) temperature will play a factor in the preservation process. Higher outside temperatures will hinder the process of cooling the carcass quickly. You may need to use one or more of the strategies listed below during those times.

Find a shady area to dress the animal. Try to keep the carcass out of direct sunlight.

Work in any area with a good breeze. Air currents will move heat away from the carcass interior.

Section the carcass if you legally can. Cutting it up into quarters allows you to deconstruct it and release internal body heat. You may be exposing more muscles to possible contamination using this method, so be careful to keep dirt and insects away.

If the carcass is sectioned, seal the meat in watertight bags. You can then place the bags in creeks or streams without contamination. Cool water will help reduce the temperature in the meat quickly.

Pack ice bags inside the dressed body cavity for transit. Keeping the interior cool will prevent internal temperatures from creating microbial havens.

Stuff the dressed body cavity with dry grass. This will help soak up any blood and will absorb some of the body heat.

Game Meat Byproducts

Early peoples used as much of the animal's carcass as possible for food, clothing, tools, weapons, bindings, and ornaments, among other things. Stomachs, bladders, and skins were fashioned into containers. Nothing was wasted following a successful hunt for meat. Today's commercial meat processors make a similar use of the entire carcass. Modern society still utilizes the nonmuscle portions and transforms them into many products.

All parts of the animal that are not included in the carcass are called byproducts. These include such parts as skin, bones, hair, teeth, feathers, claws, fat, brains, and nonconnective tissues and tendons. Your use of byproducts may depend on whether you have a need for them. Skins may be sold or tanned for leather, feathers can be used for ornaments, and fats can be used in sausage making or rendered into lard.

Three concerns you should be aware of when considering using byproducts from wild game include health issues, temperature control, and size of the byproduct.

Edible domestic byproducts typically include livers, hearts, tongues, testicles, kidneys, oxtails, stomachs (tripe), and intestines. You may use these in your meals in one form or another, although the use of the stomach and intestines from wild game is discouraged. These are sometimes referred to as variety meats. You may develop a taste for a particular byproduct part, as most can be included in specialized dishes or can be ground to include in sausage.

Domestic animals are raised under controlled environments that have protocols to guide producers in raising healthy animals for the market. Wild game does not have such guidelines and health regulations, although in some cases, such as with CWD, their management has been intensively supervised. Also, wild game will forage and eat whatever is available and to their liking. This is an uncontrolled diet that may include ingestion of liver flukes, heartworms, and other parasites living in the wild. You may put yourself at risk if you don't understand the health issues involved in using certain species such as deer, elk, or moose in your diet, particularly if you use their internal organs.

Temperature control is one of the most challenging concerns of using wild game byproducts. While you're in the field, your ability to keep them cool, fresh, and unspoiled is diminished because you are typically far away from quick refrigeration. This may be mitigated by placing the internal parts in sealed plastic bags, submerging them in cold streams or rivers, and retrieving them prior to leaving the field. It will be more difficult to cool them if no such cooling water source is available.

Lastly, the size of the internal organs varies by species. Larger species will have larger internal organs. For example, moose, elk, wild pig, and bear internal organs will be much larger than squirrel, rabbit, and most deer.

You will need to weigh the ethical issues involved in using as much of the harvested game carcass as possible against the feasibility and practicality of retaining the internal organs for later use, whether they are large or small.

Don't Use Water

Avoid using water to flush out the body cavity. This also applies to any internal organs harvested. Water in the field may contain bacteria or soil particles that can contaminate the meat and lead to spoilage. Wiping the inner cavity with a dry cloth will seal the meat with a thin film of body fluids that dries quickly. Applying water will dilute this film and introduce microbes that can create an excellent environment for bacterial growth.

Lead in Game Meat

Game harvested with lead bullets has been shown to have tiny lead particles or fragments remaining in the processed meat. These are often too small to be seen and can disperse far from the wound channel. Although lead in game meat does not rival lead paint in older homes as a health risk, the risk is not low enough to ignore. You are encouraged to use copper bullets and nontoxic ammunition for hunting.

Fishing

Fishing presents a different set of circumstances in field dressing because you want the fish to remain alive until you are ready to cut them up. Preventing bruising is an important part of having quality fish meat.

Using a stringer or placing them in an aerated tank or tub will keep most fish vigorous and free from damage.

Dead fish spoil quickly, so you will need to work diligently to remove the gills and guts to cool them as quickly as possible.

Fishing also requires that your tackle box contain a first-aid kit. Sharp hooks and multiple hook baits can cause severe punctures in the fingers and hands, especially when you are removing them from a thrashing fish. Fish teeth are also very sharp and can cause massive damage to your hand or fingers.

Keep a first-aid kit with bandages, wraps, disinfectant, and iodine. A pair of needle nose pliers can be very useful in extracting hooks that are embedded in your skin or clothing, or that are deep inside the fish.

Equipment for fish dressing includes a fillet knife, an electric blade knife, a small spoon for scraping out the bloodline, a scale scraper, and a wire mesh glove for the hand opposite your knife hand.

Tools

You will achieve more satisfactory results when butchering if you use equipment and knives that are sturdy, sharp, and appropriate for the task. You must take seriously the choice and maintenance of proper equipment and the safety issues involved. Injuries resulting from mishandled animals, inappropriate equipment, and improper knife handling can be avoided by studying and understanding the importance of each.

Knives are necessary from the start of the butchering process (which is often done in the field) until the last cut is made. The number and style of knives you use will depend on the species and size of the carcass you are working with, as well as what you deem necessary to complete the work safely

Pictured are a folding combination knife (top) with a blunt-tip blade used for slitting abdomens without puncturing intestines, a clip-point blade, and a saw for cutting through the breastbones and pelvic bones of big game. A big-game skinning knife (bottom), which has a blunt tip to avoid punching holes in the hide, is also useful in the field.

Hunting knives include general-purpose types, such as a folding drop-point (top left) and a folding clip-point (at bottom). The tip of a clip-point is more acute and curves up higher than that of a drop-point. Special-purpose types include a folding bird knife (top right), which has a hook for field dressing birds.

and satisfactorily. Knives can range from a small hand knife to a large, sturdy butchering knife, with a wide variety in between. Many different knives are available; some are better in certain locations on the carcass and some make certain cuts easier and more precise. You do not need a chef's array to do a proper job of butchering; simply use knives that fit the intended purpose, are sharp and sturdy, and are easily cleaned.

One basic rule of butchering is that sharp knives always work best. And being sharp, all knives carry safety concerns.

Simple Knife Rules

- Always use a sharp knife when cutting meat.
- Never hold the knife under your arm or leave it under a piece of meat.
- Keep knives visible.
- Always keep the knife point down.
- Always cut down toward the cutting surface and away from your body.

Safety First

Personal safety is of prime importance when handling live animals, slaughtering them, and cutting up the carcasses. Being injured by live animals can have devastating consequences. You can also be injured by unstable or inappropriate equipment, whether it is being used for slaughter or for food processing. Knife injuries can occur quickly and unexpectedly, and in severe cases may be life threatening. To help avoid serious injury, use common sense and caution, and be alert to potential dangers.

Knives and Saws

An assortment of knives and saws are available for field use and home butchering. You can buy most, if not all, of the equipment used in commercial or local slaughterhouses. Purchase what you need at hardware stores, through companies on the Internet, or at stores specializing in such equipment.

You can purchase knives for general use, or you can use knives you already have, depending on their size, condition, and intended purpose. For small-game animals and birds, you may not need or want large

Four different knives can accomplish most tasks involved in the slaughtering and fabrication of large wild game animals. These include, from left to right: a 6-inch curved (flexible) knife, a 6-inch straight (stiff) knife, an 8-inch breaking (steak) knife, and a 10-inch breaking knife.

knives or saws. You will need to use large knives and saws for big carcasses, however. You may want to have a separate knife for each task, or you may consolidate tasks by using only two or three different knives.

Take an inventory of the knives you have and gather them together. Determine which ones you'll need before you begin butchering. Identify where they can be used during the butchering process—many knives can be used for multiple tasks. Take out those that are duplicates or won't be needed. Once you begin the butchering process, you will want to work quickly and efficiently to get the meat to the freezer. Stopping to find a specific knife that is not on hand only delays the process.

Knives typically come with wooden or plastic handles, flexible or stiff blades, and in many sizes and shapes. Some meat processors prefer wooden-handled knives, which should

not be cleaned in a dishwasher. Others prefer knives with dishwasher-safe plastic handles. One disadvantage to these is that they can become slippery unless dried off prior to use. This condition can be mitigated by handles that have a gritty finish, which makes them safer to use when wet or greasy.

Buy knives that are affordable, sharp, and easy to maintain. Knives that are not sharp pose a safety hazard; they can slip, and they require more effort to pass through the muscle or bone. Make sure to keep your knives completely sanitary. If you don't keep your knives clean, they may harbor harmful microorganisms that can affect the quality of the meat and possibly your health.

Choosing the Correct Knife

The most basic answer to the question of which knife is best to use is perhaps found in the old adage: any knife is better than no knife. This is especially true when in the field and standing over your kill.

You do not need to carry an array of knives and saws into the field for dressing out an animal or bird. "Dressing" a carcass means to open it up and remove the inner organs such as the heart, lungs, liver, and the intestinal and reproductive tracts. You clean out the body cavity for two reasons: to release internal body heat to help cool the carcass, and to remove the intestinal tract to eliminate possible fecal contamination within the body.

Your main concern after a kill is to dress the carcass as soon as possible. Further breakdown of the carcass can be done later, but it is important to cool the carcass as much as possible in the shortest time to prevent it from spoiling. As mentioned earlier, once an animal is dead, some life processes stop and the muscle pH gradually drops and the muscle proteins begin to break down. As digestion stops, the intestinal tract holds the remains of unprocessed food materials that can form gases detrimental to the carcass. Removing them in the field aids in having a safe meat product later.

With a large wild animal, such as a deer, moose, elk, you are likely to use some kind of knife four or five different times before the carcass is completely broken down and ready for your freezer. The steps you'll take to break down the carcass include field dressing (removing the insides of the animal), skinning (removing the skin), caping (only if you desire to mount the head), rough-butchering (breaking the carcass down into major portions first), and the final breakdown of cuts for freezing or grinding.

For each of these steps, there are different knife sizes and blade designs that can help you do a better job than others. It mostly depends on how precise and technical you wish to be. As a general rule, field dressing knives should be short and lightweight. This allows for easy carriage to the carcass site and for extended walking.

The most commonly used knife designs are straight, drop-point, clip-point, and trailing-point. However, design should be secondary to practicality; you should choose a knife and blade you feel most comfortable with and that best suits your physical dexterity.

Hunting Knives

A good hunting knife is one of the best investments a hunter can make. Properly selected, used, and cared for, it can last a long time. A cheap knife, on the other hand, may not last a single hunting season.

When selecting a hunting knife, look closely at the materials, blade length and shape, and workmanship. The handle should

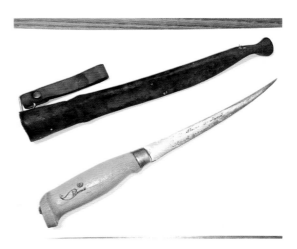

Fillet knives are long and flexible with thin blades. They are useful when trimming around bones and are preferred when skinning and cutting up fish. Fillet knives can also be used on small-game animals.

be made of hardwood, plastic-impregnated wood, or a tough synthetic. These materials last longer than brittle plastic, or wood you can easily dent with your fingernail.

Choose a knife that feels comfortable in your hand. Remember that your hands may be wet when you're using it, so look for a handle shape that's easy to hold firmly. A blade between 3 1/2 and 4 1/2 inches long is adequate for either big or small game.

Clip-point and drop-point knives are good all-purpose types. The acutely pointed tip of a clip-point is good for delicate cutting and easily penetrates the abdominal skin in field dressing. The tip of a drop-point is less apt to puncture the intestines when slitting the abdominal skin, or to punch a hole in the hide should you use it for skinning.

Many hunters prefer folding knives for convenience and safety in the field. They are shorter and easier to carry than a straight knife, and the folded blade is safely out of the way in the event of a fall.

Blade Considerations

Regardless of the different kinds of knives you use, you'll want ones that have high-carbon steel blades, which are usually most reliable at about 0.5 percent carbon. If the blade is made of too little carbon, it will be soft and the edge of the knife may bend. If it's too high in carbon, it will generally be too hard and more difficult to sharpen. The blade steel should be stainless, so it's hard but not brittle. A blade with a Rockwell hardness rating of 57 to 60 is hard enough to hold an edge but soft enough for easy resharpening at home when it does become dull.

Many knives sold through commercial outlets today are made to hold their edge, or their sharpness, for long periods of time and use. Older knives may not have those characteristics, but may be very usable if correctly sharpened. Even high-quality knives will dull and need sharpening after a period of use. You may have them sharpened by someone specializing in blades or you may sharpen them yourself.

A quick steeling of your larger knives with a steel sharpener will keep the blade edges perfectly straight and in top condition for cutting. During a butchering session, steel your large knife frequently. Hold the base of the blade against the steel at the angle at which it was originally sharpened. Draw the knife toward you in an arc from base to tip. Repeat on other side. Alternate sides until the blade is sharp.

Basic Knife Types

Use your knife only for its intended purpose. If you use it for whittling wood or to pry the lid off a jar, you can destroy the edge. When butchering, have a minimum of two types of knives available: one for skinning and one for eviscerating. The same holds true for cutting up the carcass and muscles. You should have one knife for boning or trimming, and one for breaking or cutting into bones. You may also add to this list a saw specifically designed for use on meat.

A boning knife has a long, straight edge for trimming and separating muscles from themselves and from the bones they are attached to. The tip of a boning knife may be rigid or flexible, allowing it to easily move around the bones. They usually range from 5 to 7 inches in length.

A trimming knife is a smaller, shorter version of a boning knife. It is useful for cleaning fat and tendons from small cuts, cleaning up steaks and game bird breasts, or cutting away small pieces of muscle in difficult-to-reach places.

A breaking knife can be used to reduce larger primal cuts to smaller pieces. It's essentially a longer version of a boning knife; it's thin and curves gently up to a sharp point. A breaking knife is very useful for piercing and slicing and can be used to make primal and subprimal cuts on large-bodied animals such as moose, deer, elk, and alligators.

Butcher knives are long and inflexible and are designed to allow piercing as well as cutting in a smooth, linear direction. They may have either a tapered or rounded tip.

A skinning knife is generally short with a dramatic curve to the blade and has a bulbous tip to help the blade slide easily between meat and skin without damaging either. Those used for bison or elk can be slightly more curved than the ones used for wild sheep, goats, or other small animals.

Cleavers are the heaviest of all butcher knives. They have a thick square blade that is designed to crack and split bone.

Cimeter knives are shaped like a scimitar sword, which curves along the entire length up to a fine point. These are an alternative to traditional shapes, but know that they promote a sawing motion rather than a drawing one. A cimeter knife is useful for large butchering jobs and for cutting steaks, tenderloins, and roasts.

Fillet knives are long, thin, and flexible. A good fillet knife bends easily to let you cut very thin slices of fish and meat with exact precision.

Meat saws are used to cut through bones or to sever portions of large carcasses into smaller, more manageable ones. Most meat saws are between 12 to 25 inches in length with a serrated blade. Blades should be complete, with no rust spots, chips, or missing teeth. Any meat saw should be thoroughly washed and sanitized before use. Pay particular attention to the area where the handle attaches to the metal frame—if it contains meat residue from previous usage, it may be contaminated.

Folding Knives

Folding knives, as their name indicates, are those that have blades with joints that allow them to fold over, securing the edge in a protective cover within the handle. Jack knives, Swiss Army knives, and camping knives are some of the different folding knives available. They can have single or multiple blades.

Choose folding knives carefully; check for quality construction. Folding knives are often used during hunting because they have multiple uses, are easy and safe to carry, and are sturdy enough to make quick, precise cuts. Like larger knives, they require special care. Keep the blades sharp and the knife clean.

Folding knives will have a locking device that keeps the blade from opening on its own. They also have a pivot, which is the rotation point that allows the blade to fold into the handle. When fully opened, the blade should lock in position with no trace of wiggle or sloppiness, and the back of the blade should line up exactly with the back edge of the handle.

Both the locking mechanism and the pivot need to be kept clean and free of debris to prevent contamination of the meat. Use a drop of light oil at the joint (or each joint in the case of multiple blades) to create a smooth blade action while opening and closing it. As with other knives used for butchering, your folding knives should be cleaned before and after each use.

Many folding knives come with leather pouches or sheaths. When not in use, you should store the knife and leather sheath separately because leather will absorb moisture and can rust the blade. Also, there are tanning salts and acids in leather that can rust or tarnish the steel. You can protect leather sheaths and keep them limber by using a leather preservative or mink oil.

Sharpening Knives

It bears repeating: A sharp knife is safer than a dull one. It gives you more control, and you need less pressure to cut the meat. There are three basic steps in sharpening knives: grinding, honing, and steeling. Each is a different technique, although they may seem the same to most beginners, and each is used depending on the condition of the knife.

Grinding

Grinding gives the blade its thinness and will remove part of the blade. Because of this, you will need to be cautious with any grinding so that you do not lose more of the blade than intended. Some knives need to be ground before they can be honed or sharpened. Purchased knives will come with a properly beveled blade.

Grinding produces a beveled or angled edge on the blade. In most cases, grinding is not used for sharpening but for creating a proper angle that can then be honed to sharpness. One of the easiest ways to grind an edge is to use a round stone that spins. These can be hand-turned, foot-pedaled, or electric driven; you hold the knife stationary against the turning stone.

Some professional knife sharpeners advise against using a power-driven grinding wheel because there's the potential to create too much heat from the friction of the wheel. The excess heat could cause the temper on the blade to burn. However, if you sharpen a knife slowly, in stages, you can avoid most problems with heat generated from wheels.

The purpose of the grinding process is to make one side of the blade meet the other side while pushing up a small curl of metal called a burr. If you stop grinding before the burr is formed, your knife will not be as sharp as it could be. If you grind too much, you lose any burr. As you are grinding, always check both sides of the blade all along the length. The burr tends to form quickly at the base of the blade but takes a little longer at the tip. To have fully ground one side, you must feel a burr running all the way from the heel of the blade near the handle to the tip.

Honing

Honing sharpens the beveled edge. You'll need a stone with a finer surface than a grinding stone. In honing, the stone remains stationary. It is important to keep the honing stone from moving while you apply the blade pressure. Putting it in a wood base or attaching the stone to a table with clamps will help.

Steeling

After honing, you'll need to steel the blade. Steeling makes the edge perfectly straight by removing any burrs so that they do not roll over on themselves and cause the meat to tear when cutting. A steel will realign the edge of the knife, forcing any rolled-over spots back into line and making it useable again.

Knife steels come in a variety of sizes and shapes, including round steels, oval steels, grooved steels, and several others not typically used in homes. A coarse steel texture will create more tiny points of contact with the edge of the blade, causing a more aggressive abrasion. Be careful not to apply so much pressure that you create an uneven surface.

A round steel is generally 10 to 12 inches long and can be held in one hand or placed in a vertical position with the handle up and the tip resting on a folded towel to keep it from slipping. In this position you'll be able to place the knife edge against the

1

The whetstone you use to sharpen your hunting knives should be at least as long as the blade. Place the stone on a folded towel for stability, and apply a little honing oil. Use a coarse stone first if the blade is extremely dull, then follow with a medium stone.

2

Hold the base of the blade against the whetstone at the angle at which the blade was originally sharpened (usually between 12 and 17 degrees). Push the knife away from you in a smooth arc while using moderate pressure from base to tip. Keep the edge of the blade at the same angle, in constant contact with the whetstone. Repeat this pushing motion several times.

3

Draw the knife toward you in an arc three times, maintaining the same angle. Continue sharpening alternate sides, then repeat these steps with a fine whetstone. The knife is sharp when it slices easily through a piece of paper. Clean the whetstone with soapy water before storing.

Steps for Honing a Knife Blade

- Wet the stone with oil or water and place or clamp the blade securely on a flat surface.

- Hold the knife handle. Place the end of the knife blade nearest the handle near the edge of the stone closest to you.

- Tilt the blade so the bevel lies flat on the surface, making a 20-degree angle.

- Place your fingertips on the flat side of the blade, near the back, unsharpened edge.

- Use your fingertips to apply pressure on the blade.

- With a sweeping motion, draw the knife across the stone in one direction, then turn it and draw it in the opposite direction.

steel with the blade held perpendicular at a 90-degree angle. Rotate your wrist to reduce the angle by half—45 degrees—and then rotate it again by half to about 22.5 degrees and then slightly more to a desired point at approximately 20 degrees. In general, you want to steel at a slightly steeper angle than the edge bevel of the knife.

The best result of your steeling action occurs when you lock your wrist and stroke the knife from heel to tip by moving your shoulder and slowly dropping your forearm. By locking your wrist and elbow, you will keep a stable angle from top to bottom. This is the key to maintaining a consistent angle all the way through the stroke. Standard steels do not remove metal, but only realign the cutting edge. One advantage of this method is that you won't have to apply much pressure to realign the edge. Steeling keeps the edge straight and honing sharpens it.

Sharp knives allow you to "cut" through the carcass, whereas with a dull knife you will often "push" the blade through the meat. If you learn to sharpen knives correctly, it will save wear on them. If you are unsure of your ability to sharpen knives or prefer not to, there are professional sharpening businesses that can help you.

Keep your knives sharp, clean, and dry, and avoid storing them in places where they can get nicked and damaged by other objects. Small nicks or scratches can dull even the sharpest knives.

Testing a sharpened knife should be done with paper rather than your fingers. Avoid running your finger across a newly sharpened edge to test it. A better and safer method is to cut a single piece of paper while holding it loosely between two fingers. A suitably sharp knife will allow you to cut through the paper with little motion.

Always remember that there is an inherent danger in handling, using, and sharpening knives. Knife safety, particularly during sharpening, is a matter of common sense. If you go slowly, pay attention, and stay focused, you should have little trouble. Always keep knives out of the reach of young children.

Knife Care

Clean your knives before and after each use to keep them in the best condition and promote food safety. Use mild soapy water and clean by hand. A dishwasher's hot temperatures may affect the temper of a blade so much that it will not hold its edge later when sharpened. Also, the water jets in a dishwasher can toss your knives about and cause nicks on the blades. When cleaning knives, pay close attention to the area where the blade attaches to the handle. This is the area most likely to harbor meat or blood residue after use, and it's an ideal habitat for microorganisms. A thorough washing before, after, and in between cutting will maintain cleanliness.

Washing meat saws requires more attention because of the teeth on the blade. They can be cleaned with mild soapy water but should never be washed in a dishwasher. Pay close attention to cleaning the teeth and the connecting joints where the blade attaches to the frame. Most meat saws can be dismantled for washing.

Storing Knives

Knives can be useful for years if stored properly. Keep knives or meat saws in an area that is cool with low humidity. Avoid storage areas with high relative humidity or dramatic shifts in temperature (such as attics or basements that are not insulated or heated). Wide variations in temperature and humidity can cause condensation and moisture to come into contact with exposed knives.

After washing knives, remove moisture by using a soft cotton cloth or chamois. You can protect the blades by applying drops of any quality oil or silicon treatment with a soft cotton cloth. Using a silica gel or other drying agent will help keep knives dry if you live in a humid area. Although tarnishing or oxidation is normal on high-carbon steel knives and cannot be entirely avoided, using a gel or drying agent helps protect the knife from rust. Its residue will appear as a blue-gray hue rather than red rust tones.

If your butchering knives are to be stored for long periods between use, you should check them periodically for any reddish spots that may show early signs of tarnish or oxidation—the initial rust

stages. If this is present, you should clean the blades. Stainless-steel blades are not rustproof, although most are rust and stain resistant. You can remove any stains or tarnish by using a standard metal cleaner or polish.

Aprons

Aprons made from leather, naugahyde, heavy canvass, or rubber can protect you from injury and keep your clothes from becoming soiled or bloody during the slaughtering process. A waterproof apron will also keep you dry.

A heavy apron or abdominal protection made of material impenetrable to sharp knives is a good safeguard. They may restrict some leg movement, but such aprons are an insurance against injury should your knife slip or should you accidentally draw it toward your body.

Other Equipment

Gloves are one of the best protective items you can use. Use gloves when cutting up wild game in the field. This is to protect not only your hands and fingers, but your general health as well. Gloves lessen the likelihood of cuts and contact with wild game body fluids. Some animals harbor viruses or parasites that can adversely affect your health if they enter your body. Poison oak, poison ivy, and other rash-inducing substances can also become attached to an animal's hide. Gloves act as a first-line barrier against these, but they need to be thoroughly washed and disinfected after each use.

Some simple field equipment can help make the work at hand easier and not overly burden you with extra weight. A small block and tackle may be useful for lifting a large carcass, especially if you are hunting alone.

During butchering, a heavy mesh butcher's cutting glove worn on your free hand helps protect against cuts, slashes, and punctures. Always wash and disinfect the glove before and after use and dry properly. Gloves of this type are sold in different sizes and can be used on either hand.

If you need to move a carcass over some distance, you may want to have some nylon rope available to help you drag it out of the field. A shoulder harness, to which you can attach the rope, will allow your back and shoulder muscles to bear most of the stress as you drag the animal across the ground. There are also other methods of transporting your animal over distances, and you should familiarize yourself with these prior to entering your hunt.

Plastic sealing bags are light, easy to pack, and very useful for keeping internal organs, such as the liver and heart, fresh. Also, paper towels and moist towelettes are handy items to take along.

If you plan to butcher your animal in a camp before you return home, you should have a sturdy table, cutting board, or block on which to make your primal and subprimal cuts. It is difficult to do these cuts on plastic sheeting covering the ground. Having an upright cutting surface or a plywood sheet on the back of a pickup truck will make the work easier.

If you are butchering at home, use a butchering glove. They are designed to be worn on the free hand (the one not holding a knife). They come in several sizes and are easy to wash. Some are made of thousands of braided stainless-steel threads woven into the glove; these threads resist cuts and are difficult to puncture. A heavy mesh glove is made of solid stainless-steel rings that protect hands against cuts, slashes, and laceration hazards but may not entirely stop punctures. Both types of gloves serve to reduce the chances for injury to hands and fingers. Before and after each use, you should thoroughly clean, sanitize, and dry butchering gloves.

Quick Tips

- Use knives appropriate for the situation.
- Keep knives sharp and clean.
- Wash knives and other cutting equipment thoroughly between each carcass.
- Clean knives before storing them safely.

Electric knives can be used in place of standard knives. If you're using an electric knife, be sure it has the appropriate blade for the task at hand. Electric knives may be easier to use when carving or filleting different cuts of meat, particularly if handling heavy portions is a concern. Electric knives and blades will need care and maintenance like other electric equipment and should be kept away from water sources.

Cutting Surfaces

The cutting surface you use will have a major impact on your knife blades. Cutting surfaces and boards should be made of material that is easy to clean and fairly soft. Natural wood or synthetic materials such as soft polyethylene make good cutting surfaces. Avoid using glass, ceramic, metal, marble, or any other hard material, because these can have a damaging effect on knife blades and edges.

Cutting surfaces can provide an ideal area for cross-contamination of food products, a major food safety concern. Bacteria transferred from knives to cutting surfaces to other foods can lead to food poisoning. Always clean and sanitize the surface you use for cutting meat before and after each use.

Chapter 3

BIG-GAME BUTCHERING

L arge wild game animal meat has become an attractive addition to the menu for many families. Big game animals may be hunted in the wild or sourced from commercial production facilities that specialize in raising them. Regulations apply to commercially produced big game, and if you choose to secure animals through this route, you may want to fully understand the rules and regulations governing them.

Big Game Defined

Size and weight are the determining factors that separate big-game animals from small ones. Although there is no established benchmark for this demarcation, wildlife animals that exceed 50 to 70 pounds are considered big game. That said, there are vast differences in size within the category of big game, and these differences may influence your ability to handle a carcass in the field and thus your choice of what to hunt. It is much easier to harvest, clean, and cut up a 150-pound deer than a 500-pound elk, or an even larger moose.

Some big-game animals that we will use in our butchering discussion will be deer (representing the cervids), bear, bighorn sheep (for goats too), wild boar, alligator, and bobcat/lynx.

For our discussion on butchering, big-game animals can be categorized into groups with similar skeletal structures. All big-game animals will have physiologies with common structures such as digestive, nervous, thoracic, reproductive, and pulmonary systems. By and large, they

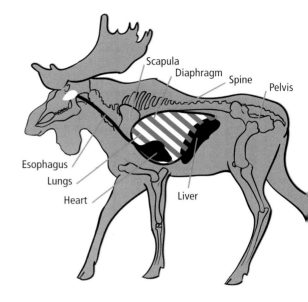

General precautions are advised when handling deer:

- Do not handle or consume the meat from any animal that exhibits symptoms of CWD.

- Do not eat the eyes, brain, spinal cord, spleen, tonsils, or lymph nodes of any deer, and minimize handling of these part while working on the carcass.

- If your deer is sampled for CWD testing, wait for the test results before eating the meat.

- Always wear disposable rubber gloves when field dressing deer or elk carcasses.

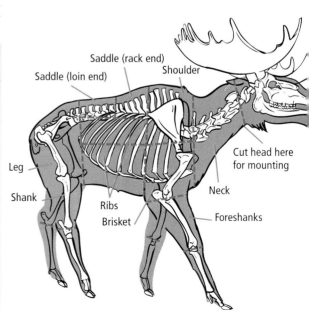

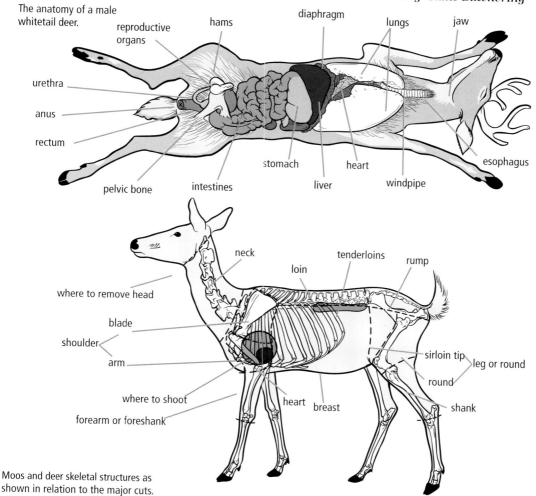

The anatomy of a male whitetail deer.

hams

diaphragm

lungs

jaw

reproductive organs

urethra

anus

rectum

stomach

liver

heart

windpipe

esophagus

pelvic bone

intestines

neck

loin

tenderloins

rump

where to remove head

blade

shoulder

arm

sirloin tip

leg or round

round

where to shoot

heart

breast

shank

forearm or foreshank

Moos and deer skeletal structures as shown in relation to the major cuts.

will also have similar muscle structures because they are quadrupeds. Their muscles are used for locomotion and work in conjunction with the rest of the body. In a basic sense, the muscles are primarily used to move the skeletal structure from feeding place to feeding place so it can satisfy the digestive system.

In each of these groups we'll look at one example of how to field dress and butcher or deconstruct them into small or more easily used portions. Dressing a carcass is simple: remove the internal organs immediately after the kill without contaminating the body cavity with dirt, hair, or contents of the digestive tract, and drain all excess from the body cavity.

Meat Volume

You can estimate the amount of edible meat that can be derived from big-game carcasses. Many factors will influence the weight of the animal, including their age and diet, but the percentages will remain fairly typical. A 100-pound field-dressed deer will typically be about 1.5 years of age and can dress out at up to 80 percent. This yields a carcass weight to cut of about 80 pounds. Roughly 50 percent of this, or 40 pounds, will be edible meat, while the other half will consist of bone, fat, and mutilated areas affected by shot and the resulting blood damage. A 1,200-pound moose dressing out at 80 percent will yield a carcass weight of about 960 pounds. Roughly half of this, 480 pounds, will be useable.

Cervid

The term *cervid* refers to any animal that resembles a deer. This includes moose, elk, caribou, deer, muskox, and antelope. For our discussion, we will include the American bison in this group as well.

These animals are all quadrupeds that nurse their young. Although some of these groups may have a larger average size than others, their muscle structures are located in the same places.

The essentials of field dressing and the steps involved will be roughly applicable to all big-game animals. We will use the butchering sequence of a deer to represent all of the cervids and other big game of like physical construction and provide further comments that may be more applicable to one group than another.

Venison Precautions

CWD is a neurological disease of deer and elk. It belongs to a family of diseases known as transmissible spongiform encephalopathies or prion diseases. The disease attacks the brains of infected animals, causing them to display abnormal behavior, lose flesh and bodily function, become very thin and

feeble, and die. This disease has been found in wild deer and elk in several U.S. states and one Canadian province. Deer population infection rates have varied from 1 to 15 percent, and infection rates in elk are much lower—often less than 1 percent.

Mutilated Areas

Portions of the carcass may have sustained damage from a gunshot or arrow wound, depending on the season. This damaged meat may have materials embedded in it such as hair, metal shards, and any mixture of blood, bone chips, and fecal matter. Damaged tissue should be cut out and discarded.

Bleeding

You can consider bleeding your deer, although it is not typically necessary. Once the animal is dead, its heart stops pumping and blood flow throughout the body ceases. If the animal is shot through the heart or lungs, this will often provide adequate bleeding. You may get a small amount of blood to drain by cutting into its jugular veins. However, for a larger animal such as a moose, you may want to try to bleed it.

Should you choose to bleed the animal, begin by either cutting the jugular vein in the neck just behind the jaw, or, in the case of a trophy-size buck, by cutting into the base of the neck several inches in front of the breast.

You can begin by inserting a hunting knife with a five-inch blade into the breast with the point of the blade aimed at the tail. Insert the blade all the way and press it downward toward the backbone and with a slicing motion withdraw it. Then elevate the hind legs to allow gravity to drain the blood.

When moving the carcass, leave the hide on to protect it from dirt and flies. An intact hide prevents surface muscles from drying too much during aging. Drag a deer with each front leg tied to an antler to keep from snagging brush, or tie a rope around the neck if anterless. In dusty terrain, you should tie the carcass shut. A bear may be dragged on a heavy tarp to avoid damaging the hair. An elk or moose may have to be quartered before transporting. Some hunters skin the carcass before quartering, so the hide can be tanned in one piece. To quarter an elk or moose, begin by bending a leg sharply. Cut the skin around the joint to remove the lower leg.

Field Dressing a Deer

There are roughly ten steps for dressing a big-game animal in the field.

1. Place the carcass on its back with the rump lower than the shoulders, and spread the legs.

2. If not mounting the head, cut from the sternum (breastbone) up the neck to the base of the jaw. Don't cut the windpipe yet; this cut will expose the windpipe and allow you to remove as much of it as possible later. The windpipe sours rapidly and is a leading cause of tainted meat.

3. Cut along the centerline of the belly from breastbone to the base of the tail. Cut the hide first and then return and make a cut through the belly muscle, along the same line, using your free hand to lift the skin and muscle away from the internal organs and intestines as you slice. Stop when you reach the aitchbone, which forms the joints in the pelvis.

4. Make a circular cut around the anus and free it from the hide. Draw it out of the pelvic cavity far enough to securely tie it shut with a heavy string. This will keep any feces from entering the body cavity when you release it.

5. Lay the carcass on its side. Loosen and roll out the stomach and intestines. Examine the liver. Keep it for sausage making if it looks healthy and free of spots, cysts, or scarring, which may indicate parasites or disease. If any are present, discard it. If clean, place the liver in a plastic bag and put it on ice as soon as possible.

6. The diaphragm separates the chest and stomach cavities. Cut around its edge and then split the breastbone. Any parts of the diaphragm that remain can be removed later.

7. Cut the esophagus near the jaw and pull the lungs, heart, and windpipe toward you and remove them from the body cavity. Cut any remaining tissues that hold it to the inside cavity.

8. Remove the heart and place it in a bag with the liver and cool as soon as possible.

9. Drain any excess blood from the body cavity by rolling the carcass over, or hanging it head-up to let it drain.

10. Use a clean cloth or paper towels to wipe down the inside of the body cavity. The carcass is now ready to be moved.

1

Field dress the animal immediately to drain the blood and dissipate the body heat. Wearing rubber gloves will make cleanup easier and protect you from any parasites or blood-borne diseases the animal may be carrying. Locate the base of the breastbone and make a shallow cut that is long enough to insert the first two fingers of your hand, being careful not to puncture the intestines.

2

Form a V with the first two fingers of your hand. Hold the knife between your fingers with the cutting edge up. Cut through the abdominal wall to the pelvic area using your fingers to keep from puncturing the intestines.

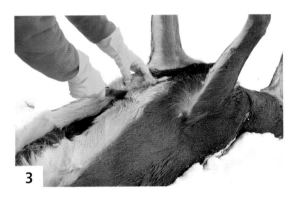

3

Straddle the animal, facing its head. If you do not plan to mount the head, cut the skin from the base of the breastbone to the jaw, with the cutting edge of the knife up. If you plan to mount the head, follow your taxidermist's instructions.

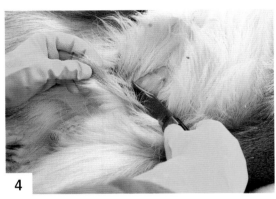

4

Separate the external reproductive organs of a buck from the abdominal wall, but do not cut them off completely. Remove the udder of a doe if it was still nursing—the milk sours rapidly and could give the meat an unpleasant flavor.

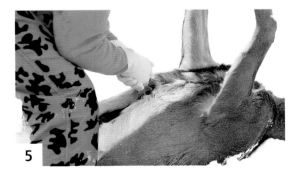

5

Cut through the center of the breastbone by bracing your elbows against your legs with one hand supporting the other; use your knees to provide leverage. An older animal may require a game saw or small axe.

6

To free a deer's urethra, split the pelvic bone (or slice between the hams on a buck). Make careful cuts around the urethra until it is freed to a point just above the anus. Be careful not to sever the urethra. Cut around the anus; on a doe, the cut should also include the vulva above the anus. Free the rectum and urethra by loosening the connective tissue with your knife. Tie off the rectum and urethra with sturdy string to prevent fecal contamination of the inside body cavity.

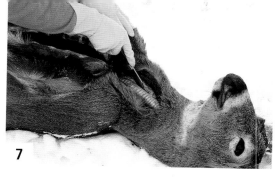

7

Free the windpipe and esophagus by cutting the connective tissue. Sever the windpipe and esophagus at the jaw. Grasp them firmly and pull down, continuing to cut where necessary, until they are freed to the point where the windpipe branches out into the lungs.

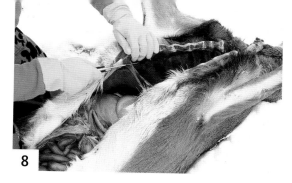

8

Hold the rib cage open on one side. Cut the diaphragm from the rib opening down to the backbone. Stay as close to the rib cage as possible; do not puncture the stomach. Repeat on the other side so that the cuts meet over the backbone.

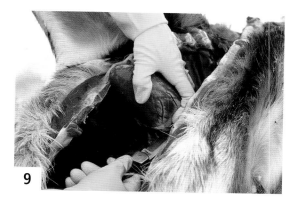

9

Remove the heart by severing the connecting blood vessels. Hold the heart upside down for a few moments to drain excess blood, then place it in a plastic bag. Some hunters find it easier to remove the viscera first before taking the heart and liver from it.

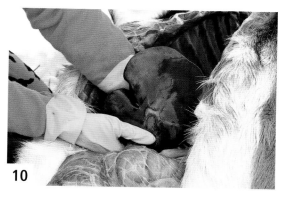

10

Cut the tubes that attach the liver and remove it. Check for spots, cysts, or scarring, which may indicate parasites or disease. If any are present, discard the liver. If the liver is clean, place into a plastic bag with the heart. Place on ice as soon as possible.

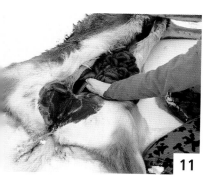

11

Pull the tied-off rectum and urethra from the pelvic bone and into the body cavity, unless you split the pelvic bone, making this unnecessary. Roll the carcass on its side so that the viscera begin to spill out the side of the body cavity.

12

Sponge the cavity clean and prop open with a stick. If the urinary tract or intestines have been severed, wash the carcass with snow or clean water. If you need to leave the carcass, drape it over brush or logs with the cavity down, or hang it from a tree to speed cooling.

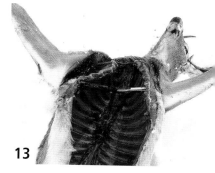

13

Firmly grasp the windpipe and esophagus; pull down and away from the body. If the organs do not pull away freely, the diaphragm may still be partially attached. Scoop from both ends toward the middle to finish rolling out the viscera.

Skinning

Skinning a carcass is easiest if it is suspended from a sturdy tree limb or, if you're at home, another stable structure. A rope is often used to hang the carcass by the hind legs, which allows you to move around it while you work. You can remove the hide more easily if the carcass is in a vertical position than if it is lying horizontally on the ground. Before raising it, cut slits in the skin between the rear leg bone and the tendon of the hock. Insert hooks, a strong piece of wood, or a metal bar into the slit. This will let you raise the carcass to a level that is comfortable to work with. If it is a buck and you wish to preserve the head, take extra care to avoid breaking the horns when you elevate the carcass high enough that the horns no longer touch the floor or ground.

The hocks should be spread apart to give you easier access to the abdominal area. You can make the first cuts for skinning before you elevate the carcass. First, make a complete circular cut around each hock just below the inserted hooks; avoid cutting into the tendons. Place the blade tip on the top of the tendon and carefully slice toward the rectum. Do not cut into the hindquarter. Then do the same for the other leg. From this point on, you will need to do very little knife work, because you can separate the skin from the carcass by sliding your fist downward between the inner hide and carcass as you pull the skin away.

Remove the forelegs by making cuts just below the knee at the smooth joints. Then begin pulling the hide from the rounds or rump and inside the rear legs with even tension. You may have to work the inside skin free before pulling from the top part of the anus. Use your hand or fist to remove the skin from the sides as you pull it down the back.

continued on page 60

Field Dressing Tips

1. A sturdy, sharp knife can usually cut the sternum and pelvic bones of a deer. For larger animals with a heavier, denser bone structure, such as moose or elk, you may need a small axe.

2. Avoid cutting, nicking, or breaking the bladder, stomach, or intestines. This can contaminate the inside of the carcass.

3. If the entrails have been punctured by a bullet or your knife, wipe the body cavity with a clean cloth or paper towels as best as possible.

4. Make your centerline cuts in the direction of the hair, from throat to tail. This will greatly reduce the amount of hair that spreads to the meat.

5. Trim all muscle that has been damaged by a gunshot or arrow puncture. If the weather is cold enough, you may be able to wait until you return home to trim damaged parts.

6. If you shoot a bull moose in Ontario, Canada, you must cut around the genitals, which must be left on one hindquarter for sex identification.

7. If the weather is warm or the animal is to be left in the field overnight (or longer), skin it except for the head and wash off any dirt or hair on the outer surface. Envelope it in a porous cheesecloth game bag that allows air circulation but is finely woven enough to protect against insects and dirt. For a larger animal it may be best to quarter it, skin it, and hang the sections in meat sacks.

8. Carcass cooling begins when the body cavity is opened. Depending on weather conditions, it may take up to 6 hours to adequately cool the carcass. A large animal cools more slowly than a small animal because of the mass involved and the difference in surface area. A squirrel cools in minutes, an elk or moose in hours. Get a large animal carcass off the ground as quickly as possible so air can circulate around it. Use tree limbs, brush, or rocks if needed. The underside of the carcass can spoil quickly lying on the ground.

9. Other than the heart and liver, which you will want to put on ice as soon as possible, don't place warm meat in plastic bags because they will trap heat and accelerate spoilage.

10. If meat is to remain at a hunting camp or in the wild overnight, place it in bags in a shaded area with good air circulation.

11. Protect the meat from rain, and never leave meat submerged in water for an extended period unless it has been cooled first and is in watertight bags.

12. Avoid transporting a carcass out in the open or in the sun. Place it inside a vehicle, covered box, or trailer. In temperatures over 50 degrees Fahrenheit, use bags of ice to cool the carcass during transport.

13. Tag the deer before you load it into your vehicle. If the carcass is too large to drag or carry to your vehicle from where you dress it, such as with a large elk, moose, or antelope, you may have to split or quarter the carcass. Knowing the laws and regulations that apply to these situations will eliminate problems later. Normally you will have a specified period of time in which to register your animal at a designated check station.

14. If you intend to process the carcass yourself, be sure to keep it in temperatures that do not exceed 40 degrees Fahrenheit while it is aging. You can age a big-game carcass for a week before cutting it up; this should improve its tenderness and palatability. If you age the meat, keep the hide on to reduce moisture loss or shrinkage and to avoid discoloration of the meat.

15. If you don't process the carcass yourself, you may be able to make arrangements with a local meat and locker service to do it. Federal and state regulations require that wild game may not be processed in conjunction with domestic animals. Be aware that a wild game carcass must be dressed before it is processed at a licensed facility.

16. All equipment that comes in contact with wild game must be thoroughly cleaned and sanitized.

17. Removal of the tarsal scent glands located on the lower legs of deer is not necessary. They will not contaminate the meat and can be discarded when the legs are removed. Elk do not have tarsal scent glands; moose have small ones, and caribou have large ones.

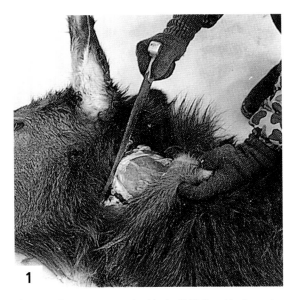

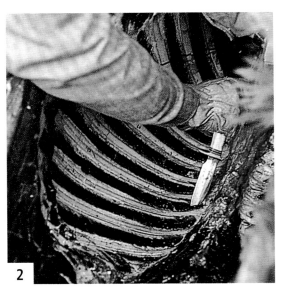

1

If you need to quarter an animal in the field, first skin the neck area before sawing off the head. Skinning the neck first will eliminate the chance of forcing hair into the meat with the saw.

2

After the viscera are removed, cut between the third and fourth ribs, from the backbone to the tips of the ribs. Make your cuts from inside the body.

3

To separate the front half of the carcass from the rear half, use your saw to cut through the backbone after making your first knife cut. A quartered hide is still suitable for tanning.

4

Split the hide along the backbone on both halves; peel it back several inches on each side of the cut to expose the spine for cleaner sawing.

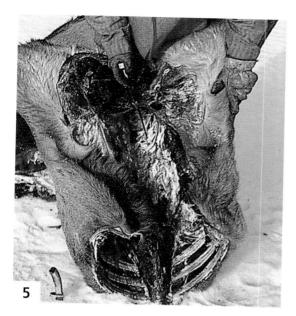

5

Begin sawing lengthwise through the backbone by propping one half against your legs. Be careful to saw down the middle of the spine and not through any of the loin.

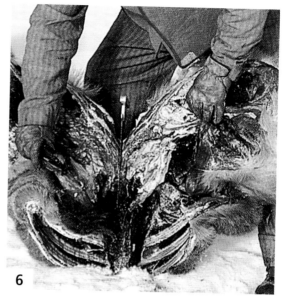

6

Keep the back off the ground as you continue cutting. Gravity will help pull the quarters apart so that your saw doesn't bind, as it would if the carcass were lying on the ground.

7

Quartered elk will look like this. Depending on the animal's size, elk quarters weigh 60 to 125 pounds each; moose quarters weigh up to 225 pounds. Where the law allows, some hunters bone the carcass in the field to reduce weight.

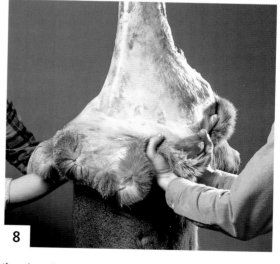

8

If you brought your carcass back whole, you'll need to skin it prior to fabrication. Start with cuts at the inner parts of the hind legs. Peel the hide away, sever the tailbone, and continue peeling with your fist along the back, using your knife only when necessary, until reaching the head, which can be cut off at the atlas joint.

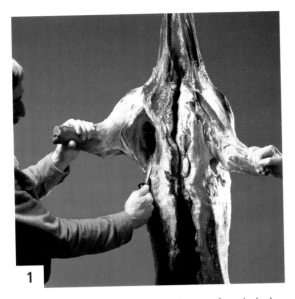

Begin fabrication by pushing the front leg away from the body and cutting between the leg and the rib cage. Continue until you reach the shoulder.

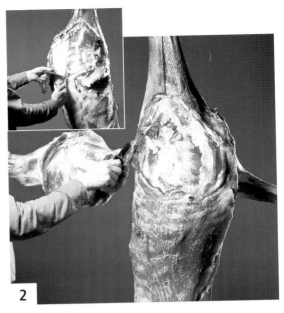

Remove the front leg by cutting between the shoulder blade and the back. Repeat with the other leg. Remove the layer of brisket meat over the ribs (inset). Moose or elk brisket is thick enough to be rolled for corning. Grind thin brisket for burger.

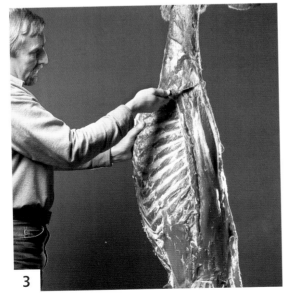

Cut the meat at the base of the neck to begin removing a backstrap. There are two backstraps, one on each side of the spine. They can be butterflied for steaks, cut into roasts, or sliced thinly for sautéing. The lower part, or loin, is the most tender.

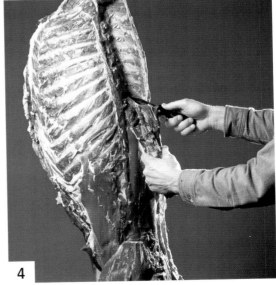

Make two cuts, one along the spine between the shoulder and rump bone and the other along the rib tops. Keep your knife close to the bones, removing as much meat as possible. Cut off this first backstrap at the rump. Repeat on the other side of the spine.

5

Begin cutting one hind leg away, exposing the ball-and-socket joint. Push the leg back to pop the joint apart, then cut through the joint. Work your knife around the tailbone and pelvis until the leg is removed. Repeat with the other leg.

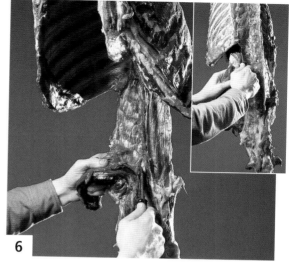

6

Cut the tenderloins from inside the body cavity after trimming the flank meat below the last rib (inset). The flank meat can be ground or cut into thin strips for jerky. Many hunters remove the tenderloins before aging the carcass, to keep them from darkening and dehydrating.

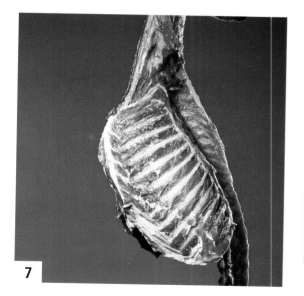

7

If desired, remove the ribs by sawing along the backbone. Cut around the base of the neck and twist the backbone off. Separate the neck and head. Bone the neck to grind for burgers or keep it whole for pot roasting.

8

Trim the ribs by cutting away the ridge of meat and gristle along the bottom. If the ribs are long, saw them in half. Cut ribs into racks of three or four. If you don't want to save the ribs, you can bone the meat between them to grind for burgers or sausage.

continued from page 54

If you plan to mount the head, you'll need to retain enough of the hide for a cape. You can open the skin on the top side of the neck and behind the shoulder to make enough for the cape. Leaving too much skin available for a taxidermist is better than too little.

To remove the head, you should cut at the atlas joint so that it and the cape of skin can be removed in one piece. After the head is removed, you can split the underside of the neck and remove the remaining esophagus, windpipe, and any other part such as the lungs and heart if this has not been done previously. Wipe the inside body cavity with clean paper towels to remove any hair or soil attached to it. After a thorough cleaning, you are ready to cut up the carcass.

If you wish to have the head mounted, you'll need to care for it and the hide before taking it to a taxidermist. To help preserve it, apply salt liberally to the head and rub salt into the skin side of the hide. Leave the salt to absorb for 24 to 48 hours before folding the skin together with the hair side out. Tie it and tag it according to the laws pertaining to your area before delivering it.

If you are skinning a deer or elk that was harvested in a CWD area, or an area known to have produced animals testing positive for CWD, be sure to minimize your handling of brain and spinal tissue. If you remove the antlers, use a saw designated for that purpose only and dispose of the blade. Do not cut through the spinal column except to remove the head. Use a knife designated only for this purpose and set it aside for special cleaning later.

Cutting the Carcass

Before you cut up the carcass, be sure to understand the risk for CWD in the area where you harvested your big-game animal. In areas affected by CWD, you will want to take special care during processing so that you and the meat you cut off the carcass do not come in contact with any spinal or lymph fluids or brain tissue.

In this case, the simplest and safest method after removing the hide is to trim all meat without making any cuts into the skeletal bones or spinal column. This may be inconvenient, but it will eliminate possible contamination. Even if there are no indications of CWD infection, the animal could be a latent CWD carrier.

If you are not in an area where CWD is a risk, proceed to cut up the carcass by using the following general steps:

- Divide the carcass by splitting the aitchbone and sawing down the center of the backbone. Remove the neck (before you split the carcass) if you plan to use the neck for pot roast or neck cuts, and you don't need to keep the head.
- Lay the carcass on its side on a clean table, abdomen-side down, and begin by

Tips

- The shanks, breast, and flank are generally boned and ground into burgers or mixed with pork fat for sausage. The neck slices can also be boned for ground meat and sausage. Venison rib chops, boneless tenderloins, round steaks, and rolled shoulder roasts are the most important cuts.

- Cut steaks to the thickness you like before freezing.

- Trim the neck muscles and meat near the joint for use in stews.

- Wrap the meat in good-quality freezer paper. Double wrap if desired, label, date, and identify package contents.

1

Cut along the back of the leg to remove the top round completely. The top round is excellent when butterflied, rolled, and tied for roasting. You can also cut it into two smaller flat roasts, cubes for kabobs, or slices for sautés.

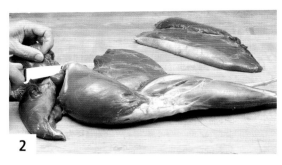

2

Remove the rump portion. Cut the rump off at the top of the hipbone after removing the silverskin and pulling the muscle groups apart with your fingers. A large rump is excellent for roasting; a small one can be cut for steaks, kabobs, or sautés.

3

Cut the bottom round away from the sirloin tip after turning the leg over and separating these two muscle groups with your fingers. Next, carve the sirloin tip away from bone. Sirloin tip makes a choice roast or steaks; bottom round is good for roasting, steaks, or kabobs.

4

Large-diameter steaks can be made from a whole hind leg by cutting across all the muscle groups rather than boning as before. First, remove the rump portion. Cut the leg into 1-inch-thick steaks. As each steak is cut, work around the bone with a fillet knife, then slide the steak over the end of the bone. Continue steaking until you reach the shank.

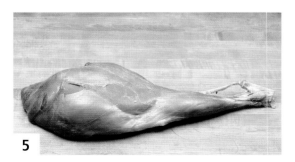

5

The hind leg consists of the sirloin tip, the top and bottom rounds, the eye of the round, a portion of the rump, and the shank. The sirloin, rounds, and rump are tender cuts for roasting or grilling; the shank is tough and best used for ground meat or soups.

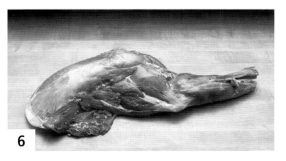

6

A front leg consists of the shoulder, arm, and shank. The meat from the front leg is less tender than that from the hind leg; it is used for pot roasting, stews, jerky, or grinding.

removing the hind legs. You can now split each side into three pieces: hindquarter, ribs, and shoulder. Make your first cut just in front of and close to the hipbone.

- Separate the shoulder from the ribs and loin by cutting between the fourth and fifth ribs.
- Remove the breast or flank by cutting across the ribs about 3 inches from the backbone, from front to back.
- Separate the ribs from the loin by cutting directly behind the last rib.
- Remove the loin strips from both sides of the spine.
- Remove the rump from the leg. Turn the aitchbone upward and make a saw cut parallel to it. Remove the flank with your boning knife.

Cleaning Up

When you have finished boning and cutting up the carcass, dispose of the hide, brain, spinal cord, eyes, spleen, tonsils, bones, and head (if not keeping for mounting) in a landfill or by other means available in your area.

Do not use household knives or utensils for processing wild game that will later be used in your kitchen. After use, thoroughly clean all knives and equipment, as well as the work areas. Soak knives for one hour in a 50/50 solution of household chlorine bleach and water. Disinfect all cutting surfaces with a fresh 50/50 solution. Wipe down the surfaces with disinfectant and disposable towels and let the surfaces dry. Do not use those towels for other purposes: throw them in the trash or burn them.

Bear

Field dressing a bear, regardless of color or habitat, is similar to field dressing a deer, only with a heavier carcass, lower center of gravity, and heavier muscling.

It's not impossible to field dress a bear weighing from 500 to 1,200 pounds by yourself, but most bear hunters prefer hunting with a group.

There are three major considerations before you field dress a bear: making certain the downed bear is dead; having additional people to help you; and tagging the bear before field dressing it.

Field Dressing a Bear

Clear an area around the bear that allows you enough room to work and to move about the carcass. Roll the bear onto its back and spread the legs. You can secure them with rope tied to trees or brush if needed.

Bleed the animal by inserting a knife into the cavity at the base of the throat and making a cut across the jugular vein. Cut a straight line from the jaw to the base of the breastbone to open the hide and expose the windpipe.

Cut along the centerline of the belly from the breastbone to the base of the anus. Cut the hide first and then return and make a cut through the belly muscle, along the same line, using your free hand to lift the skin and muscle away from the internal organs and intestines as you slice. (Some areas require hunters to leave the genitals for sex identification. If this applies, cut around the genitals to preserve them.)

Use an axe, bone saw, or heavy serrated knife to cut through the breastbone to open the chest.

Make a circular cut around the anus and free it from the hide. Draw it out of the pelvic cavity far enough to securely tie it shut with a heavy string before releasing it.

Untie the legs and roll the carcass on its side. Loosen and roll out the stomach and

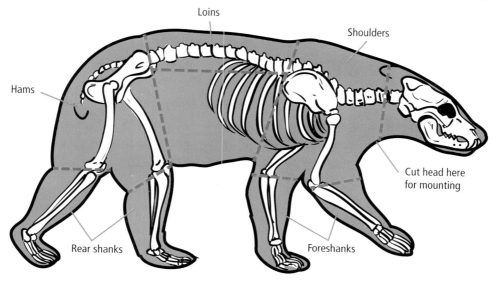

Loins

Shoulders

Hams

Cut head here
for mounting

Rear shanks

Foreshanks

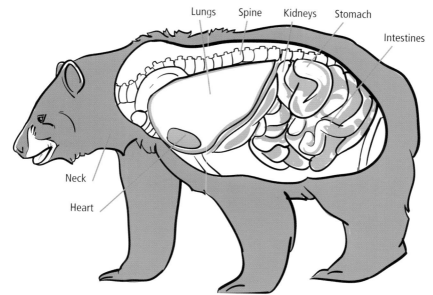

Lungs   Spine   Kidneys   Stomach

Intestines

Neck

Heart

intestines. Examine the liver—discard it if it has spots, cysts, or scarring; this may indicate parasites or disease. If it looks healthy, keep it for sausage making. Place it in a plastic bag and put it on ice as soon as possible.

The diaphragm separates the chest and stomach cavities. Cut around its edge and then split the breastbone. Any parts of the diaphragm that remain can be removed later.

Cut the esophagus near the jaw and pull the lungs, heart, and windpipe toward you and remove them from the body cavity. Cut any remaining tissues that hold it to the inside cavity.

After confirming the bear is dead, you can bleed it by making a cut into the base of the throat and across the jugular vein. Cut a line from the jaw to the base of the breastbone to open the hide and expose the windpipe. Make a centerline cut from breastbone to the base of the anus.

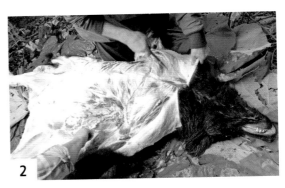

Cut the hide first and peel it back completely before cutting through the belly muscle. Unless required to retain the genital organs, remove them as you slice from the breastbone to the anus. Use your free hand to carefully lift the skin and muscle away from the internal organs and intestines as you cut.

After making a circular cut around the anus to free it from the hide, draw it out of the pelvic cavity far enough to securely tie it shut with heavy string before releasing it. This prevents seepage of the intestinal and fecal materials from contaminating the body cavity.

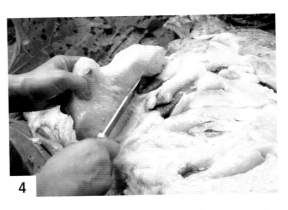

After removing the internal organs and esophagus and wiping the inside clean, you can begin to quarter the bear carcass. Begin by cutting the forelegs from the shoulder by making an incision through the joint, separating the forelegs completely. Remove as much fat as possible—fat becomes jelly-like as it cools, making it difficult to handle the rest of the carcass.

Remove the heart and place it in a bag with the liver and cool it as soon as possible.

Drain any excess blood from the body cavity by rolling the carcass over or hanging it head-up.

Use a clean cloth or paper towels to wipe down the inside of the body cavity. The carcass is now ready to be moved.

Cool down the carcass as quickly as possible.

Cutting the Carcass

Moving a large, heavy bear carcass is a difficult task, especially if it is downed in rough terrain. Most states allow for dividing the carcass up into sections, often no more

5

Cut the breastbone and split the rib cage in half. Remove the tenderloins and fillets along the spine from the bottom of the ribs to just above the hind legs. As you remove the rest of the muscle, run your knife along the edges of the bones, cutting the meat and tendons away. Finish trimming the leg bones before cubing or grinding the meat.

than five, to aid in its removal from the field. The head and neck must remain attached to one of those pieces. In most states you must remove all parts of the bear, except the entrails, from the field.

Two-thirds of the bear muscle will be in the front shoulders. The remaining third is the rear quarters and the loin. If sectioned in the field, cut at the shoulder and pelvic joints first to make the most of your pieces. These can be broken down later after registration and the return to camp.

If you take the whole carcass to your camp, follow these steps:

Skin the hide much as you would a deer, elk, or moose. Remove the feet and peel the skin away from the underlayer of fat as you slice. Once you have removed the hide, cut and shave away as much of the fat covering the carcass as possible, down to the red meat. This layer will have the consistency of jelly, while the fat layer inside the body cavity will be more like beef tallow.

Cut through the breastbone with a saw to split the rib cage in half. Remove the

Tips

1. Bear meat can be tough and strong smelling, and it dries out easily during cooking. It's usually made into ground meat or stew meat.

2. It may be preferable to cut off a little meat rather than leave excess fat on the carcass. The gelatinous fat can affect the meat quality and cause it to quickly go rancid.

3. Hunters are asked not to shoot color-tagged or collared bears used for research, although it is not illegal to do so.

4. Freeze any bear meat that you will not process immediately. Seal tightly to prevent moisture loss.

5. You will be required to provide a carcass tissue sample at the time of registration, if it is requested. Tooth and rib samples are now being requested in most bear-hunting states: one upper premolar tooth and a 2-inch-long piece of rib cut near the backbone. Check the state regulations where you hunt.

6. Bears are known to harbor trichinosis, which can damage your heart, kidneys, and muscles if ingested from undercooked meat. When cooking bear meat, be sure it attains a minimal internal temperature of 160 degrees Fahrenheit to kill larval cysts. Microwaving may not succeed in making the meat safe because of uneven heating.

7. At outside temperatures of 40 degrees Fahrenheit, you have about 12 hours to get the meat to a cooler to keep it from spoiling. At 60 degrees Fahrenheit, you have about 3 hours.

8. Use the cube meat for grinding, and slice the hindquarters into top-round and bottom-round roasts.

tenderloins or fillets located along the spine from the bottom of the rib cage to just before the hind legs. Set them aside.

Insert your knife just under the muscle on the outside of the rib cage and slice toward the spine, peeling it from the ribs.

Remove the meat from the front and rear legs by slicing your knife into the muscle and running it alongside the edges of the bones. Hold out the limbs and cut the meat and tendons away from the shoulder and pelvis joints, then saw off each limb at the exposed joint. Lay them aside for trimming.

Trim the remaining muscle from all areas of the carcass where it remains.

Trim the leg bones of all muscle.

Cube the meat or grind it for making sausage or hamburger patties.

Bighorn Sheep

Bighorn sheep are a very specialized big-game animal hunted only by permits during a restricted season. Only a few states allow their hunting. In states that do, such as North Dakota, only about three licenses are issued each year, resulting in lotteries or auctions to fill them. In the United States, the permit prices can reach into the tens of thousands of dollars.

If you secure a license and bag a bighorn sheep, it can be processed in much the same way you would handle a deer, elk, or moose. However, you need to be careful in handling the head, horns, and pelt because of their trophy value. The major considerations include minimizing damage to the pelt after your prize hits the ground, avoiding breakage of the horns during transport from the field to your vehicle, and salting the cape after removing it from the body to keep it from spoiling.

Feral Pigs

Feral pigs are rapidly becoming established throughout the United States. One estimate suggests that wild breeding populations of feral pigs are now present in at least thirty-five states. There is no specific license for hunting wild pigs, although in states that require licenses they are classified as game animals. Some states, such as Wisconsin, require only a small-game license and the permission of the landowner where you intend to hunt. Feral pigs are considered unprotected wild animals in that state, with no closed season, harvest limit, or protection of females.

The average wild pig can range from 100 to 450 pounds, with males often heavier than females, but not necessarily. Trophy-size feral pigs can stand 3 feet tall, 6 feet long, and weigh 500 pounds. An adult develops a scruffy mane covered with stiff bristles.

Although feral pigs often scurry when approached, they can be very dangerous if they attack. Males have four continually growing tusks that can be extremely sharp. The upper tusks can be 3 to 5 inches long and curl up and out along the sides of the mouth. The lower canines also turn out and curve back toward the eyes. Females don't have tusks, but do have sharp canines. Males often develop a thick, tough skin of cartilage and scar tissue around their shoulders from dominance fighting.

Field Dressing

Dressing a feral pig is very similar to dressing domestic swine. Because they can be hunted year round in some states, temperature may be one of the biggest challenges in field dressing. After you have killed a feral pig and confirmed it is dead, you can begin dressing it.

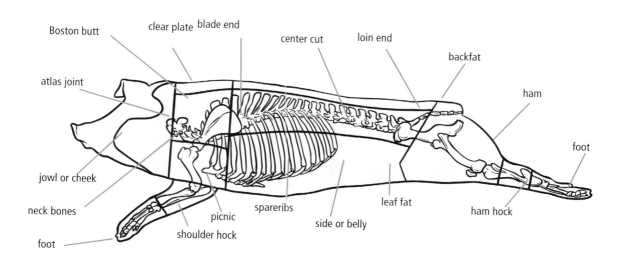

The wild pig carcass anatomy in relation to the primal cuts.

Stick your knife into the neck and cut the jugular veins to allow it to bleed. A pig will have a lot of blood and removing it will help preserve the quality of the meat.

After the bleeding has stopped, roll the pig on its back if possible. Otherwise, tie the legs to trees or brush to stabilize it for opening the body cavity.

Cut along the centerline of the belly from breastbone to the base of the tail. Make a cut through the belly muscle just posterior to the breastbone and use your free hand to lift the skin and muscle away from the internal organs and intestines as you slice toward the anus. Stop when you reach the aitchbone, which forms the joints in the pelvis.

Make a circular cut around the anus and free it from the skin. Draw it out of the pelvic cavity far enough to securely tie it shut with a heavy string. If it is a male, you will need to remove the penis and testicles. Some find these delicacies; others discard them.

Cut from the sternum (breastbone) up the neck to the base of the jaw. Don't cut

Steps for Determining Death in Big Game Animals

1. Cautiously approach the downed animal.

2. Look and listen for breathing or muscle movements.

3. If possible, and if you're unsure it's dead, prod the carcass with a long stick to see if there's a reaction.

4. Be vigilant until you're assured the animal is dead.

the windpipe yet, but this cut will expose the windpipe and allow you to remove as much of it as possible in just a few moments.

Untie and lay the carcass on its side. Loosen and roll out the stomach and intestines. If it is a pregnant female, you will have to decide whether to keep the unborn piglets. They will no longer be alive at this stage; they can be left with the entrails and scavenged.

Examine the liver. If it has spots, cysts, or scarring that may indicate parasites or disease, discard it. If it looks healthy, place it in a plastic bag and put it on ice as soon as possible.

The diaphragm separates the chest and stomach cavities. Cut around its edge and

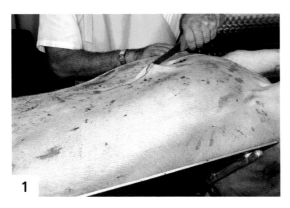

Feral pigs are dressed similarly to domestic swine, so the same steps can be used for both. Begin by making a vertical cut, knife blade out, down the midline of the carcass from the jowl to the pelvis. Avoid cutting through the abdominal wall.

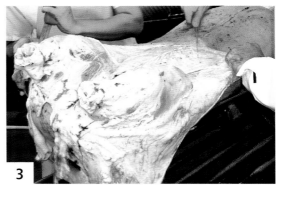

Begin the skinning process by pulling the skin up and away from the carcass; make slow, sweeping motions between the skin and body with your skinning knife. Applying an outward pressure with your knife blade will help avoid cutting into the carcass.

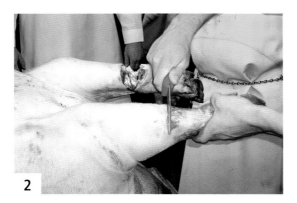

Remove the front feet by cutting at a point just below the back of the knee joint (severing the tendons will allow you to break the joint forward). Cut completely through the exposed joint to sever the foot. Do the same with the rear feet.

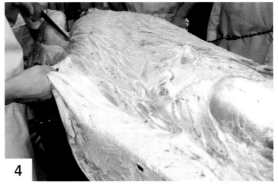

As you work the length of the carcass, avoid contaminating it with hair or dirt from the skin. Have clean water nearby to wash your free hand. Also, wash your knife frequently. If the carcass is on its back, you will need to turn it or raise it to finish removing the skin. Be sure the surface where you lay the partially skinned carcass is clean.

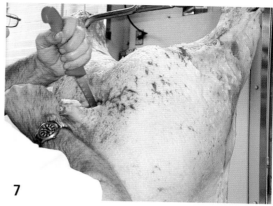

5

Use a clean chain, rope, or gambrel to lift the carcass to allow easier removal of the remaining skin. To use a gambrel, make a slit in front of the rear leg bones without cutting the tendons. Place the gambrel points in the slits and raise the carcass. The tendons are strong enough to hold the heavy carcass suspended if they haven't been cut.

7

Begin evisceration by cutting around the anus to loosen the muscles holding it. Tie the anus shut.

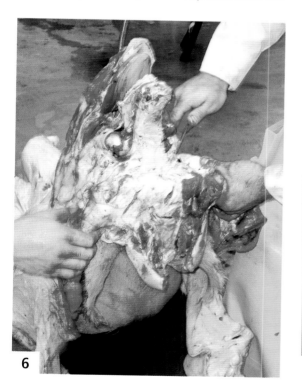

6

The head can be removed before skinning or after the carcass is raised. If left until skinning is finished, remove it by making a cut behind the ears between the axis joint (the first cervical vertebrae) and the atlas joint. Cut around the lower jaw to completely sever the head. Finish by removing the cheek muscles, tongue, and fat.

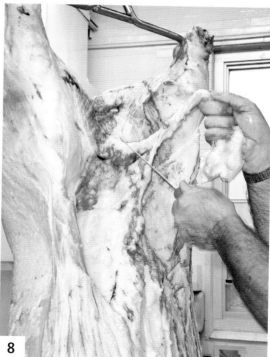

8

A male pig will have the penis, testicles, and sheath still intact. These should be removed like the skin by cutting upward toward the anus until they are severed. They can then be removed from where they are attached at the aitchbone.

then split the breastbone. Any parts of the diaphragm that remain can be removed later.

Cut the esophagus near the jaw and pull the lungs, heart, and windpipe toward you and remove them from the body cavity. Cut any remaining tissues that hold them to the inside cavity.

Remove the heart, place it in a bag, and cool it as soon as possible.

Drain any excess blood from the body cavity by rolling the carcass over. Use a clean cloth or paper towels to wipe down the inside of the body cavity. The carcass is now ready to be moved.

Cutting the Carcass

After you have returned home, you should begin cutting up the carcass. It will be easier to skin it, split it in half, and deconstruct its parts if you hang it from a gambrel hooked to a block and tackle or other means of getting it up in the air. The steps mentioned below assume that the carcass is safely suspended with its head about 6 inches or more off the floor.

Remove the head first. It gets it out of the way and aids in cooling the carcass. It also permits any residual blood to drain.

Begin with a cut above the ears at the first joint of the backbone and then move across the back of the neck. When you reach the windpipe and throat, cut through them and the head will drop. Don't slice the head off completely yet.

Pull down on the ears and continue your cut around them to the eyes and then toward the point of the jawbone. When you slice through the last part of the skin at the end of the jaw, the head will come free but the jowls will still be attached to the face. Wash the head and trim the face meat when you can.

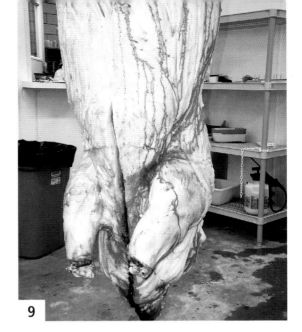

9

The sternum can be split while the carcass is on its back or after it has been lifted. These positions allow access to the thoracic cavity once the abdominal wall is opened.

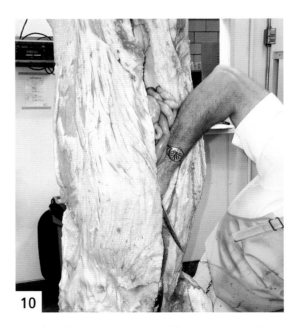

10

Open the abdomen by starting at a midline point at the pelvis. Once you carefully slice an opening large enough to insert your hand and knife, turn the blade outward while holding the heel with your hand on the inside. Use your hand to hold back the intestines as you slice down the midline in a smooth, continuous motion until reaching the opening of the thoracic cavity.

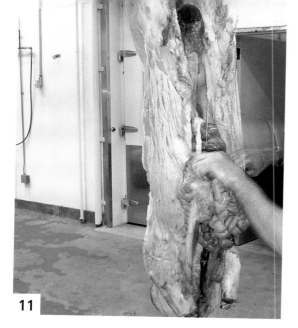

11

As you slice down, the viscera will fall down and out, but because they are held by connective tissue, they will not come out completely. Sever the connective tissues to allow the intestines and internal organs to fall free from the body cavity. Have a tub placed under the carcass before making this cut, to catch the viscera.

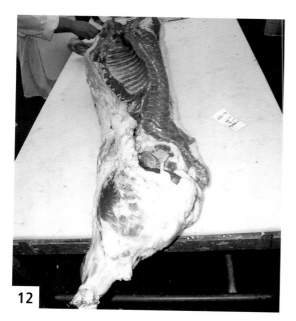

12

To begin fabrication, place one carcass side on a clean table. There are four major cuts to separate the ham, shoulder, loin, and belly. To remove the ham, make a cut perpendicular to the leg bone from 1/2 to 2 1/2 inches anterior to the aitchbone.

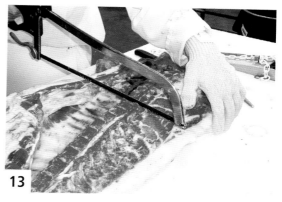

13

Separate the shoulder from the loin by sawing between the second and third rib, perpendicular to the back. This will separate the Boston butt and picnic shoulder from the belly and loin.

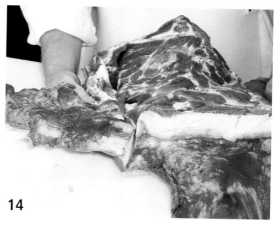

14

To remove the jowl, start cutting at the fat collar immediately above the foreshank and continue straight across the top part of the shoulder. This should be trimmed of muscle and the fat set aside for sausage making.

Split the aitchbone. This will separate the hips and make the cut down the spine easier. Sever the aitchbone with the heel of your heavy blade or with a meat saw. Use the saw to slice straight down the center of the loin areas until you reach the shoulders and separate the carcass into halves.

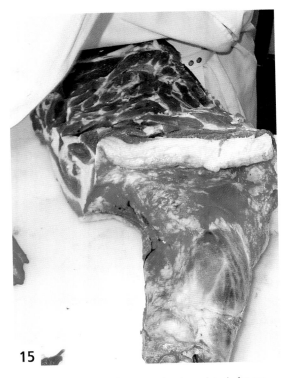

15

After removing the jowl, remove the clear plate (a fat cut much like the backfat) from the shoulder. The shoulder is composed of two wholesale cuts: the Boston butt and the picnic shoulder.

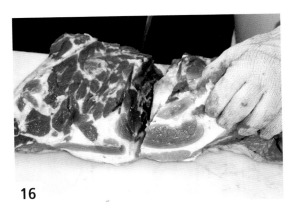

16

Separate the Boston butt and picnic shoulder by cutting 1 inch below the shoulder blade toward the leg and parallel with the sternum. Make the first cut with a knife, then continue with a saw to sever the blade bone. Trim excess fat down to 1/4 inch or less when making your cuts.

17

Separate the loin from the side (belly) by making a long, straight cut from the first rib (anterior) close to the backbone to the ham end, where the cut will be next to and closely follow the tenderloin. Avoid cutting into or scoring the tenderloin.

18

The whole pork loin is comprised of a blade section, a center section, and a sirloin section. The whole loin can be cut into bone-in pork chops or roasts, or if preferred, the bones can be removed to make boneless pork chops or loin roasts.

19

After the belly is separated from the loin, remove the spareribs. Be sure to trim out all bone and cartilage from the belly, as this is not desirable in bacon.

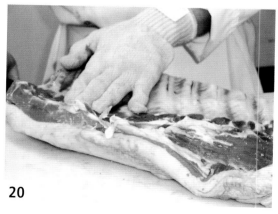

20

Bacon is made from the belly after the spare ribs have been removed. Square up the belly, trim the fat, and remove any rudimentary mammary glands and teat lines. The meat is now ready for smoking and curing.

Tips

1. If using a meat saw to make cuts on the carcass, scrape the bone dust from the cuts after sawing. This mixture of small bone particles and meat tissue can create a "crunchy" texture. Cleaning it off reduces the chances of creating a bacterial haven.

2. The hams may be too big for packaging or cooking. The bone can be trimmed out and the ham cut into smaller pieces. Bone-in roasts can be made. Also, by cutting across the face of the ham, you can make ham steaks.

3. The shoulder can be kept whole, cured, smoked, or divided into two parts. The shoulder includes the foreshank, which is high in connective tissue.

4. Wild boar meat is a lean meat with a rich, sweet, nutty flavor. Many cuts of wild boar can be cooked like domestic pork. It is low in fat, so it can be slow cooked, or seared and roasted quickly over high heat.

5. The most common use for the belly is to cure and smoke it for bacon. Most bellies are skinned before being cured and smoked.

6. Spareribs may also be cured and smoked but can also be used fresh and barbecued.

Take one side and lay it on a clean table. Remove the front and rear foot at the hock and knee. These can be trimmed later.

Remove the ham. Begin with a cut at a point about 2 1/2 inches in front of the tip of the aitchbone and then cut through the fifth and sixth lumbar vertebrae. Use a knife to finish after sawing through the bone. Trim off most of the fat, but leave about 1/4 inch on the whole ham.

Saw off the shoulder at the third rib, counting from the neck. The Boston butt and picnic shoulder are two primal cuts from the shoulder.

The clear plate is a fat cut much like backfat. Remove it from the top part of the shoulder by trimming close to the Boston butt. This large piece of fat can be discarded or rendered.

Divide the shoulder into picnic and Boston butt by cutting about 1 inch below the shoulder blade and parallel with the breast.

Remove the loin, which is the most tender cut in the pig. Separate it from the shoulder by sawing across the third rib. To separate the loin from the ribs, make a straight cut from a point close to the lower edge of the backbone at the shoulder to a point just below the tenderloin muscle from which the ham was cut. The spareribs and belly are now separated from the loin. You can trim the ribs of meat for stews or ground pork.

The belly or side is left. This will contain parts of the ribs, which must be trimmed. Use a straight knife to cut between the backfat and the belly to remove the ribs.

With the spareribs removed, you can slice the belly or side into strips for bacon. Square up the belly by trimming the outside parts evenly to remove any rudimentary mammary glands and teat lines that remain.

Alligator

Alligators are only native to the United States and China. They have been around for about 150 million years and are among the few animals to have been saved from the endangered species list. Alligator populations have grown exponentially in states such as Alabama, Georgia, and Louisiana due to protective legislation. They can be legally hunted by landowners on their own property, or by licensed residents with permission from the landowner of the property on which they're hunting. Licenses for hunting alligators on public lands are administered through a lottery program.

The daily or season limit is equal to the number of alligator tags that a licensed alligator hunter possesses. The limit is set by state fisheries and wildlife departments and is dependent upon several factors, including the estimated alligator population. A yearly lottery program is used for hunters who don't own private land or have permission to hunt on private land. There are no size restrictions on wild alligators taken during the general open season. An adult American alligator can reach a weight of 800 pounds and a length of 13 feet.

Skinning is the first step in processing an alligator carcass. The steps below will summarize the general concept of skinning, but remember that the hide is valuable. If you are inexperienced, have someone with experience do the skinning. Minor knife cuts, holes, and poor skin preparation can dramatically decrease an alligator hide's value.

Alligators have body armor. There are bony plates inside the skin called scutes that make the skin very hard to penetrate. Inside each little spike on the alligator's back is a piece of bone that helps protect it from attack. These horny scales are arranged in rows, parallel to the body.

Set the alligator on a sturdy table in good light. Begin with a cut along the sides between the first and second row of scutes on the back.

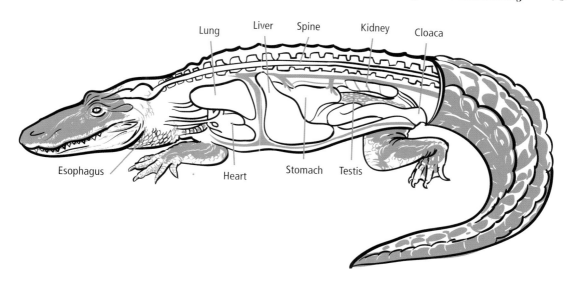

Lung   Liver   Spine   Kidney   Cloaca

Esophagus   Heart   Stomach   Testis

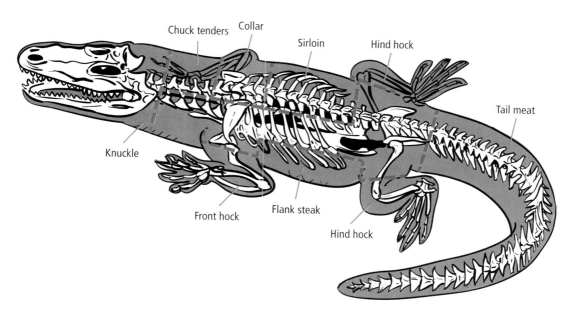

Chuck tenders   Collar   Sirloin   Hind hock

Tail meat

Knuckle

Front hock   Flank steak   Hind hock

Alligators have a very complex muscle structure. The two main muscle contributors are in the jaw and the tail, which contains the choicest cut of white meat. The tenderloin comes from a cylindrical tube inside the tail. Although there is meat in the body midsection, it has a stronger taste and slightly tougher texture (similar to a pork shoulder) because of the muscle activity. Meat can also be found in the feet.

Tips

1. Once skin is scraped and cleaned it must be salted. Salt removes moisture and helps cure the skin. Rub a fine-grade salt into all parts of the skin.

2. Use dull scrapers on the skin to avoid cutting or tearing it as you remove the fat and muscle left on it.

3. The choice cuts of the alligator are the tail and the jaw. Body and leg meat can be used in special recipes and mixed with pork and spices.

4. Meat from the legs, ribs, and midsection of the body is more strongly flavored when compared to alligator tail meat, and is said to taste somewhat similar to pork shoulder.

5. Some enjoy the meat found in the feet, sometimes called alligator wings. The flavor and texture resembles frogs' legs.

6. Alligator meat is extremely low in cholesterol and high in iron.

Make a straight cut through the largest scales from the body along the top of each leg. Make a circle cut around each foot at the wrist or ankle.

Cut a line on the tail just below the top row of tail scutes. When the cut reaches the single row of tail scutes midway along the tail, cut through the base to the end of the tail. Skin the tail completely along the sides.

Skin the body section with the front legs and adjacent side skin. Slowly cut the skin away from the front legs and side of body. You may need to pull on some upper leg portions. Continue until you finish skinning the rest of the carcass on top, leaving the belly portion.

Turn the alligator on its side after you finish skinning the sides and legs. Make outline cuts along the lower jawbone.

Pull on the jaw muscle to tighten the flesh, which will allow for easier skinning. After the skin is cut from the lower jaw and neck, you can skin down the belly.

Cut carefully around the anus to avoid tearing the skin if pulled. You can pull and cut skin from the remaining tail section. The skin should now be free of the carcass. Be sure to scrape all meat and fat off the skin until the hide is white in appearance.

Wash the skin in clean, fresh water to remove blood and other fluids.

Hang the skin in a shaded area and allow it to drain.

Trim the fat and muscle. The tenderloin comes from a cylindrical tube inside the tail and runs next to the tailbone and spinal column. It is the most tender of cuts. The alligator tail is a lean white meat that is firm and light-grained, with a mild flavor.

Roasting Big Game

The two basic ways to roast big game are with dry and moist heat. Dry-heat roasting, which can use high or low temperatures, is for tender cuts of meat. Moist-heat roasting, which uses low temperatures, is for less tender cuts. The most common method of moist-heat roasting is braising, which includes pot roasting.

Use only prime roasts—such as top round, sirloin tip, backstrap, and rump roasts—for dry-heat, high-temperature cooking. Tenderloins from moose, elk, or deer may be used; typically they do not need long, slow cooking because they are naturally tender.

High-temperature cooking requires a hot oven (between 400 degrees Fahrenheit and 450 degrees Fahrenheit), but roasts should only be cooked to rare or medium; well-done cooking will dry them out and cause shrinkage. Low-temperature roasting can be used for prime cuts too. This involves using a slow oven (300 degrees Fahrenheit to 325 degrees Fahrenheit). Low heat allows for roasts to be cooked rare, medium, or well-done. Use a meat thermometer to check for doneness when roasting with dry heat.

Internal Temperature of Meat at Various Degrees of Doneness

Degree of Doneness	Internal Temperature (F)
Rare	130° to 135°
Medium-rare	135° to 140°
Medium	140° to 145°
Medium-well	150° to 155°
Well-done	155° to 160°

Big-Game Substitution Guide

Although there are differences in flavors, texture, and fat content among the meats from the various hoofed big-game species, you can successfully substitute them for deer in a recipe, keeping in mind the tenderness of the specified cut and that of the substitute. The following chart shows the various big-game cuts you can substitute for the most common deer cuts.

Deer Cut	Tenderness	Substitute	Cooking Method
Tenderloin (Whole)	Very Tender	Tenderloin Portion from Moose, Elk, or Caribou Loin Portion from Caribou, Deer or Antelope	Oven Roast, Grill
Loin (Portion)	Tender	Loin Portion from Moose, Elk, or Caribou Tenderloin (Whole) from Moose, Elk, or Caribou	Oven Roast, Broil, Grill, Pan-Broil, Panfry
Loin Steak	Tender	Loin Steak from Moose, Elk, or Caribou Tenderloin from Moose, Elk, Caribou, Deer, or Antelope	Broil, Grill, Pan-Broil, Panfry
Loin Chop	Tender	Loin Chop from Any Big-Game Animal	Broil, Grill, Pan-Broil, Panfry
Rump Roast	Intermediate Tender	Rump Roast from Any Big-Game Animal Deer Sirloin Tip Rolled, Tied Bottom Round from Deer or Antelope Eye of Round from Moose, Elk, or Caribou	Oven Roast, Grill, Braise
Round Steak	Intermediate	Round Steak from Any Big-Game Animal Sirloin Steak from Any Big-Game Animal Loin Chop from Moose, Elk, Caribou, Deer, or Antelope	Broil, Grill, Pan-Broil, Panfry, Stir-Fry (Strips)
Boneless Rolled Shoulder Roast	Less Tender	Boneless Rolled Shoulder Roast from Any Big-Game Animal Rolled Rib Roast from Moose, Elk, or Caribou	Braise
Bone-In Chuck Roast	Less Tender	Bone-In Chuck Roast from Any Big-Game Animal Blade Pot Roast from Moose, Elk, or Caribou	Braise

Venison and Beans

1/2 lb. ground deer, antelope, elk,
    or moose
6 slices bacon, chopped
1 medium onion, chopped
16 oz. (1 can) pork and beans
16 oz. (1 can) kidney beans, drained
16 oz. (1 can) butter beans, drained

1/3 c. brown sugar
1 c. ketchup
2 tbsp. vinegar
1 tbsp. Worcestershire sauce
1/2 tsp. salt
1/4 tsp. prepared mustard

Heat oven to 350°F. Cook bacon until crisp. Remove with slotted spoon; set aside. Add meat and onion to pan with 1 tablespoon bacon fat. Cook over medium heat, stirring occasionally, until meat is no longer pink and onion is tender. Add reserved bacon and remaining ingredients to pan; mix well. Cook and bake until bubbly around edges, about 45 minutes. Serves 8 to 10.

Venison Meatloaf

2 lbs. ground deer, antelope, elk,
    or moose
2 c. soft breadcrumbs
1/2 c. beef broth or venison stock
1/2 c. chopped onion
2 eggs, slightly beaten
1 tsp. salt
1/2 tsp. Worcestershire sauce

1/4 tsp. sugar
1/4 tsp. celery salt
1/4 tsp. dried crushed sage leaves
1/4 tsp. dried oregano leaves
1/4 tsp. pepper
2 small tomatoes, peeled, halved,
    and seeded

Heat oven to 325°F; grease 9x5-inch loaf pan; set aside. In large mixing bowl, combine all ingredients except tomatoes; mix well. Pat half of meat mixture into prepared pan. Arrange tomatoes on meat mixture, leaving 1/2 inch around edges of pan. Spread remaining meat mixture over tomatoes, pressing well around edges to seal. Bake until well browned, about 1 1/2 hours. Let stand 10 minutes. Remove to serving platter. Serves 6 to 8.

Venison Steak

3 lbs. venison steak
Sliced onions
1 c. tomato soup
1 tbsp. vinegar

1 tbsp. Worcestershire sauce
2 tbsp. salt
1 tbsp. brown sugar
1/2 c. water

Fry steak until well done. Cover steak with onions; simmer for 1 hour. Mix soup with vinegar, Worcestershire sauce, salt, brown sugar, and water. Pour over steak and onions. Bake at 350°F for 1 hour. Add more water if needed. Serves 8.

Fillet of Venison, Moose, Antelope, or Elk

1 whole tenderloin, 1 to 3 lbs.
1 to 2 tbsp. butter or margarine
1 tbsp. olive oil or vegetable oil

Salt and freshly ground black
    pepper

Remove all surface fat and silver skin from tenderloin. Slice across grain into fillets, 1 inch thick. In medium skillet, melt butter in oil over medium-low heat. Add fillets; cook to desired doneness over medium-high heat, turning once. Salt and pepper to taste. Serves 2 to 3.

Venison Breakfast Sausage

1 lb. trimmed deer, antelope, elk,
    or moose meat
6 oz. lean bacon ends or slab
    bacon

3/4 tsp. salt
1 tsp. dried crushed sage leaves
1/2 tsp. ground ginger
1/4 tsp. pepper

Cut meat and bacon into 3/4-inch cubes. Place in medium mixing bowl. In small bowl, mix salt, sage, ginger, and pepper. Sprinkle over meat; mix well. Chop or grind to desired texture. Shape into thin patties and fry over medium heat until browned and cooked through, turning once. Sausage can also be frozen uncooked.

Roast Leg of Venison

Leg of venison	Salt and pepper
1/4 c. fat salt pork	Flour

Wipe carefully and remove dry skin. Lard the lean side of the leg with strips of pork. Soften fat, rub it over the meat, and coat with salt, pepper, and flour. Lay the leg on rack of roaster, sprinkling bottom of pan with flour. Roast uncovered at 300°F, allowing 20 to 22 minutes per pound. When flour in the bottom of pan is browned, add boiling water to cover bottom. Baste venison frequently, renewing water in pan as often as necessary. Serve with gravy made from the juices in the bottom of the pan. Always serve venison with a tart jelly like currant, wild grape, or plum. Allow 1/2 pound per person.

Big-Game Baked Round Steak

2 to 3 lbs. boneless deer, antelope, elk, or moose round steak, 1-inch thick	2 to 3 tbsp. olive oil or vegetable oil
	3 tbsp. finely chopped onion
	Brown sugar
1/2 c. flour	Ketchup
2 tsp. salt	Dried basil leaves
1/4 tsp. pepper	1 tbsp. butter or margarine, cut up
1 to 2 tbsp. butter or margarine	1/4 c. venison stock or beef broth

Heat oven to 350°F. Trim meat; cut into serving-size pieces. Pound to 1/2-inch thickness with meat mallet. On a sheep of waxed paper, mix flour, salt, and pepper. Coat steaks on both sides in flour mixture. In large skillet, melt 1 tablespoon butter in 2 tablespoons oil over medium-high heat. Add coated steaks; brown on both sides. Arrange browned steaks in baking pan. Sprinkle with onion. Top each steak with 1 teaspoon brown sugar and 1 teaspoon ketchup. Sprinkle lightly with basil. Dot with 1 tablespoon butter. Add stock to drippings in skillet. Cook over medium heat for about 1 minute, stirring to loosen any browned bits. Add to baking pan. Cover with aluminum foil. Bake for 45 minutes. Remove foil; add water or stock to pan if dry. Bake until browned on top, about 15 minutes longer. Serves 6 to 8.

Moose Roast

3 lbs. moose meat
1 package (1oz.) onion soup mix
1 can (11oz.) golden mushroom soup

1 can (11oz.) water
1 c. sherry

Trim all fat and tallow from roast. Place in roaster; cover with all other ingredients. Roast, covered, 20 minutes per pound at 325°F. Baste occasionally. Gradually add 1 cup sherry during bastings.

Bear Stew

1 1/2 to 2 lbs. bear stew meat
1/4 c. flour
1 tsp. dried marjoram leaves
1 tsp. salt
1/8 tsp. pepper
2 tbsp. vegetable oil
16 oz. (1 can) whole tomatoes,
    undrained
1 c. water

1/4 c. white wine or water
1 tbsp. vinegar
1 medium onion, cut in half
    lengthwise and thinly sliced
1/2 c. chopped celery
2 cloves garlic, minced
1 bay leaf
2 medium baking potatoes

Remove all fat and silver skin from meat. Cut into 1-inch pieces. Combine flour, marjoram, salt, and pepper; shake to mix. Dip pieces in mixture, coating all sides. In large saucepan, heat oil over medium-high heat until hot. Add meat and flour mixture. Brown, stirring occasionally. Add remaining ingredients except potatoes; mix well. Heat to boiling. Reduce heat; cover. Simmer 1 hour, stirring occasionally.

Cut potatoes into 1-inch pieces. Add to saucepan. Heat to boiling. Reduce heat; cover. Simmer until meat and potatoes are tender, about 1 hour, stirring occasionally. Discard bay leaf before serving. Serves 4 to 6.

Peppered Antelope Roast

**3 to 5 lbs. boneless rolled antelope
or deer top round roast
2 medium cloves**

**Vegetable oil
Cracked black pepper
8 to 10 slices bacon**

Heat oven to 325°F. Cut each garlic clove into four or five slivers. Make eight or ten shallow slits in roast and insert a garlic sliver into each slit. Place roast on rack in roasting pan; brush with oil. Sprinkle pepper over roast. Cover roast with bacon slices. Roast to desired doneness, 22 to 32 minutes per pound; remove roast when temperature is 5 degrees less than desired. Allow meat to rest for 10 to 15 minutes before carving. Serves 2 to 4 per pound. You can substitute a deer or small elk sirloin tip, or deer, elk, or moose backstrap or rump roast.

Elk Tenderloin Sauté

**1 1/2 lbs. elk tenderloin, thinly sliced
2 c. water
1 tsp. salt
1/2 lb. fresh pearl onions (about 1 1/2 c.)
1/4 c. flour
1/2 tsp. salt
1/4 tsp. pepper
2 tbsp. butter or margarine
2 tbsp. vegetable oil
1 3/4 c. beef broth**

**16 oz. (1 can) whole tomatoes, cut up
and drained
1/2 c. burgundy
1/4 c. tomato paste
1 tsp. Worcestershire sauce
1/4 tsp. dried thyme leaves
1 or 2 cloves garlic, minced
2 bay leaves
1/2 lb. fresh mushrooms, cut into halves
Hot cooked rice or noodles**

Heat water and 1 teaspoon salt in small saucepan to boiling. Add onions. Return to boiling. Reduce heat; cover. Simmer onions 15 minutes or until tender. Drain and rinse under cold water. Set aside.

Combine flour, 1/2 teaspoon salt, and pepper; mix. Add elk slices and coat all sides. In large skillet, melt butter in oil over medium heat. Add elk slices, then cook over medium-high heat until browned but still rare, stirring occasionally. Remove with slotted spoon; set aside. Add remaining ingredients except mushrooms and rice to cooking liquid in skillet; mix well. Add mushrooms and reserved onions. Heat to boiling. Reduce heat; cover. Simmer 10 minutes. Stir in elk slices. Cook, uncovered, over medium-heat until slightly thickened, about 5 minutes. Discard bay leaves before serving over rice or noodles. Serves 4 to 6.

Chapter 4

SMALL-GAME BUTCHERING

❖

Hunters typically refer to small game animals as those not raised in domestic settings. There are a number of wild species that can be harvested for home use, including rabbits, hares, raccoons, opossums, squirrels, muskrats, beavers, groundhogs (woodchucks), turtles, frogs, and snakes. These can be found in many different ecosystems, including grasslands, forests or woodlands, and wetlands. These diverse locations can add to the challenges and rewards of a successful harvest.

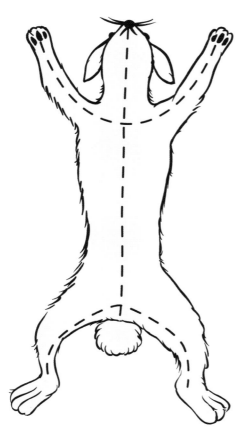

Small furred game can be skinned in one of two methods: open or cased skin. The cut marks on the rabbit show an open-pelt method.

Hunting in grasslands can be dramatic, with grouse unexpectedly exploding from the cover and wily pheasants moving silently through it. Hunters in forests or woodlands must mimic the elusiveness as the animals they hunt, from chattering squirrels that become silent and blend into the foliage to bears and deer that run at the faintest scent. Wetland birds and animals, such as muskrats or beavers, have the edge over hunters because they are better adapted to their surroundings than humans.

1

To skin a rabbit or hare by the open-pelt method, start by pinching the hide up and away from the middle of the rabbit's spine. Slit the hide from the spine down the sides, being careful not to cut the meat. When handling rabbits, wear rubber gloves not only while dressing and skinning, but also during all stages of kitchen preparation to avoid contracting any bacterial disease from the carcasses.

2

Grasp the hide with both hands and pull in opposite directions. Keep pulling until all the legs are skinned up to the feet, then cut off the head, feet, and tail. If you did not field dress the rabbit before skinning, slit the underside from the vent to the neck and remove all internal organs. Check the liver for white spots, which could indicate disease.

3

Clean the body cavity, removing any material left after dressing. Rinse briefly under running water and pat dry. Squirrels can also be skinned this way, but not as easily.

4

To portion a rabbit, begin by cutting into the rear leg at a point near the backbone. When you come to the leg bone, stop cutting. This portioning method works with squirrels, rabbits, hares, and raccoons.

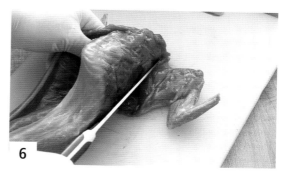

6

Remove the front legs by cutting close to the rib cage and behind the shoulder blades—the legs come off more easily this way because you don't cut through joints. On a large animal, cut each leg in two at the elbow. The ribs contain very little meat, but they can be used for soup stock.

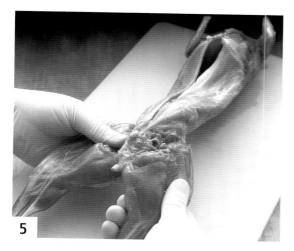

5

Bend the leg back to pop the ball-and-socket joint. Cut through the joint to remove the leg. Repeat with the other leg. On a large rabbit, hare, or raccoon, each rear leg can be split in two at the knee. The rear legs are the meatiest pieces, followed by the saddle or loin portion.

7

Cut the back into two or three pieces, depending on the animal's size. If you choose, remove the rib cage. When portioning a raccoon or large hare, split the back along the spine to make four to six pieces.

Each of these ecosystems offers challenges, and that's one reason hunters are drawn back to the wild time and again.

Rabbits/Snowshoe Hares

Wild rabbits and hares have darker meat than domestic rabbits, largely due to diet and exercise. They are susceptible to a communicable disease known as tularemia, or rabbit fever. This is a very infectious disease that can be transmitted from one rabbit to another by lice or ticks, or to humans by handling the flesh of an infected animal, inhaling the bacteria during the skinning

Rabbit Tips

- It is illegal to hunt rabbits out of season; check local laws.

- Hunt rabbits when they're most active: in early morning and at sunset.

- Cold weather may reduce the number of parasites but not eliminate them completely.

- Always wash your hands before and after preparing food, and keep raw meat away from other food.

- Dipping rabbits in boiling water may help remove parasites in the fur or hide.

- The rear legs contain the most meat, followed by the loin and front legs.

- Always cook rabbit meat thoroughly to a minimum of 180 degrees Fahrenheit.

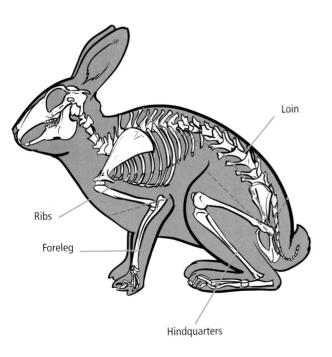

Loin

Ribs

Foreleg

Hindquarters

process, or through a tick bite. Since its entry is through cuts, abrasions, or inhalation, you need to take precautions when skinning a wild rabbit carcass.

Wear rubber or latex gloves when dressing and skinning rabbits, as well as during the preparation for cooking. Always handle the rabbit carcass with care to prevent bruising.

Begin by making an incision at the rear hocks between the leg bone and the tendon to suspend the carcass by hooks through the hocks. This makes skinning easier.

Sever the head by making a cut where the vertebrae joint meets the base of the skull. Remove the tail and the forelegs at the knee joints.

To skin the rabbit, make a cut on the rear side of one leg, slicing to the base of the tail and back up the other leg. Pull the pelt away from the muscle and down the carcass. They should separate without needing to make any further cuts in the skin.

Open the abdomen by cutting the midline of the belly from the anus to the rib cage, making sure not to puncture the intestines. Pull out the viscera before cutting off the other rear leg.

Inspect the liver for white, yellow, or any other spotting, which could indicate tularemia. Wash and rinse the carcass thoroughly with cold water to remove any materials on it.

If you can't skin the animal right away, at least remove the entrails before continuing your hunt. If you're field dressing the carcass, use paper towels to clean the body cavity before you return home.

Place the carcass in a cool water bath or ice chest during transport, particularly if hunting during warm weather.

Place the rabbit carcass on its back on a clean surface. You can cut the carcass into three sections: forequarters, loin, and rear quarters. Cut into the rear leg at a point near the backbone but stop before cutting through the bone. Bend the leg back to pop the ball joint of the hip. Cut through the joint to remove the leg.

The front legs can be split at the shoulders by cutting through the shoulder joints and severing them. The loin can be portioned by cutting off the shoulder and at the hip joint. The ribs can be trimmed because they contain very little meat, but they can be used for soup stock. There should be seven meat pieces when finished: four legs, saddle or loin from each side, and ribs.

Squirrels

Squirrels are considered rodents and three major types can be used for meat: red or brown, gray, and fox squirrels. Skinning a squirrel is similar to skinning rabbits because the pelt can be easily stripped off rather than trimmed.

Begin by making a cut through the base of the tailbone, on the underside of the tail. Stop when the bone is severed and make a circular cut around both rear legs. Do not cut the skin on the top side of the tail.

Securely suspend the hind legs and peel the skin inside out down the body, like peeling a banana, until reaching the front

1

Start skinning a squirrel by cutting through the base of the tailbone on the underside of the tail. Stop when the bone is severed. Do not cut the skin on the top of the tail.

2

Place the squirrel on the ground and set your foot on the base of the tail. Pull up on the rear legs, peeling the skin all the way to the front legs.

3

Peel the skin off the rear legs to the ankle joints. Keep your foot firmly on the base of the tail until all skinning is complete.

Squirrel Tips

1. Dipping the squirrel carcass in a bucket of water will help decrease hair-to-skin contact.

2. When you're finished cutting up the carcass, you should have six pieces of meat: four legs and the saddle or loin from each side.

4

Remove the squirrel's back feet by cutting through the ankle joints with a knife, always cutting away from yourself.

6

Cut the head off. Remove any glands and clean out the body cavity just as you would a rabbit. Remove any remaining long hairs with a knife or game shears.

8

You can quarter a large squirrel by cutting each half apart. Quartered squirrels are easier to fry than halved ones, and they look more attractive when served. You can snip the meat around the bone if you are using game shears, an excellent tool for cutting up squirrels, rabbits, and hares. You may need a heavy knife to cut through the thick backbone of a raccoon.

5

Pull each front leg out of the skin, as far as the wrist joint. Use your free hand fingers to help loosen the skin at the elbow, then cut each front foot off at the wrist joint.

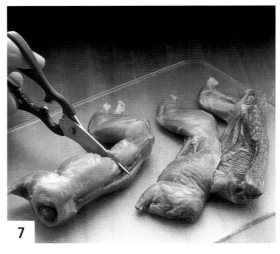

7

To portion a squirrel, begin by cutting it in half behind the ribs or along the backbone. If the squirrel is small, no further cutting will be necessary.

legs. Peel the skin on the rear legs back to the ankles.

Remove the hind feet by cutting through the ankle joint. Pull each front leg out of the skin, as far as the wrist joint, then cut each front foot off at that joint.

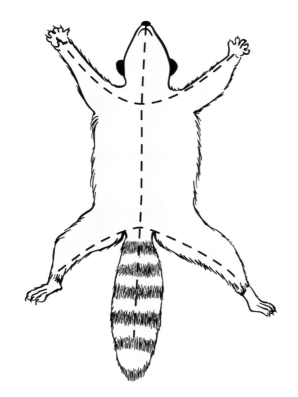

An open-pelt method for a raccoon.

A case-pelt method for a raccoon.

Finish pulling the skin down to the head; in most cases this will also remove it. If not, then when you cut the head off, you will remove the pelt with it. You can open the body cavity, clean it, and make the cuts as you would with a rabbit.

Raccoons

Raccoons can yield two useful products: meat and pelts. The price of pelts can vary considerably depending on market conditions; the meat can be used at home. The most important cuts are found in the hind legs.

The steps required to skin and cut up raccoon and opossum carcasses are very

similar, so the following list can be used for both. However, if the raccoon pelt is to be sold, you need to carefully skin its carcass.

Begin by suspending the carcass by the hind legs and making circular cuts just above the hocks. Cut along the inside of each leg to a point below the tail, then make a circular cut around the anus to free all the skin on the rump.

Peel the skin down the hind legs with even tension until you reach the tail. Cut through the tailbone close to the rump, leaving the tailbone inside the pelt.

Continue peeling off the pelt until you reach the shoulders. Make circular cuts above the knee joint on both front legs and

1

Raccoons can be skinned to keep the pelt saleable. Begin by hanging the carcass by the rear legs and cutting the skin around the rear feet. Raccoon hunters should wear rubber gloves while dressing and skinning the carcass—some raccoon populations carry a roundworm that may be found in the droppings and on the pelt. In very rare circumstances, this parasite can be transmitted to humans.

2

Cut along the inside of each rear leg to the base of the tail. Peel the pelt back to the base of the tail. Begin peeling the skin off the abdomen.

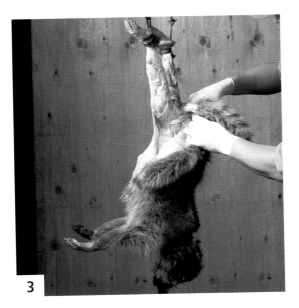

3

Use your knife to skin the pelt from the spine above the tail. Cut through the tailbone close to the rump, leaving the tailbone inside the pelt.

4

Continue peeling off the pelt until you reach the shoulders, using your knife only when necessary. Cut the skin around the front feet.

5

Pull the pelt off the front legs and off the head, cutting carefully at the eyes and rear base of the ears. Cut the pelt off at the nose and turn it right-side-out to dry. Cut and peel the tail skin to remove the bone.

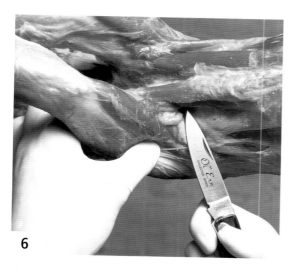

6

Remove the glands that lie under the front legs and above the base of the tail. Cut off the head and feet. Slit the abdomen from vent to neck. Remove the internal organs, rinse the raccoon, and pat it dry. This method of skinning can also be used for opossums and muskrats.

make an incision on the inside of each leg to a point at the brisket.

Make a singular cut from the brisket to the tip of the lower jaw. Make circular cuts around the eyes and the rear base of the ears to free the skin from the sockets and ears. Peel the skin down the front until the head, where you will need to skin the face with a knife. The pelt should then be free.

Remove the viscera by cutting down the centerline of the abdomen, being careful not to puncture the intestine or internal organs. Once they are removed, you can wash the carcass with clean water.

Raccoons have several small scent glands (located under the front legs and above the base of the tail) that need to be removed. Use your knifepoint to trim them away from the flesh, being careful not to puncture them or break them open with your fingers.

After removing these glands, cut through the flank to the backbone, then cut through the hip joints to remove each hind leg. The rest of the carcass will contain little meat and can be discarded or composted.

Rinse the legs in clean water and place in salt brine for several days before use.

Opossum

The opossum is a large rodent-like animal found in North and South America. In recent decades they have been expanding their territory to include urban areas. Depending on their age and sex, opossums can range from 5 to 15 pounds. Their meat is fine-grained and light in color, but tends to carry a lot of fat. This can make them difficult to cook. Skin them the way you'd skin raccoons, rabbits, squirrels, and other small furred game.

Muskrat

The muskrat is a medium-size semiaquatic rodent native to North America. It is found in wetlands but can range over different climates and habitats.

You can skin muskrats the way you would skin other furred game. Be sure to check for any county or state regulations that may apply to hunting or trapping them.

Muskrats can be case-skinned. This means you can make one or two cuts on the feet and then pull the carcass inside out, similar to peeling a banana.

Lay the muskrat on its back and make circle cuts around the hocks of the rear feet. Make a long cut from one rear leg to the other, passing in front of the anus, so that you can peel the skin from the legs.

Work your hand under the hide and loosen the skin from the belly, then slip your hands between the skin and the backbone. Pull the loosened hide forward, pushing on the head to peel the hide to the front legs.

Work the front legs out of the skin and pull hard to loosen it from the front feet. You can also cut off the front feet before you do this.

Pull the skin forward to the head; cut the ear cartilage and the skin at the eyeholes. Cut the nose cartilage on the inside but leave the nose on the skin.

Trim all fat and flesh from the skin and hang to dry if keeping it. Trim all meat off the front and rear legs and the loin areas.

Groundhog (Woodchuck)

The groundhog is also known as a woodchuck or whistle pig because of its ability to whistle to other groundhogs when it is alarmed or senses danger.

Groundhogs can reach weights of 4 to 9 pounds or more. They are covered with two coats of fur: a dense gray undercoat and a longer coat of banded guard hairs. They are burrowing animals, but typically remain solitary.

Opossum Tips

1. After skinning and eviscerating the carcass, remove as much of the fat as possible.

2. Before storing or cooking, remove the reddish glands located under the forelegs and at the small of the back. The carcass can then be placed in a salt brine of 1 tablespoon salt in 1 quart of water to remove some of the meat's strong flavor.

Muskrat Tips

1. After it has been eviscerated and washed clean, you can roast the carcass whole or cut into pieces for cooking.

2. The meat from muskrats can be fried, broiled, made into casseroles or sausage, or used in other recipes for small-game animals.

Woodchuck Tips

1. Woodchuck meat is dark but mild flavored and tender. It does not require soaking, but may sit in saltwater overnight before use.

2. If a woodchuck is caught before it begins its winter sleep, there will be an insulating layer of fat that will need to be removed.

3. There are seven to nine scent glands in the small of the back and under the forearms that will need to be removed.

Because groundhogs have a body structure similar to a muskrat, they can be case-skinned using the method mentioned above.

Beaver

Beavers are the largest rodents in North America. Many adults weigh 45 pounds or more. Their fur has been valued for generations: it consists of coarse guard hairs and silky, dense, waterproof underfur. Use an open-skinning method on a beaver.

Clean and dry the animal before laying it on its back. Cut off all four feet where the fur and bare skin meet.

Make a circle cut around the tail but leave it on the body to use to turn it over. Skin up the center of the belly from the tail to the lower lip, holding the knife upward.

Separate the skin by pulling it at one side of the belly cut. Use short strokes to shave the skin from the fat and muscle. Continue until you reach the head and middle of the back, then work the other side.

Remove the head skin last. It will be tight to the head, so take care not to slice the pelt. Cut the ear cartilage with your knife tip tight against the head. When free, pull the skin forward to the eyes and use the knife tip to cut around each eye. Cut the cartilage on the inside of the nose to free the skin.

Place skin on a flat surface to scrape off all fat and meat. Eviscerate like other small-game animals. Cut off the legs and trim the body. Trim meat from legs, ribs, and loin area.

Snakes

Most common snakes are unprotected and can be used for meat. Many rattlesnakes are protected; check your local or state regulations before capturing any wild snakes.

Beaver Tips

1. Properly treated, the beaver's pelt will be marketable and its flesh edible.

2. Many hunters like beaver meat. It makes good jerky and can be roasted like beef and pork.

3. If the beaver was trapped in cold water and recovered within 36 hours, the meat will likely not have deteriorated. Any animal left in a trap longer than that should not be eaten, although the pelt should still be recoverable.

4. It may take a week or more to dry the hide. Stretch and nail it hair down on plywood or other flat surface. Use nails or staples to hold it in place.

Since some snake species are venomous, you'll need to use great care in capturing or handling them.

Begin by removing the head. Snakes have been known to strike even when they are considered dead, and those with fangs can still be dangerous.

Wash the outside of the snake thoroughly and lay it on a clean, flat surface, belly-side up. Use the knife tip to cut an incision down the center from the head to the tail. Cut only through the skin—avoid cutting into the body.

Use your hands to pull the skin from the flesh with even tension, beginning at the head. The hide should be loose enough to detach it from the carcass. Trim areas if the flesh begins to tear as you peel off the skin.

Remove the tail and skin by severing them just in front of the cloaca. Remove the viscera by hand after making a centerline cut the length of the body and into the flesh.

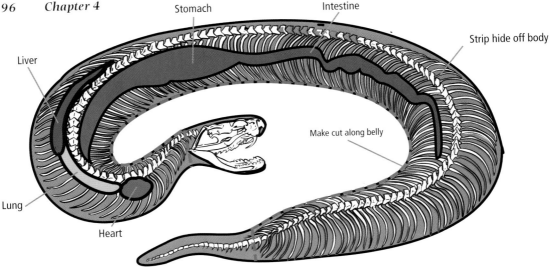

Stomach   Intestine   Strip hide off body

Liver

Make cut along belly

Lung

Heart

Snake Tips

1. Reptiles are known to spread salmonella. Be sure to wash your hands and equipment thoroughly after handling.

2. Use caution initially, as snakes have been known to strike even when they are considered dead. Those with fangs can still be dangerous.

3. If you are bitten by a snake, particularly a venomous one, seek medical treatment immediately.

4. The flavor and texture of snake is somewhere between chicken and fish. The pieces may be placed in salt water for a day or two before cooking to remove any remaining blood or reduce the wild flavor.

5. Although cooking should remove all venom contained in any snake, you should check for any signs that the snake has been bitten by another snake. If you see snake bite marks, be careful with those areas of the meat, and even consider discarding the snake.

Avoid making deep cuts at the lower end of the digestive tract.

After the viscera are removed, rinse the carcass in cool water and cut it into segments. When cutting segments, make sure your cuts are between the ribs and not across them. This will avoid severing the ribs, which may be difficult to remove from the meat after it is cooked.

Turtle

Turtles are vertebrates that have two skeletons: an endoskeleton that consists of all the internal bones, and an exoskeleton, which is its outer shell. The endoskeleton is divided into two subsections, called the axial and appendicular skeletons. The axial skeleton is made up of the skull and both the cervical and thoracic vertebrae; the appendicular skeleton consists of the remaining bones, including the legs.

There are two parts to the shell: the carapace, which is the hard upper part, and the plastron, which sometimes is referred to as the belly. Both shells are made of many fused bones. A turtle has the ability to pull

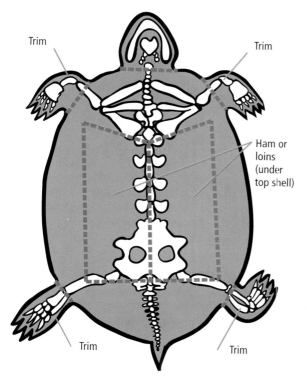

Trim

Trim

Ham or
loins
(under
top shell)

Trim

Trim

The turtle anatomy includes four different types and numbers
of vertebrae: cervical (eight), dorsal (ten), sacral (two), and
caudal (twenty to thirty).

Turtle Tips

1. You do not need to debone the legs, neck, or tail before you cook them as pieces in stews or soups, but you can boil the bone-in pieces and then separate the bones from the meat before cooking.

2. Harvesting wild turtles is legal in many states. Check state regulations about bag limit, season dates, and licensing.

3. Alligator snapping turtles look superficially similar to other common snapping turtles but are a threatened or endangered species and have federal protection. Be sure you recognize the differences, and only harvest common snapping turtles.

the carapace and plastron together tightly while it retracts its body into the shell. This is the joint where you will cut to open up the shell.

Begin by decapitating the turtle, but realize that its reflexes will still be working; avoid the head and feet so you don't get bitten or clawed. Place the body upside down in boiling water for five minutes to loosen the exterior layer of the skin.

The tail, neck, and all four legs are attached to the carapace. Separate them from the bottom shell (the plastron) by turning the turtle on its back and making

a circular cut at the joint between them. As the plastron is loosened, trim until it is completely free from the body. This should expose the viscera, which can be removed by hand.

Most of the meat will be located in the carapace and includes the legs, shoulders, loins, and neck. First, remove the legs by severing them at the shoulder and pelvic joints. Then remove the neck and tail. These can be boned later because the skin is inedible.

The loins or hams are located in the top part of the carapace, protected by a rib-like structure made of hard cartilage. You will need sturdy shears to cut through them before you can remove the loins.

After you have removed as much of the muscle as possible, separate it from the fat particles and wash all the pieces in clean, cool water.

Frogs

Frogs and other amphibians are cold-blooded animals. A number of frog species, including the green frog, leopard frog, and pickerel frog, are harvested from the wild and sold as luxury food in restaurants. The common bullfrog is the largest native North American species, often reaching 8 inches in length, which makes it best for human consumption.

Kill the frog by inserting your knife into its lower jaw and thrusting up into its cranial cavity. Make a circular cut behind the ears, which appear as round spots behind each eye.

Pull the skin out below the jaw and grasp it with your fingers or pliers. While holding the head, pull the skin down with your free hand. It should slip free of the front legs.

Continue pulling until you reach the hips at the top of the hind legs. The skin is constricted at this point, so either cut a small incision in the skin or slowly work it over the hips with your fingers.

Once past the hips, continue to pull the skin off the back feet. Now the skin should be completely removed.

Remove the four feet by cutting at the joint where each foot bends at the tip. Remove the head by cutting just behind the skull and around the bottom jaw. Either sever it or pull the head apart from the body.

To open the abdomen, insert the tip of your knife at a point slightly anterior to the pelvis and slice up to the ribs. A little pressure with a sharp knife should split the rib cage up through the breastbone.

Remove the viscera and esophagus, if it does not come out with the head. Rinse the carcass with clean, cool water before you cook or refrigerate it.

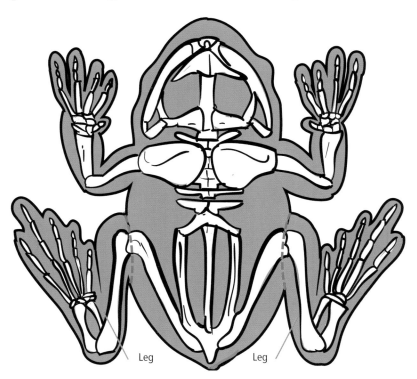

Leg   Leg

Final Thoughts

Small furred animals can provide meat for exotic or adventurous tastes, but hunters should give some thought to the effect harvesting has on local wildlife populations. The diversity of species in the wild is dependent upon their ability to sustain their populations. Overhunting or trapping can decimate populations to the point that they become unsustainable. If you decide to pursue these game animals, use as much of their carcasses as possible, so they are not wasted.

In many states, it is lawful to capture and possess no more than a few wild native animals or amphibians for private use. It is not lawful to sell, barter, or trade any that you hunt or trap.

Small-Game Cooking Considerations

Simplicity is the greatest asset in obtaining good taste from small game. Follow several basic principles of small-game cooking to determine how your game tastes and how it should be prepared to maximize flavor.

The chronological age of the game animal has a great influence on the flavor and cooking method used. Young animals born within the year (yearlings) can be cooked by roasting, broiling, or frying. Older animals, large adults, or animals that have been subjected to a chase require slow cooking, either in stews, pot roasts, or fricassees.

Secondly, fat typically needs to be added during cooking to bring out the flavor and compensate for the leanness of most game meat. Very active small-game animals, such as squirrels and rabbits, typically have fat reserves that only accumulate during certain seasons. The result is a lean, muscled animal that will make tough chewing at certain times of the year unless some fat is added. Some animals, such as opossum, possess a natural oiliness that helps the cooking process.

Adding fat to small-game cooking is referred to as "oiling," and is most generally done by rubbing the individual cuts with pork fat. Bacon can be used when it is cut into slabs or small pieces and laid over the small-game cuts.

The taste of game meat is also influenced by the food habits of the animal. Most are favorable and become characteristic of regions and times of year. This may influence the method of cooking used for a specific species at a particular time of year; roasting may be more favorable at one time and stewing at another.

Canning Small Game

For canning, use only good-quality game meat that has been properly cleaned and cooled. You *must* process these meats in a pressure cooker to reach sufficient temperatures for a long enough time to kill all bacteria that cause spoilage or food poisoning. The meat can be raw packed or hot packed.

Soak dressed meat for one hour in water containing 1 tablespoon of salt per quart; rinse.

Remove excess fat and cut meat into suitable sizes.

Can, with or without the bone.

For hot pack—Boil, steam, or bake meat until about two-thirds done. Add 1 teaspoon salt per quart, if desired. Fill jars with pieces and hot broth, leaving 1 1/4 inch headspace.

For raw pack—Add 1 teaspoon salt per quart, if desired. Fill jars loosely with raw meat pieces, leaving 1 1/4 inch headspace. Do not add liquid.

Smoking Small-Game Animals

Smoking can add flavor and increased shelf life to your small-game meat. Choose freshly killed and dressed healthy birds for smoking.

Soak dressed meat for 1 hour in water containing 1 tablespoon of salt per quart; rinse.

Remove excess fat and cut meat into suitable sizes for canning.

Can, with or without the bone.

For hot pack—Boil, steam, or bake meat until about two-thirds done. Add 1 teaspoon salt per quart, if desired. Fill jars with pieces and hot broth, leaving 1 1/4 inch of headspace.

For raw pack—Add 1 teaspoon salt per quart, if desired. Fill jars loosely with raw meat pieces, leaving 1 1/4 inch of headspace. Do not add liquid.

Follow proper canning recommendations.

Recipes

For small-game dinners, you will need about 3/4 pound of dressed game meat per person. Gray squirrels dress out at about 3/4 pound, fox squirrels 1 pound, cottontail rabbits 1 1/2 to 2 pounds, snowshoe hares 2 1/2 to 3 pounds, and young raccoons 3 to 6 pounds.

Small-Game Substitution

Small-game flavors vary greatly. Although you can substitute different species, remember that the final dish may taste quite different. Be particularly careful when substituting raccoon for rabbit or squirrel; its strong taste can overwhelm a mildly seasoned dish. Hare is tougher than rabbit or squirrel and requires longer cooking. Domestic rabbit will probably need less cooking time than wild rabbit.

If your recipe calls for a particular leftover or cooked small game, you can substitute any type of cooked small game, or even cooked pheasant, chicken, or turkey. Cuts of fresh upland game birds can be easily substituted for small game of similar size.

Species	Approximate Dressed Wt.	Number of Servings	Substitute	Cooking Method

squirrel	3/4 to 1 lb (gray)
	 1 to 1 1/2 lb (fox)
		1
		 1 to 1 1/2
			cottontail rabbit
			   (1 rabbit to 2 squirrels)
			 half of young snowshoe
			   hare
			 portion of young raccoon
			 portion of domestic rabbit
			 pheasant or substitute
			   (1 pheasant to 2 squirrels)
				panfry, bake, stew, braise, pressure-cook

cottontail rabbit	1 1/2 to 2 lbs.	2	2 squirrels young snowshoe hare portion of young raccoon portion domestic rabbit 1 pheasant or substitute	panfry, bake braise, stew, pressure-cook

snowshoe hare	2 1/2 to 3 lbs.	2 to 3	2 small cottontail rabbits
			 2 to 3 squirrels
			 domestic rabbit
			 half of young raccoon
			   (or portion of large
			   raccoon)
				braise, stew, pressure-cook

raccoon	3 lbs. of pieces	3 to 4	snowshoe hare, qtrd. 2 cottontail rabbits, qtrd. 3 or 4 squirrels, qtrd. domestic rabbit, cut into pieces	braise, stew, pressure-cook

Snapping Turtle Stew

2 pounds turtle meat, trimmed
    and cut into 1-inch cubes
4 c. seeded chopped tomatoes
4 1/4 c. water, divided
1 c. chopped onion
1/2 tsp. salt
1/2 tsp. dried thyme leaves
1/4 tsp. dried rosemary leaves

1/4 tsp. pepper
1/4 tsp. ground nutmeg
1/8 tsp. ground cloves
1 tbsp. lemon juice
2 tbsp. all-purpose flour
1/2 c. snipped fresh parsley
1/4 c. dry sherry

In a 6-quart Dutch oven or stockpot, combine turtle meat, tomatoes, 4 cups water, the onions, salt, thyme, rosemary, pepper, nutmeg, cloves, and lemon juice. Bring to a boil over medium heat, stirring occasionally. Reduce heat to low. Simmer, uncovered, for 2 1/4 to 2 1/2 hours, or until meat is tender, stirring occasionally.

In a small bowl, combine flour and remaining 1/4 cup water. Blend until smooth. Add to stew, stirring occasionally, until mixture thickens and bubbles. Just before serving, stir in parsley and sherry. Serves 4.

Hasenpfeffer

1 rabbit
1 qt. vinegar
2 tbsp. salt
1 tbsp. pickling spices
1 tbsp. peppercorns
2 large onions, sliced

2 tbsp. fat (bacon grease)
2 tbsp. flour
1 c. cold water
1 tsp. cinnamon
1/2 tsp. allspice

Cut rabbit into serving portions. Place in crock and cover with vinegar, combined with salt, spices, peppercorns, and 1 onion. Let stand in cool place for 24 hours. Drain, cover with boiling water, and simmer until tender, about 1 1/2 hours. Remove meat and strain broth. Melt fat or bacon grease in frying pan. Blend in flour and add water, stirring constantly. Cook until thickened. Add rabbit, strained broth, cinnamon, allspice, and remaining onion; simmer for about 1 hour. Serves 4.

Grilled Marinated Frog Legs
6 pairs frog legs (about 2 pounds), skin removed

MARINADE

1/2 c. vegetable oil
3 tbsp. finely chopped red onion
2 tbsp. snipped fresh parsley
1 tbsp. grated lemon peel
1 tbsp. plus 1 1/2 tsp. lemon juice

1 tsp. salt
1 tsp. dry mustard
1 tsp. dried basil leaves
1/4 c. butter or margarine
1 clove garlic, minced

Arrange frog legs in single layer in 11x7-inch baking dish. In small mixing bowl, combine marinade ingredients. Reserve 1/3 cup marinade. Cover with plastic wrap. Chill. Pour remaining marinade over frog legs, turning to coat. Cover with plastic wrap. Chill 3 hours, turning legs over occasionally.

Spray cooking grate with nonstick vegetable cooking spray. Prepare grill for medium direct heat. Drain and discard marinade from frog legs. Arrange legs on prepared cooking grate. Grill, covered, for 3 minutes. Turn legs over. Grill, covered, for 3 to 5 minutes longer, or until meat is no longer pink and begins to pull away from the bone.

In 1-quart saucepan, combine reserved marinade with butter and garlic. Cook over medium heat, stirring frequently, for 1 to 2 minutes, or until mixture is hot and butter is melted. Before serving, pour marinade mixture over frog legs. Serves 4 to 6.

Roast Rabbit

1 rabbit
Salt and pepper
Sausage stuffing

Poultry fat or oil
Currant jelly

Wash the dressed rabbit under running water. Dry it, then season with salt and pepper. Stuff it and sew shut. Roast uncovered at 325°F for 1 1/2 to 1 3/4 hours or until tender. Baste with fat. Serve on hot platter with brown gravy and currant jelly. Garnish with parsley or watercress. Serves 4 to 6.

Squirrel

3 small squirrels	1/2 tsp. salt
3/4 c. salad oil	1/8 tsp. pepper
1/4 c. lemon juice	1/2 tsp. onion juice
2 c. breadcrumbs	4 tbsp. olive oil or bacon fat
1/2 c. milk or cream	1 tsp. Worcestershire sauce
1/2 c. mushrooms, diced and sautéed	Paprika

Wash and clean squirrels in several cups of water, then dry. Cover with salad oil mixed with lemon juice and let stand for 1 hour. Combine breadcrumbs with just enough milk or cream to moisten, mushrooms, salt, pepper, and onion juice. Stuff the squirrel with this mixture, skewer, and truss. Brush with olive oil or bacon fat and roast uncovered at 325ºF for 1 1/2 to 1 3/4 hours or until tender. Baste every 15 minutes with fat from bottom of pan. When tender, make gravy with remaining broth, adding Worcestershire sauce and paprika to taste. Serve gravy in separate dish. Serves 6.

Roast Raccoon

1 raccoon

DRESSING

8 to 10 slices dry bread	1/2 tsp. ground cloves
Stock from raccoon	1 tbsp. salt
2 eggs	2 tbsp. sage

Cut raccoon into small pieces and salt to taste. Cook in inset pan of pressure cooker for 1 hour at 15 pounds pressure. Cook longer if the meat is tough. When tender, arrange pieces in baking dish and cover with dressing. Mix ingredients and put on top of cooked raccoon meat. Bake at 350ºF until dressing is browned. This method can also be used for opossum.

Brunswick Stew

2 squirrels
1 tbsp. salt
1 minced onion
2 c. fresh lima beans
6 ears corn
1/2 lb. salt pork

6 potatoes
1 tsp. pepper
2 tsp. sugar
4 c. sliced tomatoes
1/2 lb. butter
All-purpose flour

Cut squirrel into serving pieces. Add salt to 4 quarts of water; when boiling, add onion, lima beans, corn cut from the cob, pork, potatoes, pepper, and squirrels. Cover and simmer 2 hours; add sugar and tomato, and simmer 1 hour more. Ten minutes before removing from heat, add butter cut into walnut-size pieces and rolled in flour. Bring to a boil. Serve in soup plates for 6.

The characteristic Brunswick stew is made with squirrels. Chickens and rabbits can be used in place of squirrels.

Stuffed Opossum

1 opossum

The opossum is a very fat animal with a peculiarly flavored meat. Wash thoroughly inside and out with hot water after dressing and skinning. Cover with cold water to which 1 cup of salt has been added and let stand overnight. Drain off the salted water and rinse with clean, boiling water.

DRESSING

1 large onion, minced
1 tbsp. fat
Opossum liver, chopped
1 c. breadcrumbs

1 sweet red pepper, chopped
Dash Worcestershire sauce
1 hard cooked egg, chopped
Salt

Brown the onion in fat. Add liver; cook until liver is tender. Add breadcrumbs, pepper, Worcestershire sauce, egg, salt, and water to moisten.

Stuff opossum and place in roaster; add 2 tablespoons water and roast at 350°F for 1 1/2–1 3/4 hours or until tender. Baste every 15 minutes with drippings. Skim fat from pan gravy; serve gravy separately with baked yams or sweet potatoes. Serves 10.

Chapter 5

GAME BIRDS & WATERFOWL

Birds are a diverse group. The planet has approximately 9,000 bird species, and the U.S. Fish and Wildlife Service estimates that between 12 to 15 percent of these bird species call the United States home at some point during the year. That equals between 1,100 and 1,400 species in the fifty states, Puerto Rico, and other U.S. territories.

About 700 species regularly settle in the continental United States; about 90 percent of those, or 650 species, have active breeding populations here. About 250 of these are migratory bird species that nest in the United States and Canada and fly south to winter in Mexico, Central and South America, or the Caribbean.

The 700 continental bird species can be divided into those identified as game birds, numbering about 58, and nongame birds. Conservation efforts have mostly focused on bird species that are hunted. Except for the American bald eagle, nongame species have received little conservation attention compared to game birds, although that is beginning to change.

Upland Game Birds

Game birds are generally divided into two categories: upland birds and waterfowl. *Upland* means "high ground" and refers to birds found there.

Upland birds are most likely to be found on dry land areas with heavy vegetative cover, such as grasslands, prairies,

Ring-necked pheasants are only one type of wild game bird that can make delicious meat dishes. Unlike domestically raised fowl, game birds are regulated. Be sure to check state rules and regulations before hunting.

or fencerows along cultivated fields. Some upland birds can be found in lowlands or marsh areas. Upland birds have excellent eyesight and sharp hearing, which makes them difficult (but rewarding) to hunt.

Meat from upland birds can vary greatly in color and flavor. As mentioned earlier, muscles that get extensive use, whether in game animals or game birds and waterfowl, are laced with blood vessels that supply oxygen. This enables them to fly longer distances. For example, the woodcock and sharptail grouse both have dark breast meat and can fly greater distances than ruffed grouse and wild turkey, which have white breast meat with fewer blood vessels throughout.

Waterfowl

Game waterfowl are birds that live in or near water. They are good swimmers and have medium to large bodies with webbed feet. Ducks and geese are waterfowl.

The U.S. Fish and Wildlife Service has the primary responsibility for protecting these birds, because ducks and geese migrate through many states. This agency establishes

Wild turkeys are often found in abundance in the Midwest. That does not mean they are easy to hunt. Wily creatures, they may take longer to successfully harvest because they can be very elusive. However, they yield a large amount of tasty meat.

hunting seasons and bag limits for each state. These laws may change from year to year depending on a variety of factors, including population estimates.

There are about 50 different waterfowl species. Ducks and geese are the most prevalent. Geese are larger than ducks and can weigh up to 15 pounds. Aside from their smaller size, ducks differ from geese in that the sexes vary in color. Males have a more colorful plumage, while the females' subdued color helps camouflage them from predators. Geese have a slower wing beat than ducks—geese are very good for the long flight, ducks for the sprint.

There are physical differences between duck species that help them adapt in different ways. For example, puddle ducks are adept at walking and feeding on land and diving ducks are not. Diving ducks possess legs and feet that are positioned farther back on their bodies, and this helps them dive and swim below the water's surface. Puddle ducks have legs positioned near the center of their body, which gives them better balance for walking on land. Sea ducks spend most of their time in sea or estuary areas.

These differences in physical characteristics help with identification, but aren't major concerns when field dressing waterfowl.

Health Concerns

All wild birds and waterfowl are susceptible to a variety of diseases and parasites just as wild game animals are. These include avian influenza, duck virus enteritis (duck plague), avian cholera, botulism, aspergillosis, sarcosporidiosis (rice breast), and lead poisoning.

Avian influenza, or bird flu, is an illness caused by several different strains of influenza viruses that adapt to specific hosts. Humans can be infected through contact with an

Most Prevalent Upland Game Birds
- blue grouse
- bobwhite quail
- California quail
- Chukar partridge
- doves
- Gambel's quail
- Hungarian partridge
- mountain quail
- pigeons
- prairie chicken
- ptarmigan
- ring-necked pheasant
- ruffed grouse
- sage grouse
- scaled quail
- sharptailed grouse
- wild turkey
- woodcock

infected bird—usually during the handling of infected dead birds or by contact with infected fluids. No known instances of bird-human transmission have been reported in the United States as of this writing, but hunters must be careful when handling birds. Be sure your game bird appears healthy before dressing it. Birds infected with avian flu may exhibit symptoms such as nasal discharge, diarrhea, and a purple discoloration of the wattles, combs, and legs.

Duck plague is caused by a herpes virus and can be spread through contaminated water or direct contact between birds. It has a 90 percent mortality rate when it affects ducks, geese, and swans. Listless birds that are unable to fly should be examined closely if shot. There may also be discoloration in the esophagus or blood in the digestive

Most Prevalent Waterfowl for Hunting

Puddle Ducks—Feed by tipping down to reach aquatic plants and invertebrates below the surface. Take flight by springing into the air.	Diving Ducks—Dive and swim underwater for food. Need a running start on the water to get airborne.	Sea Ducks—Expert divers that feed on crustaceans, mollusks, and fish.	Geese—The largest members of the duck family. They will graze on grasses and other land plants as well as aquatic plants.
• American black duck • American wigeon • blue-winged teal • cinnamon teal • gadwall • green-winged teal • mallard • mottled duck • northern pintail • northern shoveler • wood duck	• canvasback • common merganser • greater scaup • lesser scaup • hooded merganser • red-breasted merganser • ring-necked duck • ruddy duck	• Barrow's goldeneye • black scoter • bufflehead • common eider • common goldeneye • harlequin duck • king eider • long-tailed duck • surf scoter • white-winged scoter	• Brant geese • Canada geese • Ross's geese • snow geese • white-fronted geese

tract that is not attributable to being shot. If you suspect you've harvested a bird with these symptoms, contact your local, state, or national wildlife office to report it.

In the wild, avian cholera is a bacterial disease caused primarily by one strain. It is transmitted by direct contact between birds. Sick birds appear lethargic or fly erratically, and when captured may die within minutes. Humans are not at risk for infection from the bacterial strain that causes avian cholera. Nevertheless, wear gloves and wash your hands if you handle birds with this appearance, as they may harbor other avian viruses. It is a good sanitation practice to use gloves to prevent the possible spreading of any bacteria or viruses to other domestic birds, such as poultry, that you may have at home. Be sure to thoroughly sanitize them after each use or dispose of them carefully.

Aspergillosis is a fungal disease affecting the lungs and bronchial areas of ducks. It mostly affects mallards; they may ingest it when they eat moldy grains or grasses that harbor the fungus.

Sarcosporidiosis is a parasitic infection that enters the muscle tissue in the host bird and can be ingested by another predator. Human infection is rare, but it can occur if undercooked meat is eaten. Prevent this by always fully cooking waterfowl before you eat it.

Botulism is deadly and can be transmitted to humans. Birds become infected by feeding on invertebrate carcasses that harbor the toxin produced by botulism bacteria. The toxin attacks the bird's nervous system, causing paralysis. Symptoms include paralysis of the legs—a bird may try to propel itself across water with only its wings. A bird may drown because it can't hold its head above water. Don't eat any bird that displays these symptoms, as the bacteria can be transmitted to humans.

Lead poisoning occurs when wild waterfowl ingest spent lead shot from hunters' guns. Lead shot can be picked up from lake or marsh bottoms or in low feeding areas. Birds exhibiting lead poisoning will have difficulty flying or be unable to fly. They may also be so weak that you can easily catch them, or they might have a staggering or unbalanced walk on land.

A ban on the use of lead shot for hunting waterfowl was phased in starting with the 1987–1988 hunting season. The ban became nationwide in 1991. However, nontoxic shot regulations apply only to waterfowl such as ducks, geese, swans, and coots. Hunters still use lead shot to kill other species, so it can still be ingested by waterfowl.

Whenever you encounter diseased animals or birds, contact your local office of the Fish and Wildlife Service. Reports like this alert them to potential widespread problems.

Equipment for Processing

There is more than one way to butcher wild game birds and waterfowl. You can make the process as elaborate as you wish, but a simple procedure is explained here. Processing these birds requires four basic steps:

1. Field dressing
2. Removing feathers
3. Breaking down your bird
4. Chilling and packaging

If properly done, your processing can be a pleasant experience. To help move the process along swiftly and safely, arrange your work area prior to starting.

If you're handling just a few birds, you will probably need fewer tools, knives, and equipment than if you were handling many

Quick Tips
- Wear latex or rubber gloves to field dress and clean wild birds.
- Don't eat sick birds or birds that act abnormally.
- Cook bird meat to a minimum internal temperature of 165°F.
- There is little evidence of hunters getting West Nile virus from handling or eating infected birds.

birds. The processing principles are the same, however.

In the most basic operation, you'll need knives for eviscerating and cutting, an axe and chopping block for removing the heads, several five-gallon pails, a scalding tub, a heating coil, a propane tank, a canvas or tarpaulin, and a sturdy table. Your chopping block will work best if you pound two large nails into it about 1 or 2 inches apart, depending on the size of the birds. For ducks and geese you may want to increase that width an inch.

The area you use for processing should be clean, have plenty of water available, and be as free from flies and insects as possible. Working early in the morning is often a good idea if you expect flies and insects to be a problem later in the day. Scrub tables with soap, water, and a diluted chlorine solution prior to use. If this is not possible, use a disposable plastic cover.

Sharpen and sanitize all knives before starting. Keep them in a clean and accessible area.

You can use galvanized or plastic garbage cans or pails to hold the cooling water. Be sure these containers have been thoroughly washed, sanitized, and rinsed with clean water each time they are refilled with carcasses to be

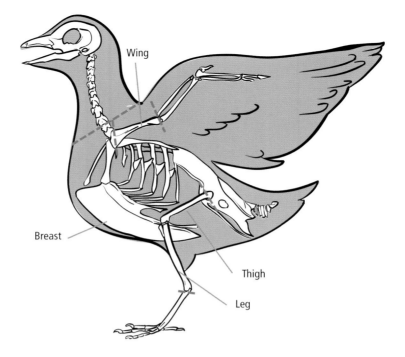

Wing

Breast

Thigh

Leg

chilled. Set up similar cans, pails, or plastic-lined boxes to use for feathers and unwanted body parts. While you're butchering, keep a water thermometer handy for checking the scalding water.

Keep your packing materials close by. Have plastic-lined boxes or portable coolers filled with ice where you can cool the eviscerated carcasses quickly.

Make a list of all the necessary butchering steps. This will allow you to envision the process from beginning to end. It is better to make adjustments at this stage than when the processing begins. Identify areas where the potential for contamination may exist and keep these in mind as you are working, so you can avoid them.

Once all your equipment is clean and set out, you are ready to begin.

Dressing Your Bird

Initial cooling of the bird is an important part of field care. Try to cool the carcasses as quickly as possible and keep them at a constant temperature until they are cleaned.

1

To field dress a wild game bird, begin by cutting the skin from the vent toward the breastbone. Some hunters pluck the feathers between the vent and breastbone before cutting.

Taking a cooler full of ice to the hunting area helps with this.

Dressing your bird is a simple process and takes little time once you become experienced. It's usually better to field dress

2

To pull out the windpipe, make a short slit above the breast toward the chin. Remove the crop (a flexible sac that lies between the bird's breast and chin) and any undigested food it may contain.

3

Remove the entrails, including the lungs. If you choose to save the heart, gizzard, and liver, store them in a plastic bag (be sure to trim the green gall sac from the liver). Wipe the inside of the bird with paper towels.

4

Another method for removing entrails is with a special bird-gutting knife. Insert the knife into the body, rotate it, and pull it out. The entrails will twist around the hook. A small forked stick can be used in the same way.

5

To field dress a wild turkey or large sage grouse, make a large cut so you can insert your whole hand inside the body cavity (left). This makes it easier to pull out the entrails (right).

birds before you pluck them, but to do this you'll need to remove some feathers along the line of incision.

If there are still feathers on the carcass, begin by pulling out the feathers from below the breastbone to the anal opening.

Make a cut through the skin and muscle starting below the breastbone and continuing to the anus.

Remove the internal organs by pulling them toward the anus, taking care not to puncture the intestines. Be sure to remove

1

To skin a wild game bird, begin by cutting off the last two joints of the wing with game shears or a knife. Cut off the feet, removing the leg tendons.

2

Place your fingers in the slit where the crop was removed during field dressing; pull to skin the breast and legs. If the crop is still intact, slit the skin and remove it first before removing the skin.

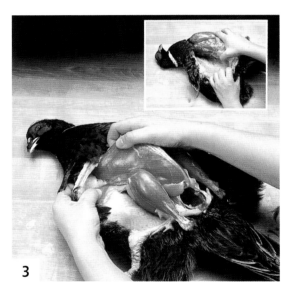

3

Pull the skin away from the wing joints, turning the skin inside-out over the joints as if peeling off a stocking. Free both wings and peel the skin off the back of the bird (inset).

4

Remove the head and tail with game shears. If the bird wasn't dressed before skinning, pull out the windpipe and entrails. Clean the body cavity thoroughly, rinse, and pat dry.

the crop and windpipe. The crop is located at the front of the breastbone. It is a transparent sac that holds undigested food. Slice open the skin on the lower neck to remove the crop and windpipe.

Remove the oil gland on the top side of the tail bulb. This gland contains the oil that birds use to coat their feathers—it can cause off flavors in the meat.

Probe the shot holes in the bird and use your knife tip to remove any pellets.

Wash with cold water. Use vinegar if it is heavily soiled or bloodstains have set, then rinse again in clear, cold water before using or freezing.

1

To breast a wild game bird while retaining the legs, begin by cutting off the feet and pulling the skin off the breasts and legs. Do not yet skin the wings.

2

Use a fillet knife to slice the breast halves away from the breastbone. Keeping the blade as close to the bone as possible, cut the meat away from the wishbone to free it completely.

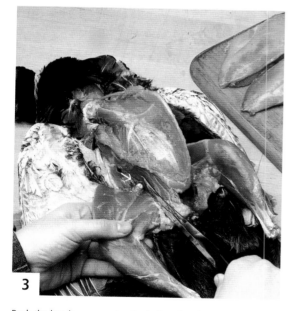

3

Push the leg down, popping the ball-and-socket joint (arrow). Cut through the joint to remove the leg. Repeat on the other leg. If the bird wasn't field dressed, remove the liver, heart, and gizzard if they appear healthy and you want to save them.

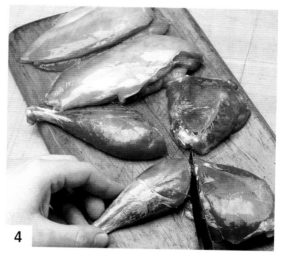

4

Cut apart the thigh and drumstick if desired. You can dispose of the rest of the carcass. With this method of breasting, the only meat discarded is on the back and wings. The boneless breast halves are easy to cook.

Pack with ice if available. Clean paper towels or dry grass packed into the cavity will help absorb blood residue and keep flies out, especially in warm weather.

Removing Feathers

One of the challenging steps in game bird hunting is removing the feathers. Feathers can be difficult to handle, whether on small birds like quail or large birds like turkeys, but they must be removed before the carcass can be completely broken down and disjointed.

There are four basic ways to remove feathers from game birds and waterfowl: dry picking, wet picking, wax picking, and skinning. Be aware that some bird parts (such as heads) may be needed for identification, so be sure to check the applicable state laws where you hunt.

Choose a Method

Some hunters cool birds in the field by removing any feathers that can be pulled out easily, then finish the rest at home. If you dress a bird and remove its feathers as soon as it's shot, you'll reduce skin loss.

Dry picking is pulling out the feathers while the bird is still dry. Begin by grasping the bird by the neck or feet with one hand. Pull the feathers with the other hand. Pull the feathers in the direction that they lay, as this will reduce skin tears.

Dry picking tends to work best if you do it soon after field dressing the bird. There is less chance of tearing the skin, because it hasn't had time to shrink or loosen after the bird's death.

Start with the underside of the bird, then turn it over to finish its back, legs, and finally the neck.

Wing feathers can prove a challenge. If they are small birds you can simply cut the wing off flush to the body, using a knife or pruning shears. There will be little meat to save on these small wings.

Short, hard-to-grasp feathers can be pulled by pinching them between your thumb and forefinger. Extremely short or stubborn feathers may need to be plucked with a tweezers or pliers.

Young birds and birds in the initial stages of molt may have hairlike pinfeathers growing under their developed feathers. Pinfeathers probably won't come out, so you may need to use a flame, such as a propane torch, to burn them off. Be sure to burn these feathers off outside your house

1

Dry picking is one method used to remove wild game-bird feathers. Grasp only a few feathers at a time and pull gently in the direction in which they grow. Drop into a paper bag to minimize the mess.

2

If necessary, use pliers to pull out the wing and tail feathers. Some hunters cut off the outer two joints of the wings, losing little meat in the process.

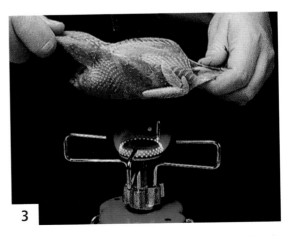

3

Use a gas burner to singe any downy feathers or "hair." Finish by rubbing off any leftover feathers.

1

Wet picking is used with the aid of heated water. Begin wetting the bird thoroughly by holding it underneath a running faucet. If wet picking waterfowl, rub the breast with your thumb to ensure the thick down feathers are saturated with water.

2

Dip the bird several times in simmering (160 to 180 degrees Fahrenheit) water. For waterfowl, add a tablespoon of dishwashing liquid to help saturate the feathers. Rinse any soapy water from the body cavity of a field-dressed bird.

3

The body feathers should strip off easily when you rub them with your thumb. If they don't, dip the bird in hot water again but do not scald. Pull out the large wing and tail feathers, using pliers if necessary.

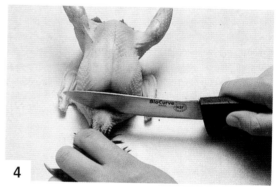

4

Cut off the head and tail. Slice off the feet, removing the leg tendons. Clean the body cavity and take out the windpipe if it is still present. Rinse the cavity thoroughly and pat the bird dry.

or building—it's safer and it keeps foul odors (resulting from burning feathers) outdoors. To prevent scorching, scalding, or burning of the skin, don't hold the flame too close to the bird or for too long in any one spot.

Wet picking or scalding can be used when feathers are too difficult to pull by dry picking. However, you should dry pick as many feathers as you can before using the wet picking method.

If you plan on wet picking, you'll need to have everything set up before you begin. You'll need a tub of water heated to between 160 and 170 degrees Fahrenheit. This is about 10 degrees hotter than you would

use for domestic birds such as chickens. Waterfowl and game birds have natural water-repellent oils in their feathers, and this higher temperature helps the water penetrate the feathers.

Once the water has reached this temperature, you can begin. Start by holding the bird tightly by its legs and immersing it neck first into the scalding water. It is important to get enough water into the feathers.

Move the bird up and down and from side to side to get an even and thorough scalding, which will make the feathers easier to remove. Repeated dips may be necessary, but be careful not to burn the bird.

One simple rule to follow when scalding is that less immersion time is needed when the water temperature is higher. Avoid overscalding by following the temperature and time factors for the birds you're using. Overscalding causes the skin to tear and discolor and gives the bird a cooked appearance; the carcass will lack bloom and turn brown rapidly, or bright red when frozen.

To wax pick waterfowl, begin by heating a large pot of water to a gentle boil. Melt several chunks of special duck-picking wax or paraffin in the water. The floating layer of melted wax should be at least 1/4 inch thick.

Hot scalding, with water temperatures above 160 degrees Fahrenheit, is an easy, quick method to remove feathers. Water temperature and length of time immersed largely determine the speed at which the feathers are loosened from the body. The hotter the water, the quicker the feathers are loosened, although another method that involves immersing the carcass for longer periods at lower temperatures can be successful too.

Water this hot will cause the outer cuticle layer of the skin to slough off as the feathers are plucked from the carcass. The use of high temperature for a shorter period of time increases the ease of plucking but risks the loss of this outer layer of the skin, which may result in the skin tearing more easily. If you choose not to keep the skin, this may not be a concern.

Rough-pluck the larger feathers from the body, legs, wings, and tail. Pull only a few feathers at a time. Leave the smaller feathers on the bird, since they make the wax adhere better.

Wax picking works well to remove small feathers and down from ducks and geese after most feathers have been removed and the carcass has dried for a short time. Paraffin wax can be heated in a tub separate from the scalding water to about 135 to 160 degrees Fahrenheit to create a liquid bath. Dip the bird into the wax bath for 30 to 60 seconds, then dip it into cold water to set the wax. The wax will adhere to the dry feathers, down, and stubs, which are very short broken feathers. You may need to dip the bird a second time if it's not completely covered the first time.

While the wax is still flexible, you can begin to peel it off. This will remove any

After covering a table with newspapers, dip the bird in the wax and water. Swish it around gently, then slowly remove it from the wax. Hold the bird up until the wax hardens enough that you can set it down on the newspapers without it sticking. You can also hang it by wedging the head between closely spaced nails on a board.

4

Allow the bird to cool until the wax is fairly hard. To speed the process, dip the bird in a bucket of cold water. Repeat the dipping and cooling until a layer of wax has built up at least 1/8 inch thick. Allow the wax to cool completely and harden.

5

Peel the hardened wax off the bird. The feathers will come off with the wax, leaving the skin smooth. You can reuse the wax if you melt it again and strain it through cheesecloth to remove the feathers.

6

Cut off the head, feet, and tail. Remove the windpipe and entrails if the bird was not dressed before waxing; remove the wax from the cavity of a dressed bird. Clean the cavity thoroughly, rinse the bird, and pat it dry.

Quick Tips

- Field dress game birds promptly.
- Cool carcasses quickly.
- Keep birds cool during transport.
- If the bird can't be skinned within several hours, place it on ice or in a refrigerator.
- If the bird can't be skinned within 24 hours, wrap it in an airtight plastic bag and freeze whole; thaw slowly in a refrigerator before skinning.
- Abide by game regulations for hunting, transporting, and storing birds.

feathers, pinfeathers, hair, and down that has adhered to the wax. Finally, rinse or wash the carcass to remove any remaining wax particles and to moisten the carcass again.

Skinning the bird is a method you can use if you don't wish to save the skin. You can remove it along with the feathers, which saves you the scalding and feather-plucking steps. In most cases, the skin can be torn off the carcass, leaving the muscles intact. Some birds have a tough, close-lying skin that will need to be opened first with a knife.

Begin with a cut into the skin at the bottom of the breastbone with the carcass on its back and its head away from you. Lift the skin and cut it forward to the front of the neck. Peel the skin and feathers back with your hands and expose the breast muscles. Use your hands to work the skin loose from the thighs. Cut through the hock joint after the skin has been pushed back to expose it. Remove the skin from this area on each foot.

Next, loosen the skin to the joint between the first and second section of the wing. Remove the last two sections of the wing, along with the skin.

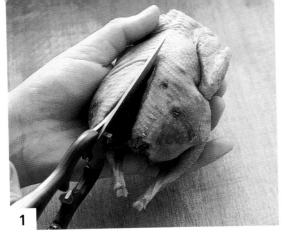

1

To split your bird into halves, begin by cutting along one side of the backbone with game shears. If you want to remove the backbone, cut along the other side to remove it.

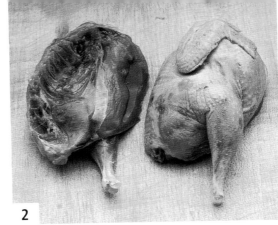

2

Cut along one side of the breastbone and through the wishbone. You can remove the breastbone by making a second cut along the other side of it.

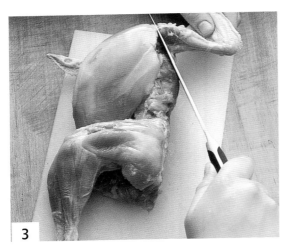

3

To cut up your bird, begin by removing the wings by cutting through the joint next to the breast. You can save wings to make excellent soup stocks.

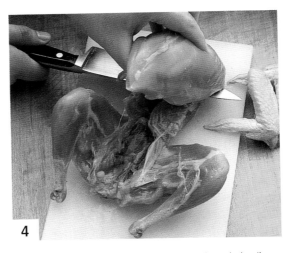

4

Separate the breast from the back by cutting through the ribs. When you reach the shoulder, grasp the breast in one hand and the back in the other, bending the carcass as if it were hinged. Continue to cut the breast and back apart.

Loosen the skin at the base of the neck and cut the meat around the base of the neck near the shoulders. Twist or cut the neck off the carcass. The final cut is the removal of the tail and the attached skin with feathers, which will include the oil gland.

The carcass is now skinless, neckless, and tail-less. Place the carcass in a pan of clean water while you clean and sanitize your table or cutting surface before going on to the next bird.

Breaking Down Your Bird

To butcher your bird after the feathers have been removed, you can use the following easy steps if you do not want to roast or cook the bird whole. Older birds tend to be larger and may need to be cooked for longer periods,

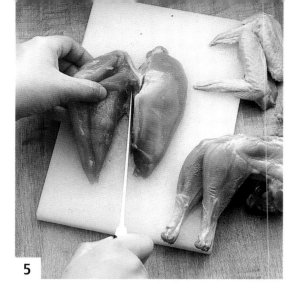

5

Divide the breast into halves by cutting along one side of the breastbone, then cutting away the wishbone. You can also cut along the other side of the breastbone and remove it.

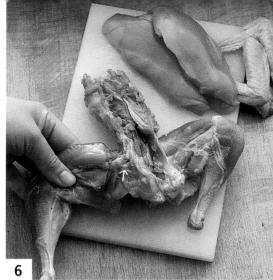

6

Begin cutting the leg away from the backbone, then bend it back to expose the ball-and-socket joint (arrow). Cut through the socket to remove the leg. You can also separate the thigh from the drumstick by cutting through the knee joint.

especially the legs and thighs. Younger or smaller birds may be better if the whole carcass is roasted or cooked.

Remove the head by locating the notch where the neck joins the body. Use a kitchen shears or knife to cut through.

Make cuts along the inside of each leg next to the body. Then move each leg back so the joints pop out. Sever the joint and remove the legs.

Cut the wings at the first joint.

Create two breast portions by cutting along one side of the keel bone. This bone separates the two breast sides and is easy to locate.

Slice along the keel bone to remove one breast and then finish the other side.

To keep the breastbone intact for roasting, cut through the mid-line of the keel bone, separating the bird into halves.

Rinse in cold water to remove residual clots or body parts.

Wipe dry with paper towels. The bird parts are now ready for cooking or freezing.

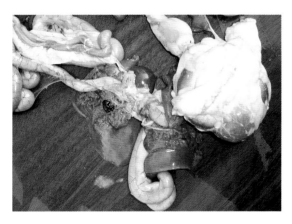

The heart, liver, lungs, gizzard, and other organs and viscera should have a healthy look. Examine them. If they appear off-color or any lesions are noticeable, it may indicate an unhealthy bird, which you should consider disposing of. A healthy bird will have bright-colored, vibrant organs and viscera.

Viscera

Look at the heart, liver, gizzard, and other internal organs after you have removed them from the bird. Check to see that they appear healthy. If they appear off-color or show any spots or lesions, you may have an unhealthy bird and you should consider discarding it. A healthy bird will have bright-colored, vibrant organs and viscera.

Remove the green gallbladder from the liver, either by cutting or pinching it off, and discard it. Since it stores and concentrates bile, the gallbladder has little use in a meal. However, the gizzard, liver, and heart can be removed and eaten.

Cut the gizzard from the intestines and stomach. It can be split lengthwise and the contents washed away. Peel away the lining inside the gizzard and remove it using your fingers.

The gizzard is highly prized by some people. Slice it in half and remove any feed contents that may remain. The lining on the inside is easily peeled off and should be removed before cooking.

You may decide not to cut up the carcasses until all the dressing, feather plucking, and viscera removal is completed for all the birds. If you wait to cut up the birds, you need to place the whole eviscerated carcasses in cold water to remove any remaining body heat.

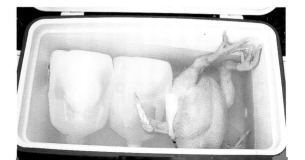

Quick Tips

- Birds generally don't require aging.
- Don't cross-contaminate during processing.
- If not used immediately, refrigerate birds at 40 degrees Fahrenheit or lower, and use within 3 days
- Freeze whole, cleaned carcasses or individual parts at 0 degrees Fahrenheit or lower for long-term storage up to 1 year.

Remove the heart and cut it open to release any remaining blood. Rinse it and the gizzard well and place them in a pan of cold water. These can be cooked or saved for sausage making.

A word of caution: If your wild bird was not eviscerated soon after it was killed, the giblets—heart, liver, gizzard—may not be safe to eat and should be discarded.

Chilling the Carcass

Unless you immediately proceed to cut up the carcass, put it in a cold water bath with temperatures between 32 and 36 degrees Fahrenheit. Birds should never be frozen before being chilled down because the meat will be less tender later as the muscle fibers slide and lock together. Placing the birds in an icy slush will rapidly cool them.

Some hunters like to age their birds by hanging them for several days. Depending on your tastes, you can age them for 24 to 48 hours at 35 to 45 degrees Fahrenheit. If you don't cook the birds within that time, you should freeze them.

You can freeze your birds with their feathers still on. This will help keep them from drying out, but it is typically not done.

Game Bird Preparation

A distinction must be made between white meat and dark meat in cooking game. Quail and partridges are white meat and, like chicken, must be thoroughly cooked.

Ducks, pigeons or squabs, grouse (prairie chicken), snipe, and woodcock are dark meat and are cooked rare and served very hot.

Turkeys and geese can be considered white meat for the most part, because their largest muscles are located in the breast area. The birds use these muscles less than their wing muscles. The legs can be considered dark meat.

All these birds may be cooked by the same methods, varying only as to the degree of rareness desired. Pick out shot from birds with a sharp pointed knife and wash quickly under running water. Small birds may be skinned when they are clean.

Canning Game Birds

Soak dressed meat for 1 hour in water containing 1 tablespoon of salt per quart, then rinse. Remove excess fat. Cut meat into suitable sizes. Can game bird meat with or without the bone.

Smoking Game Birds

If you don't have a special smokehouse, you can process game birds in a salt brine (in which the salt has been smoked or to which liquid smoke has been added) and cook them in your home oven. You can also cure the meat in a sugar and salt brine, then smoke it using hardwoods or wood chips. Smoking will give the game birds a light brown color and smoky aroma. Smoked birds may keep for up to 3 to 4 weeks in a refrigerator. If you don't consume it immediately, you can freeze smoked meat for up to 6 months. If you are using a smokehouse, follow these steps:

- Heat carcass to 140 degrees Fahrenheit for 30 minutes, then turn on smoke.
- Increase humidity by placing pans of water over heat source.
- Heat at 150 degrees Fahrenheit for 1 hour.
- Turn off smoke and heat at 170 degrees Fahrenheit for 2 hours, followed by 185 to 200 degrees Fahrenheit smokehouse air temperature, until internal meat temperature reaches 165 degrees Fahrenheit.
- After smoking, you must refrigerate the bird at temperatures less than 40 degrees Fahrenheit.

Waterfowl Substitution Guide

With more than twenty species of ducks and geese on the chart below, you can take a "mix-and-match" approach to substitutions. The chart is broken into four areas: large geese, medium-size geese, small geese/large ducks, and small ducks. If the recipe calls for a mallard, you can find it on the chart and then substitute any of the other ducks from that same area of the chart.

Breast meat from any of these birds can be substituted for mallard breast in recipes. Domestic ducks are generally too fatty to substitute for wild ducks. Upland game birds with dark meat also make good substitutes for duck if the cuts are the same size.

If the recipe calls for a whole Canada goose, you can substitute any wild goose of similar size. You can also substitute a domestic goose of the proper size, but the flavor won't be as rich as that of wild goose. You will have to prick the skin of a domestic goose frequently during roasting to allow the excess fat to drain off. Be sure to skim the fat from the pan juices prior to making gravy or sauce.

Species		Approximate Dressed Weight	Number of Servings	Cooking Method
large geese	giant Canada (young)	4 to 6 lbs.	4 to 6	oven roast, grill, panfry
	giant Canada (mature)	6 1/2 to 10 lbs.	6 to 10	parboil/roast, braise, stew
	interior Canada (mature)	4 3/4 to 6 lbs.	5 to 10	parboil/roast, braise, stew
medium-size geese	lesser Canada	3 to 4 1/2 lbs.	3 to 6	oven roast, grill, panfry
	snow or blue goose	3 to 4 lbs.	3 to 5	oven roast, grill, panfry
	white-fronted goose	3 1/2 to 4 3/4 lbs.	3 to 5	oven roast, grill, panfry
	interior Canada (young)	3 1/2 to 4 1/2 lbs.	4 to 5	oven roast, grill, panfry
small geese/large ducks	cackling Canada	2 to 2 1/2 lbs.	2 to 3	oven roast, grill, panfry
	brant	1 3/4 to 2 1/2 lbs.	2 to 3	oven roast, grill, panfry
	canvasback	1 3/4 lbs.	2	oven roast, grill, panfry
	mallard	1 1/4 to 1 1/2 lbs.	2	oven roast, grill, panfry
	black duck	1 1/4 to 1 1/2 lbs.	2	oven roast, grill, panfry
	redhead	1 1/4 lbs.	2	oven roast, grill, panfry
	greater scaup (bluebill)	1 1/4 lbs.	2	oven roast, grill, panfry
small ducks	goldeneye (whistler)	1 to 1 1/4 lbs.	1 to 1 1/2	oven roast, grill, panfry
	pintail	1 to 1 1/4 lbs.	1 to 1 1/2	oven roast, grill, panfry
	gadwall	3/4 to 1 lb.	1 to 1 1/2	oven roast, grill, panfry
	lesser scaup	3/4 to 1 lb.	1 to 1 1/2	oven roast, grill, panfry
	widgeon (baldpate)	3/4 to 1 lb.	1 to 1 1/2	oven roast, grill, panfry
	ring-necked (ringbill)	3/4 lb.	1 to 1 1/2	oven roast, grill panfry
	wood duck	1/2 to 3/4 lb.	1	oven roast, grill, panfry
	bufflehead	5 oz. to 3/4 lb.	1	oven roast, grill, panfry
	blue-winged teal	1/2 lb.	1	oven roast, grill, panfry
	cinnamon teal	5 oz. to 1/2 lb.	1	oven roast, grill, panfry
	green-winged teal	5 to 6 oz.	1 or less	oven roast, grill, panfry

Upland Game Birds Substitution Guide

As with small-game animals, there are noticeable differences in meat color and flavor among upland game birds. The subtle berry flavor of a ruffed grouse, for example, may be overpowered in a recipe with strong flavors, just as a strong-flavored sharptail may not work in a lightly seasoned dish.

Game-farm birds, such as pheasants, Chukar partridge, quail, and turkey, can be easily substituted for wild birds in recipes. A game-farm bird will probably have more fat than a wild one, so remove the excess fat before cooking.

Species	Approximate Dressed Weight	Number of Servings	Substitution	Cooking Method
wild turkey (whole)	8 to 16 lbs.	5 to 10	domestic turkey of similar weight (not prebasted type)	oven roast
wild turkey (any pieces)	3 to 4 1/2 lbs.	6 to 8	2 pheasants, quartered 3 ruffed or sharptail grouse (halved) 3 or 4 Chukar or Hungarian partridge (halved) 3 lbs. domestic turkey pieces, no excess fat	panfry, braise, bake
pheasant (whole)	1 1/2 to 2 1/4 lbs.	3 to 4	2 ruffed or sharptail grouse 2 Chukar or Hungarian partridge	oven roast, pan-broil, panfry braise, bake
2 pheasants (cut up)	3 to 4 1/2 lbs.	6 to 8	thighs and legs from wild turkey 3 or 4 ruffed or sharptail grouse (quartered) 4 Chukar or Hungarian partridge (quartered) 8 quail (halved)	panfry, braise, bake
pheasant (2 whole breasts, boneless)	1 lb.	4	boned breast portion or thighs from turkey boned breast and thighs from 2 ruffed or sharptail grouse 2 Chukar or Hungarian partridge boned breasts from 4 quail boned breasts from 6 or 7 doves	panfry, bake deep-fry, grill, braise
ruffed or sharptail grouse (whole)	1 to 11/4 lb.	2 to 3	1/2 pheasant 1 Chukar or Hungarian partridge	oven roast, panfry, bake, braise, grill
Chukar or Hungarian partridge	3/4 to 1 lb.	2	1/2 pheasant 1 ruffed or sharptail grouse	oven roast, panfry, bake, braise
quail	4 quail (4 to 6 oz. each)	4	1 pheasant, cut up 1 1/2 ruffed grouse, cut up 2 Chukar or Hungarian partridge (quartered)	oven roast, panfry, bake, braise, grill

Upland Game Birds Substitution Guide *continued*

Species	Approximate Dressed Weight	Number of Servings	Substitution	Cooking Method
woodcock	5 to 6 woodcock (5 oz. each)	4	1 pheasant, cut up 1 1/2 ruffed grouse, cut up 2 Chukar or Hungarian partridge, cut up 4 quail (halved)	panfry, braise, bake
dove	6 or 7 doves (2 to 3 oz. each)	4	1 pheasant, cut up, breast section 1 1/2 ruffed or sharptail grouse, cut up, breast sections halved 2 Chukar orHhungarian partridge, cut up, breast sections halved 4 quail, halved	panfry, braise, bake

Roast Duck

1 5-pound duck	**Salt and pepper**
Apples (optional)	**Garlic**
Celery (optional)	**Currant or cranberry jelly**
Onions (optional)	

Some believe ducks have too strong a flavor, and so to absorb this flavor, they lay cored and quartered apples inside the body. These are removed before the duck is put on the table. Celery and onions may also be placed inside the duck to season it and improve the flavor. Use 2 tablespoons of chopped onion to every cup of chopped celery.

Wash and clean the duck, season with salt and pepper, rub with garlic, and fill with apples, if desired. Place in pan and roast uncovered at 325°F, allowing 20 to 30 minutes per pound. Baste every 10 minutes using 1 cup of orange juice, if the flavor is desired. Serve with currant or cranberry jelly. Serves 5.

Roast Goose

1 8-pound goose
Salt and pepper
Flour

Rinse goose with cold water and dry on outside. Roast at 325°F for 45 minutes on rack in uncovered roasting pan. Remove from the oven, pour off fat, season with salt and pepper, dredge with flour, and return to oven.

When the flour is browned, pour 1 cup hot water into pan and baste the goose often, dredging each time with a slight sifting of flour to absorb fat. Allow 20 minutes per pound for a young goose, and 25 minutes for an older goose. Remove from pan and add 1 cup hot water to gravy and thicken, if necessary, with browned flour. Serves 5.

Salamis of Goose

To 4 cups sliced roast goose add 2 tablespoons each of lemon juice and Worcestershire sauce, and 2 cups goose gravy; simmer 20 minutes. Add 1/2 cup sherry and twelve ripe, sliced olives, and reheat. Garnish with parsley and serve on hot buttered toast.

Roast Turkey

Place the fresh turkey breast up on rack of a shallow pan. Brush with melted butter and cover with aluminum foil, making sure the breast, wings, and legs are well covered, and roast at 300°F until tender. Allow 20 minutes per pound for birds under 12 pounds, and 25 minutes per pound for larger birds. Baste several times with melted butter or drippings in the pan. Season when half-done. Allow 3/4 to 1 pound per serving. Any frozen turkey must be properly thawed prior to baking. Thaw in cold water or in refrigerator overnight before use.

Roast Canadian Goose

1 5-pound wild goose
Lemon juice
6 c. dressing

Salt and pepper
2 tbsp. melted butter
2 c. water

Prepare goose. Brush cavity with lemon juice. Insert dressing (see recipe below) and sew the cavity shut. Mix salt and pepper in melted butter and brush on the outside of goose. Heat oven to 450°F. Pour water in roasting pan. Place goose on a rack in pan. Turn oven down to 350°F and cook 20 minutes per pound or until tender.

Dressing

Giblets
Giblet stock
2 1/2 qts. dried bread, chopped
1 large onion, chopped

2 diced apples
Salt and pepper
Sage
Garlic

Boil giblets until tender; reserve stock. Remove skin from giblets and chop fine. Combine bread, onion, and apples; mix well. Add salt, pepper, sage, and garlic to taste. Moisten with giblet stock.

Rub cavity of goose with 1/8 teaspoon salt per pound. Bake at 375°F for 15 to 20 minutes. Dip out fat and stuff the bird. Prick fat on back, around the tail, and the skin around the wings and legs. Cover and roast at 325°F for 4 hours for an 8-pound goose; 4 1/2 hours for an 11-pound bird. If goose is very fat, remove excess fat from pan during roasting.

Braised Duck

1 4-pound duck
4 slices bacon
1 onion, minced
1 carrot, diced
1/2 tsp. powdered thyme

2 tbsp. minced parsley
Salt and pepper
4 c. boiling water
4 tbsp. flour
1/4 c. cold water

Prepare duck as for roasting and sauté in bacon fat until brown. Add onion, carrot, thyme, parsley, salt, and pepper; cover with water. Simmer until the duck is tender, then remove from stock. Blend flour and cold water together until smooth and add gradually to stock, stirring constantly. Pour gravy over the duck. Serves 4.

Braised duck with mushrooms—Omit bacon and carrot. Use 1/2 pound of sliced mushrooms and sauté in fat.

Broiled Birds

Season with salt and pepper and dust with flour. Brown the bird on both sides, allowing 8 to 12 minutes for quail and 25 to 40 minutes for partridges and pheasants. A strip of bacon, smoked ham butt, or salt pork may be placed over the top of each bird. When done, brush with melted butter. During broiling, if the breasts are quite thick, cover the broiling pan with another pan, lower the temperature, and lengthen the cooking time.

Roasted Birds

Clean and stuff the birds. Brush with unsalted melted fat. If the birds do not have a lot of fat, lay strips of salt pork across the breasts. Roast uncovered at 350°F until the meat is tender and the bird is well browned. Baste every 30 minutes with butter and water. Season the bird with salt when about half-done. Place on a warmed platter and cover with gravy made from pan drippings. Garnish the platter with parsley. Allow 1/2 to 1 bird per person.

Roast Wild Duck

Clean the duck by wiping the inside and outside with a damp towel. Tuck back the wings and truss. Dust with salt, pepper, and flour. If there is not a lot of fat on the duck, cover breast with 2 thin slices of salt pork. Place duck in a pan and add 1 cup of water and 2 tablespoons of fat. Roast uncovered and breast down at 350°F, allowing 20 to 25 minutes per pound, according to rareness desired. Baste frequently. Turn the duck to breast side up when half done. Serve with slices of lemon or orange and a brown gravy. Wild ducks are served rare and are seldom stuffed when roasted.

Roast Pheasant with Sauerkraut

1 whole pheasant, skin on	2 c. pheasant stock or chicken broth
2 tbsp. butter, softened	1/4 c. cognac or brandy
2 slices bacon, cut up	1/3 c. canned cranberries, rinsed
1 can (16 oz.) sauerkraut, rinsed and drained	3 tbsp. butter or margarine

Heat oven to 375°F. Rub softened butter over pheasant. Place in small roasting pan; cover. Roast until pheasant is tender and juices run clear when thigh is pricked, about 35 to 45 minutes.

Prepare remaining ingredients while roasting pheasant. In medium skillet, cook bacon over low heat until lightly browned. Add sauerkraut and 1 cup pheasant stock. Cook over medium heat until most liquid evaporates, about 12 to 15 minutes. Remove from heat, set aside, and keep warm.

When the pheasant is done, transfer from roaster to heated platter; set aside and keep warm. Pour drippings from roaster into small bowl; set aside. In small saucepan, heat cognac gently over low heat until warm. Remove from heat and carefully ignite the cognac with a long match. When the flame dies, add 1 cup pheasant stock and cranberries. Cook over high heat until liquid is reduced by half, about 10 to 15 minutes.

Skim fat from reserved drippings. Add drippings and 3 tablespoons butter to cranberry mixture; cook, stirring occasionally, until butter melts, about 2 minutes. Serve cranberry sauce with pheasant, sauerkraut, and crusty French bread. Serves 2 to 3.

Sautéed Partridge Breast with Figs

4 boneless breast halves from
    partridge or ruffed grouse
6 dried figs, chopped
1 c. partridge stock or chicken broth
1 tbsp. butter or margarine

1 tbsp. balsamic vinegar
1/4 tsp. dried thyme leaves
1/4 c. butter, cut into 4 pieces
Salt and pepper

In small saucepan, heat figs and stock to boiling. Reduce heat; simmer until stock thickens and darkens slightly, about 15 minutes. Remove from heat and set aside.

In medium skillet, melt 1 tablespoon butter over medium-low heat. Add breast halves. Cook until well browned on both sides but still moist in the center, 6 to 10 minutes. Remove from skillet. Set aside and keep warm.

Add balsamic vinegar after wiping skillet clean with paper towels; swirl vinegar around skillet. Add the reserved fig mixture. Cook over high heat until mixture is thick; stir in thyme. Remove skillet from heat. Add butter, 1 tablespoon at a time, stirring well between each addition. Add salt and pepper to taste. Slice the reserved breasts; pour sauce over breasts. Serves 2.

Doves or Quail in Cornbread Stuffing

8 dove breasts

STUFFING
1/2 c. celery, chopped
1/4 c. green onion, sliced
2 tbsp. snipped fresh parsley if
    available

1/4 c. butter or margarine
3 c. cornbread stuffing mix
1 c. game bird stock or chicken broth
1/2 tsp. dried marjoram leaves
1/2 tsp. salt
1/8 tsp. pepper

Heat oven to 350°F. Lightly grease 2-quart casserole; set aside. In medium skillet, cook and stir celery, onion, and parsley in butter over medium heat until tender. Add remaining stuffing ingredients. Mix until moistened. Place half of stuffing mixture in prepared casserole. Arrange dove breasts over stuffing. Cover completely with remaining stuffing mixture. Bake, uncovered, until dove is cooked through and tender, about 1 hour. Serves 4. To substitute quail for doves, use 6 quail and split in half. Proceed as above.

Stewed Partridge with Sage Dumplings

3 partridge, whole or cut up
1 1/2 qts. water
2 bay leaves
1 tsp. dried thyme leaves
1 tsp. dried rosemary leaves
1 tsp. dried summer savory leaves,
    optional

2 tsp. salt
1/8 tsp. pepper
4 carrots, cut into 1-inch pieces
3 stalks celery, cut into cubes
2 medium onions, cubed

In saucepan, combine partridge, water, bay leaves, thyme, rosemary, and savory leaves. Heat to boiling. Reduce heat; cover. Simmer for 1 1/2 hours. Add salt, pepper, carrots, celery, and onions; cook until partridge and vegetables are tender, about 45 minutes. Remove from heat. Remove partridge and bay leaves from stock and vegetables; discard bay leaves. Cool partridge slightly.

Skim fat from broth. Remove partridge meat from bones and any skin. Tear meat into bite-size pieces and return to broth. Discard bones and skin.

SAGE DUMPLINGS

1 1/2 c. flour
2 tsp. baking powder
1/2 tsp. salt

1/2 to 3/4 tsp. crushed sage
2/3 c. milk
3 tbsp. butter or margarine, melted

In saucepan, combine partridge, water, bay leaves, thyme, rosemary, and savory leaves. Heat to boiling. Reduce heat; cover. Simmer for 1 1/2 hours. Add salt, pepper, carrots, celery, and onions; cook until partridge and vegetables are tender, about 45 minutes. Remove from heat. Remove partridge and bay leaves from stock and vegetables; discard bay leaves. Cool partridge slightly.

Skim fat from broth. Remove partridge meat from bones and any skin. Tear meat into bite-size pieces and return to broth. Discard bones and skin.

To make dumplings, combine flour, baking powder, salt, and sage in medium mixing bowl; stir with fork to combine. Add milk and melted butter; stir until flour is moistened. Set aside.

Heat meat, vegetables, and broth until the broth boils. Drop dumpling dough by heaping tablespoons onto broth mixture. Cook over medium-high heat for 5 minutes; cover and cook until dumplings are firm, about 10 minutes longer. Serves 4 to 6.

Pigeon and Squab Cooking

Domestic pigeons are the most desirable. Wild pigeons are likely to be tough. Squabs are the nestlings of pigeons, usually marketed at about 4 weeks of age. They are tender and delicately flavored. Both are prepared by the same methods as chicken, though pigeons need a long, slow cooking time.

Broiled Squab

6 squabs
Salt and pepper

Butter
Toast

Wash birds quickly under running water. Split down the back, flatten the breast, season, and broil. When browned, brush with melted butter and serve on toast. Serves 6.

Pigeon and Mushroom Stew

3 pigeons
1 tbsp. fat
2 c. stock or gravy
Salt, pepper, cayenne pepper

2 tbsp. mushroom ketchup
1/2 c. mushrooms
2 tbsp. cream

Clean and cut pigeons into serving portions. Sauté in fat but do not brown. Add stock or gravy, salt, pepper, cayenne, and mushroom ketchup. Simmer 1 hour, or until tender. Add mushrooms, simmer 10 minutes more, and stir in cream. Serve on hot platter with mushrooms arranged around pigeons. Serves 3.

Chapter 6

FISH

F ish, like wild game, have been part of the human diet for thousands of years. Fish meat is high in protein and contains nine amino acids our bodies require but can't produce for ourselves. Fish is a good source of vitamin B_{12}, and most fish are rich sources of iron. They also contain omega-3 fatty acids, which support brain and neural development.

Most fish are cold-blooded animals, meaning their internal body temperature is about the same as the surrounding water. However, tuna, swordfish, and a few shark species are warm-blooded.

Fish make up the largest and most diverse class of vertebrates (animals having a spine). The kinds of game fish that swim in

Initial care of caught fish is important to ensuring a great-tasting meal. Proper care ensures firm flesh for cooking. Clip-type stringers are preferable to the rope style because the fish are not crowded. However, rope stringers are better for very large fish.

Wire baskets or net bags hung over the side of the boat keep small fish alive. The fish should have ample room to move around.

Aerated live wells in many boats keep bass, northern pike, and other hardy fish alive. Limit the number of fish and remove dead ones to ice immediately.

freshwater in North America vary in size. They range from small types, such as bluegills and crappies, to large ones, such as muskellunge, sturgeon, and catfish.

There are three basic classes of fish: cartilaginous, with bony skeletons and a body frame of cartilage (sharks and rays are in this group); ray-finned, which have

Popular Freshwater Game Fish

- bass (largemouth and smallmouth)
- bass (rock, spotted, striped, white)
- bluegill
- carp
- catfish
- crappie
- eel
- gar
- grayling
- muskellunge
- perch
- pickerel
- pike
- salmon (Atlantic, coho, Pacific, pink, sockeye)
- sturgeon
- sunfish
- trout (brook, brown, lake, rainbow)
- walleye
- whitefish

fins composed of rays of bony spines, such as panfish and sturgeon; and lobe-finned, a group of bony fish that have paired fleshy fins at the base of fleshy lobes (lungfish and coelacanths are in this group).

Fish can also be grouped as freshwater or marine. Some species, such as salmon, will migrate from the sea into freshwater rivers to spawn. Others, like freshwater eels, will migrate from a freshwater environment to the sea to spawn. We will focus on freshwater game fish that inhabit the United States and Canada, namely those belonging to the ray-finned class.

Ray-finned fish are the most diverse group of fish and include almost 24 thousand species divided into 431 families. In North America, freshwater game fish can be divided further into two groups: large fish (such as sturgeon and muskellunge) and small fish, referred to as panfish because they can fit in a normal cooking pan. These include crappies, bluegill, and perch.

Initial Care

Fish are extremely perishable. Properly caring for, cleaning, and preserving your fresh fish is critical to ensuring your catch becomes a great-tasting meal. The quality of a fish begins to decline as soon as it is caught. Handle them with care to avoid bruising and keep them out of sunlight to prevent further deterioration. Discard any that do not have a fresh odor, clear eyes, or red gills, as they are likely not good for eating.

The secret to preserving your catch is to keep it alive and cold until just before cleaning and dressing it. Attach your caught fish to a stringer or place them in a wire basket in the cool surface water to keep them alive while you continue fishing. Remove them from the water if you move to another spot and then return them back to the water when you have stopped. This will help keep them alive and fresh until you make shore.

Many boats have aerated water wells to keep fish alive. Check your fish often whether they are on a stringer, in a wire basket, or in an aerated well. If any die, remove them and place on ice immediately until you can clean them. Dead fish left in water will spoil quickly.

Fish meat bruises easily, so avoid letting them flop around inside your boat after you reel them in or against your boat if they're on a stringer.

It is difficult to keep fish in good condition on long trips if they are not frozen. They don't need to be frozen, but they need to be kept cold. If you're traveling longer than two days, consider freezing or smoking them for transport. If you ship your fish by plane or overland express, be sure to pack them securely in ice and send them in an insulated container that is labeled with proper handling instructions.

Avoid placing fish in the sunshine or in nonporous wrapping such as plastic bags or rubberized pouches—fish spoil quickly without air circulation.

Wicker creels are used by wading anglers. Place layers of moss, ferns, or grass between the fish to provide ventilation. Transfer your catch to ice as soon as possible.

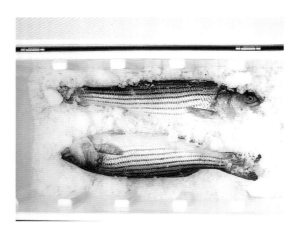

Coolers filled with ice keep fish cold. Crushed ice chills fish faster than a solid block. Drain the cooler often so the catch does not soak in water.

Burlap bags, newspapers, moss, and other materials that allow air in help preserve fish when ice is not available. Keep the covering moist because evaporation helps cool fish.

Field Dressing

There are several ways of cleaning and cutting up fish, and no one method is better than another if properly applied.

Fish should be cleaned as quickly as possible once they are removed from the water. For best quality and flavor, clean out the gills, viscera, and kidneys first, because these spoil rapidly in dead fish.

It's easy to dress or clean a fish if you have the right equipment and a convenient location. A sharp knife, whetstone, spoon,

Different techniques for dressing fish are used for different species, generally related to size and whether they will be cooked with their skin on or not. A basic approach starts with removing the gills by cutting the throat connection. Continue by cutting along both sides of the arch so that the gills pull out easily.

Quick Tips

- Keep fish alive as long as possible.
- Keep fish covered during winter fishing to prevent freezing and drying.
- Check for signs of disease and/or parasites.
- Follow all applicable fishing regulations.

mesh glove, and cutting board are the basics. A scaling tool can be useful too. The mesh glove is for your protection and will prevent hand or finger lacerations if you slip while cutting with your knife.

Cleaning and cutting up fish is easier and more efficient if you have a sharp knife. Dull knives can be useful for removing scales, but they don't do a very good job of cutting the meat. Cutting through the skin and bones,

especially if a large number of fish are being dressed, can dull a knife. A whetstone can keep your blade edge sharp.

Some anglers like to remove the scales from their fish first. This is usually done if the fish are to be cooked with their skin on, but only if they have large scales. Panfish have large scales, which should be removed if the skin is kept on for cooking. Largemouth bass have a strong-tasting

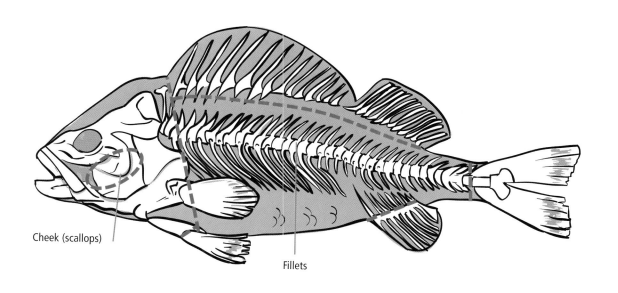

Cheek (scallops)

Fillets

Insert the knife in the vent and run the blade tip to the gills. Pull the viscera and gills out of the cavity. Most fish that are filleted do not need to be scaled, but those that are cooked whole or with their skin on should have their scales removed.

Cut the membrane along the backbone. Scrape out the kidney or bloodline underneath the membrane. Use a mesh glove on your free hand to prevent accidental cuts from your knife and to protect it from the external spines.

Anglers use a variety of filleting techniques. One way is to begin by lifting the pectoral fin with your knife and angling it toward the back of the head to start your cut to the backbone.

Turn the blade parallel to the backbone and cut toward the tail with a sawing motion until the fillet is cut off. Having a sharp knife is essential to making easy cuts.

Remove the rib bones by sliding the blade along the ribs. Turn the fish over and remove the second fillet. Cutting through rib bones will dull knives quickly, so keep a steel handy to touch up your knife when necessary.

Remove the thin strip of fatty belly flesh on oily fish such as salmon and large trout. Any contaminants the fish ingests will settle into this fatty tissue. Discard the viscera and belly.

skin, so many anglers remove it. Keep the skin on the fish if it is to be charcoal grilled, as this will prevent the meat from falling apart or sticking to the pan or grill.

To dress or scale your fish, place it on newspaper over a cutting board to make cleanup easier. Wipe the fish with a paper towel to remove slime and make it easier to hold firmly.

Basic Filleting

There are a variety of filleting techniques; the following is one example. A fillet board with a clip to hold the head can be a useful aid, as it holds the fish while you are slicing in the opposite direction. Applying salt to your opposite hand will also help to hold a slippery fish while you are filleting.

7

Skin the fillet, if desired, by cutting into the tail flesh to the skin. Turn the blade parallel to the skin. Keep the skin on fillets that will be charcoal grilled—this helps prevent the flesh from falling apart, sticking to the grill, and overcooking.

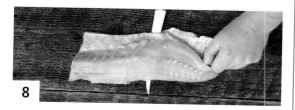

8

Finish by pulling the skin firmly while moving the knife in a sawing motion between the skin and the flesh. Clean the fillets by wiping with paper towels or rinsing quickly under cold water, then dry thoroughly.

9

Northern pike, muskellunge, and pickerel have a row of Y-shaped bones that float just above the ribs and run lengthwise along the fillet, ending above the vent. They can be cut out by guiding the knife blade along the bones and scraping lightly. (See next three photos.) Some flesh is lost when Y-bones are cut out, but this step may make for more pleasurable dining. The bones can also be left intact and removed after cooking.

Y-Bones

Y-bones are the skeletal bones that run lengthwise along the fillet, starting just above the ribs and ending above the anus. Northern pike, muskellunge, and pickerel have a row of Y-shaped bones on each fillet side.

10A

To remove the Y-bones, begin by slicing through the flesh along the right edge of them (the fillet at left will be boneless).

10B

Cut the flesh from the Y-bones by guiding the knife blade along the bones (arrow) with a light scraping motion.

10C

Remove the triangular strip of bones and flesh, saving them for stock if desired. This leaves two long boneless fillets.

Many anglers remove Y-bones before cooking, even though some meat is lost. The easy alternative is to pull these bones out after cooking.

Canadian Filleting

Some fishermen find the Canadian style of filleting an easy method to use, especially with a fish that has a heavy rib structure

Quick Tips for Large Fish

1. Oily fish such as salmon and large trout will have a thin strip of fatty flesh running along the bottom of their belly. Remove this. Fish can contain a variety of environmental contaminants, which often settle in the fat cells. Any contaminants in the fish will likely be found in the belly fat.

2. Begin by making your first cut just behind the gill behind the head. Turn your knife at an angle and slice down the backbone, using the heel to guide your cut.

3. As your knife slides along the backbone, it will cut through the ribs until you reach the tail. If you skin the fillet, you can stop your cut at the tail, leaving a portion of skin attached to the fish.

4. Turn the fillet over (skin-side down), flatten the knife on the skin, and run it forward to separate the flesh and skin.

5. Do the same for the other side. If done properly, the end result will be an entire carcass left without the meat fillets.

6. To clean the fillets, use paper towels and wipe dry or rinse in clean, cold water, then dry. To keep the fish whole, you will only need to remove the viscera or guts and wash the fish inside and out with clean water.

7. After handling fish, be sure to rinse your hands with clean water, then with soap. To remove the fishy smell you can use vinegar and salt, lemon juice, or toothpaste.

8. You can make fish steaks by using the dressing procedures, then cutting the body crosswise into portions about 1 inch thick. Generally, steaking is only done with large fish such as northern pike and salmon.

9. It is often easier to fillet large fish (such as walleye, northern pike, or bass) if you retain the head to use as something to hold on to while cutting the fish. The fish are also easier to cut if the viscous covering is thoroughly washed off the scales.

(such as white bass and large black bass). This method takes a little longer and may leave more flesh on the bones, but it eliminates the extra step of cutting the rib bones from the fillet.

U.S. fishermen transporting their legal catch across the border from Canada need to be aware that a certain portion of the skin needs to remain attached to each fillet. This allows for proper fish identification, which corresponds to the allowable bag limit. Be sure to check the regulations that apply before completely filleting and skinning your Canadian-caught fish.

Filleting with an Electric Knife

An electric knife is useful for filleting panfish, catfish, and any large fish that has heavy rib bones. If the skin is retained for cooking, scale the fish before filleting.

Pan Dressing Fish

Panfish, including bluegills, crappies, and yellow perch, are often too small for filleting. They are usually pan dressed instead. Scales, fins, guts, and head are always removed. The tail is quite tasty and can be left on. Most of the tiny fin bones in a fish are removed by pan dressing.

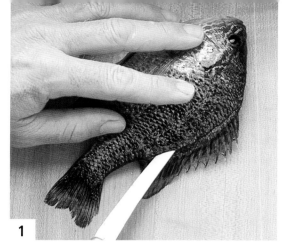

1

Panfish, including bluegills, crappies, and yellow perch, are often too small for filleting. They are usually pan dressed instead. Begin by slicing along the dorsal fin of the scaled panfish. Make the same cut on the other side, then pull out the fin.

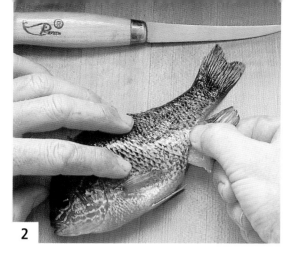

2

Cut along both sides of the anal fin. Remove the fin by pulling it toward the tail.

3

Remove the head. Angle the blade over the top of the head to save as much flesh as possible.

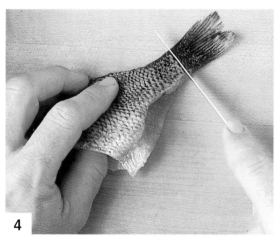

4

Slit the belly and pull out the viscera. Slice lengthwise along the spine to separate into halves. Trim out the small rib cage by using a smooth scraping motion. Refrigerate or freeze fish if not using immediately.

Storing Fish

A fish will taste best if it is cleaned and cooked within two hours after it's caught. Of course, you may have to keep it longer than that.

If fish are handled and cleaned properly, they can be refrigerated for twenty-four hours with little flavor loss. The key is temperature:

Quick Tips for Panfish

1. Begin by slicing the throat where the lower jaw connects to the gill membrane.

2. Insert the blade tip into the anus and run it up the stomach to the gills. Try to avoid puncturing the intestines.

3. Push your thumb into the throat. Pull the gills and guts toward the tail. Scrape out the insides with a spoon if necessary.

Quick Tips

- Clean and cool fish as soon as possible. Heat and time rob the fish of freshness.

- Clean knives after each use so you don't cross-contaminate.

- Store cleaned fish at 40 degrees Fahrenheit or lower and use within two days.

For top flavor, clean and cook your fish within two hours after catching it. To properly store cleaned fish, wipe or pat the fillets, steaks, or whole fish with paper towels.

the colder the storage temperature, the longer the fish can be held.

Fish stored in crushed ice will remain fresh for two to three days, but must be drained often. Superchilled fish can be kept up to seven days (see below). Lean fish can be stored longer than oily fish, and whole fish longer than fillets or steaks.

Storage Preparation

Rinse the fillets with clean, cold water. If you plan to store the whole fish, thoroughly wash the body cavity and remove any remaining residue; wipe dry with paper towels.

Superchilling involves storing fish in crushed ice and covering them with a salt-ice mixture. This will hold the fish at about 28 degrees Fahrenheit. This is colder than refrigeration and is especially helpful when freezing facilities are not available.

Wrap the whole fish, fillets, or steaks in aluminum foil or plastic wrap before superchilling. As the ice melts, you can add more of the salt-ice mixture.

Tagging Programs

As an angler, you may on occasion catch a fish that has been tagged. Tagging programs help monitor and manage available stocks. They provide population estimates and other information on game fish to help improve

The colder the storage temperature, the longer the fish will keep. You can refrigerate fish on paper towels or cover them tightly in a pan using plastic wrap or aluminum foil. Lean fish can be stored longer than oily fish, and whole fish longer than fillets or steaks.

Fish can be transported in crushed ice. A mixture of 1 pound coarse ice cream salt into 20 pounds of crushed ice makes an excellent salt–ice mixture. This will keep temperatures colder than refrigeration if long trips are required and freezing facilities are not available. Layer the fish and salt–ice mixture for even freezing.

the management of fisheries resources. These tags typically have a number, tag date, location, species, and size when released. If you catch a tagged fish, you should report the location and date of capture as well as the measurement of the fish.

By working with conservation efforts, you will help to preserve fishing as a viable sport and recreation activity.

Freezing, Pickling, and Canning Fish

Fish tends to dry out more quickly than other meats. Glazing with ice or freezing in water are good preservation methods for fish, as are pickling and canning.

Freezing and Thawing Fish

Freezing is a convenient way to preserve the quality of fish. Freeze them immediately after cleaning unless they will be eaten within 24 hours. Proper packaging shields the fish from air, which causes freezer burn. Air cannot penetrate ice, so fish frozen in a solid block of ice or with a glaze are well protected. A double wrap of aluminum foil or plastic wrap and freezer paper is added insurance against air penetration.

Cut fillets into serving-size pieces before freezing. Be sure fillets are suspended in the middle of the ice block and not at the top or bottom. Store fish in a 0°F freezer. A frost-free freezer is not recommended, because the fan pulls moisture from wrapped fish and quickly causes freezer burn.

You can treat fish fillets and steaks to extend their freezer life. Mix 2 tablespoons of ascorbic acid in 1 quart water. Place fish in the mixture for 20 seconds. Double wrap and freeze immediately.

Never thaw fish at room temperature. Bacteria flourishes in warm temperatures. Place wrapped packages on a plate in the

A Pickling Checklist

- Use only potable water approved for drinking purposes. Avoid using "hard" water, as the minerals (such as iron, calcium, and magnesium) interfere with the curing process and can cause off flavors.

- Use only high-quality distilled vinegars (white) of 5 percent acidity. Check labels and avoid using any vinegars of unknown acidity. Avoid using ciders or fruit vinegars, which may give fish an off color and flavor.

- To avoid bitter flavors and discoloration of the fish, use only high-quality, pure, granulated salt that's free from magnesium compounds. For pickling, noniodized salt is best.

- Use normal table sugar (cane or beet).

- Use high-quality, fresh, whole spices for best results. Mix only at the time it is to be used.

- Mix a weak brine of 1 cup salt to 1 gallon of water and soak fresh fish in it for one hour.

- Drain. Mix a strong brine (2½ pounds salt to 1 gallon water) and pour it over fish packed into glass jars, heavy food-grade plastic, or enamel. Soak for 12 hours. Refrigerate at 40 degrees Fahrenheit or lower.

refrigerator for a day. Larger pieces may need even longer to thaw.

Pickling Fish

Fish can be cured in a brine—this is known as pickling. Commercial pickling is only done with a few types of fish, but almost any fish species can be pickled for home use.

When using the vinegar-spice cure, preserve only the freshest and best-quality fish. Other factors that will affect the texture, flavor, color, and preservation quality include the water, salt, sugar, vinegar, and herbs used.

Canning Fish

Canning offers some advantages over freezing if you lack freezer space. The safest way to process fish for canning is with a pressure cooker. Fish that has been frozen can be safely canned by thawing in a refrigerator and canning promptly. Always follow proper canning procedures carefully.

Fish may be canned with bones intact. However, it is recommended that you use only pint or smaller containers for canning fish. The best fish for canning are those with a relatively high fat content, like salmon, trout, or mackerel.

To can fish:
- Eviscerate fish within two hours after they are caught.
- Keep cleaned fish on ice until ready to can.
- Remove head, tail, fins, and scales.
- Wash and remove all blood.
- Cut cleaned fish into 3 1/2-inch lengths.
- Fill pint jars, skin side next to glass. Leave 1-inch headspace.
- Add 1 teaspoon of salt per pint, if desired.
- Do not add liquid.
- Adjust lids and process according to table recommendations.

Freezer Storage Chart for Fish

FISH TYPE	WHOLE	STEAKS	FILLETS
Large Oily	2 months	1 1/2 months	1 month
Small Oily	1 1/2 months	1 month	1 month
Large Lean	6 months	4 months	3 1/2 months
Small Lean	4 months	3 months	2 1/2 months

Time Table for Canning Fish

Pack	Jar Size	Time (Min.)	Pounds Pressure–Dial Gauge		
			0–2,000 ft.*	2,001–4,000 ft.	4,001–6,000 ft.
Raw	Pints	100	11	12	13

Pack	Jar Size	Time (Min.)	Pounds Pressure–Weighted Gauge	
			0–1,000 ft.	Above 1,000 ft.
Raw	Pints	100	10	15

Time Table for Canning Smoked Fish

Jar Size	Time (Min.)	0–2,000 ft.*	Pounds Pressure-Dial Gauge		
			2,001–4,000 ft.	4,001–6,000 ft.	6,001–8,000 ft.
Pints	110	11	12	13	14

Jar Size	Time (Min.)	Pounds Pressure–Weighted Gauge	
		0–1,000 ft.	Above 1,000 ft.
Pints	110	11	15

*Local altitude
Source: U.S. Department of Agriculture Extension Service

Fish Substitution Guide

All of the game fish listed can be replaced by other fish in these recipes. For best results, use a fish from the same grouping on the fish substitution chart below. For example, northern pike, walleye, or muskellunge can be substituted in a recipe that calls for largemouth bass.

Type	Species Name	Other Common Names
large oily (2 pounds or larger)	salmon:	
	Chinook	king salmon, Tyee
	coho	silver salmon
	sockeye	red salmon
	pink	humpback
	chum	dog salmon
	Atlantic	landlocked salmon, Sebago salmon
	trout:	
	brook	squaretail, speckled trout
	brown	Loch Leven trout, German brown
	rainbow	steelhead, Kamloops
	cutthroat	Yellowstone trout
	lake	gray trout, togue, mackinaw
small oily (up to 2 pounds)	salmon:	
	kokanee	sockeye, red salmon
	trout:	
	brook	squaretail, speckled trout
	brown	Loch Leven trout, German brown
	rainbow	steelhead, Kamloops
	cutthroat	Yellowstone trout
large lean (2 pounds or larger)	black bass:	
	largemouth	black bass
	smallmouth	bronzeback, black bass
	muskellunge	muskie
	northern pike	jack, pickerel, snake
	striped bass	rockfish, striper
	walleye	walleyed pike, pickerel, dore
	white bass	striper, silver bass
small lean (up to 2 pounds)	panfish:	
	bluegill	bream, sunfish
	yellow perch	ringed perch, striped perch
	crappie	papermouth, speckled perch
	pumpkinseed	bream, sunfish
	black bass:	
	largemouth	black bass
	smallmouth	bronzeback, black bass
	white bass	striper, silver bass
catfish and bullheads	catfish:	
	flathead	yellow cat, mud cat
	channel	fiddler
	blue	white cat, silver cat
	bullhead	horned pout

Salmon Quiche

CRUST

3 c. flour
1 tsp. salt
2/3 c. vegetable oil
1/4 c. plus 2 tbsp. milk

FILLING

1 to 1 1/2 c. salmon, cooked and flaked
1 c. shredded Monterey Jack cheese
5 eggs
2 c. half-and-half
3/4 tsp. salt
1/8 tsp. pepper
Dash ground nutmeg
2 tbsp. parsley flakes

Heat oven to 350°F. In medium mixing bowl, mix flour, salt, oil, and milk lightly with fork until blended. Pat into 13x9-inch baking pan, patting dough 1 inch up side of pan; bake for 8 minutes.

Sprinkle cheese over hot crust, then sprinkle with fish. In small mixing bowl, blend eggs, half-and-half, salt, pepper, and nutmeg. Pour over fish. Sprinkle with parsley. Bake until knife inserted in center comes out clean, 30 to 35 minutes. Cool for 10 minutes. Cut into 1 1/2 to 2-inch square pieces. Serves 36 as appetizers.

Salmon Salad

2 c. salmon, cooked and flaked
1 c. small shell macaroni, uncooked
1/3 c. black olives, sliced
1/4 c. green pepper, finely chopped
1 tablespoon onion, grated
1/4 c. vegetable oil
2 tbsp. red wine vinegar
1/4 tsp. dried oregano leaves
1/4 tsp. salt
1/8 tsp. pepper

Prepare macaroni as directed on package. Rinse under cold water; drain. In medium bowl, combine macaroni, salmon, olives, green pepper, and onion. In small bowl, blend oil, vinegar, oregano, salt, and pepper. Pour dressing over salad, tossing to coat. Refrigerate at least 1 hour before serving. Serves 4 to 6.

Baked Walleye and Ratatouille

2 to 3 lbs. walleye
1 medium onion
2 cloves garlic, minced
1/4 c. olive or vegetable oil
1 eggplant (about 1 pound)
3 medium zucchini (about 1 pound)
1 medium green pepper

2 c. mushrooms, sliced
1 (16 oz.) can whole tomatoes,
    drained and cut up
1 tsp. salt
3/4 tsp. dried basil leaves
1/2 tsp. dried oregano leaves
1/4 tsp. pepper

Heat oven to 350°F. Cut onion into thin slices and separate into rings. In saucepan, cook and stir onion and garlic in olive oil over medium heat until onion is tender, about 5 minutes. Peel eggplant and cut into 3/4-inch cubes. Cut zucchini into 1/4-inch slices. Core and seed green pepper; cut into 1/2-inch strips. Stir eggplant, zucchini, green pepper, mushrooms, tomatoes, salt, basil, oregano, and pepper into onions. Cook over medium heat, stirring occasionally, for 10 minutes. Set aside.

Place fish on large sheet of heavy-duty aluminum foil. Spoon vegetables over and around fish. Wrap tightly. Place on baking sheet. Bake until fish flakes easily at backbone, about 35 minutes. Serves 2 to 4.

Lemon Fried Panfish

1 1/2 lbs. panfish or other lean fish
    fillets
1 c. all-purpose flour, plus more
    for coating
2 tsp. lemon peel, grated

1/2 tsp. salt
1/4 tsp. pepper
1 c. water
Vegetable oil

In medium bowl, combine 1 cup flour, lemon peel, salt, and pepper. Blend in water, then cover. Refrigerate 30 minutes.

In deep-fat fryer or deep skillet, heat oil (1 1/2 to 3 inches) to 375°F. Coat fish with flour, then dip in chilled batter. Fry a few pieces at a time, turning occasionally, until light brown, about 3 minutes. Drain on paper towels. Keep warm in 175°F oven. Repeat with remaining fish. Serves 4 to 6.

Creamy Northern Pike Casserole

2 c. flaked, cooked northern pike or
    other lean fish
1 c. thinly sliced celery
1 tbsp. butter or margarine
1 (10 3/4 oz.) can condensed cream
    of shrimp soup
1 c. green beans (use fresh if available)

1 (5.3 oz) can evaporated milk
1 (4 oz.) can sliced mushrooms,
    drained (use fresh if available)
1 (3 oz.) can French-fried onion
    rings, crushed
1/8 tsp. pepper

Heat oven to 350°F. In small skillet, cook and stir celery in butter over medium heat until tender, about 6 minutes. Set aside.

In 2-quart casserole, mix fish, cream of shrimp soup, green beans, evaporated milk, mushrooms, 1/2 cup of crushed onion rings, and pepper. Stir in celery.

Bake for 30 minutes. Top with remaining onion rings. Bake until hot and bubbly, 15 to 20 minutes. Serves 4 to 6.

Pickled Fish

10 lbs. fish
1 oz. whole allspice
1 oz. mustard seed
2 oz. regular mixed pickling spice
1/2 lb. onion, sliced
1/2 oz. bay leaves

1 1/2 qts. distilled (white) vinegar
2 1/2 pints water
1 oz. white pepper
1 oz. hot ground or dried pepper
    (if desired)

Rinse fish in fresh water. Combine the recipe ingredients in a large pan or kettle. Bring to a boil and add fish. Simmer for 10 minutes, or until fish is easily pierced with a fork. Remove fish from liquid and place in a single layer on a flat pan and refrigerate for rapid cooling to prevent spoilage. Pack cold fish in a clean glass jar, adding a few spices, a bay leaf, and freshly sliced onions.

Strain the vinegar, bring to a boil, and pour into jars until to cover the fish. Seal jars with lids. Must be stored in a refrigerator at 40°F or lower and should be used within 4 to 6 weeks. Serves 18 to 20.

Chapter 7

FREEZING, CANNING &COOKING

When you butcher wild game, it is likely you will have more meat available than you can eat at one meal. You'll want to preserve the rest for later use. Different preservation methods serve different purposes. Before you begin processing, decide how much meat you want to preserve using one or several of these methods. Do you want to freeze all or part of the carcass that is not used immediately? Do you want to make some into sausages? If you develop a plan before you begin, you'll reduce waste and save time.

Preservation Options

Preservation, in relation to meat products, is the process of handling meat in a way that stops or retards the growth of microorganisms, making it safe for long-term consumption. There are many forms of meat preservation, including freezing, canning, curing, pickling, and drying, to name the major processes used in homes. Large commercial applications employ methods such as vacuum packaging, irradiation, and sugaring, as well as using lye, modified atmosphere, and high pressure, but those will not be discussed here. In this chapter, we'll discuss freezing and canning, as well as some basic methods for cooking meat and how to handle byproducts. In chapter 9, we'll discuss curing (including pickling and corning), drying, and smoking.

Freezing, one of the most commonly used preservative methods, has several advantages. It is a fast and simple way to stop microbial growth. The nutritional value of the meat does not deteriorate with freezing, although texture and quality can suffer if long-term storage results in freezer burn. Freezing is discussed in greater detail below.

Canning involves cooking food to a boiling point for a specified time as a form of sterilization. This is done while sealed cans or jars are submerged in boiling water or placed in a pressure cooker. Canned meat offers several benefits: It's a useful alternative if you don't have enough freezer space for all your meat; it's a good backup in case of freezer malfunction; and it offers a ready-to-heat meal in as much time as it takes to open a can or jar.

Curing draws moisture out of tissue through a process of osmosis. Salt or sugar can be used separately or in a combination. Salted fish or meat was a staple in the diets of

Pickling involves the use of brines or vinegars to preserve meat products through fermentation. It is mostly used for fruits and vegetables, but it can be used for animal and fish products, such as pig's feet, pork hocks, corned beef, herring, northern pike, or other large game fish.

many early settlers who were on the move or lacked other methods to preserve food.

Pickling is the use of a brine, vinegar, or other spicy edible solution to inhibit microbial action. Pickling can involve two different forms: chemical pickling or fermentation pickling. The edible liquid used in chemical pickling typically includes agents such as a high-salt brine, vinegar, alcohol, and vegetable oils, particularly olive oil. The purpose is to saturate the food being preserved with the agent. This may be enhanced in some cases by heating or boiling. Common foods that are chemically pickled include corned beef, peppers, herring, eggs, and cucumbers. Fermentation pickling is generally not used with meat, but it can be used with foods that are served with meat, such as sauerkraut.

With fermentation pickling, the food is preserved by lactic acid bacteria.

One variation of pickling involves the combination of two methods: dry cure and pickle cure (sometimes referred to as sweet pickle cure). Dry-cured meats are typically not injected with sweet pickle. However, when temperature control is difficult or impossible, injecting "pickle" into the meat helps to ensure a safe, high-quality product. This works well with wild game or game birds and waterfowl.

Injecting or pumping this brine into the meat will distribute pickle ingredients throughout the interior of the meat so that curing begins on the inside and moves outward at the same time that curing begins on the outside and works inward. This protects the meat against spoilage and provides a more even curing.

Drying is perhaps the oldest method of food preservation and involves dehydration of the meat. The removal of water from the meat significantly reduces the water activity to prevent, inhibit, or delay bacterial growth. Reducing the amount of water in meat also reduces the total weight, making it easier to transport. Much of the drying of wild game meat today involves making jerky.

Freezing

Freezing remains one of the best preservation methods available for long-term storage because it doesn't destroy the meat's vitamins or nutritional value. Freezing meat almost completely inactivates enzymes and inhibits the growth of spoilage organisms.

To water pack fish, cut-up game birds, or small game in meal-sized portions, you can use washed milk cartons or plastic containers. Choose containers based on the size of the game you are freezing. Half-gallon cartons work well for ducks, while pint-sized cartons are better for partridge. Tiny game birds, cut-up game, fish fillets, or game-bird giblets can be frozen with a number of pieces in each container. Add cold water to cover the meat, then jiggle to eliminate air bubbles. Freeze on a level surface until completely solid.

Once the meat is frozen, check to be sure it is completely covered with ice. If not, add a layer of cold water and repeat freezing. If the meat sticks out of the ice it will quickly develop freezer burn, which diminishes the quality.

Quick Tips

- Set freezer temperature at -10 degrees Fahrenheit at least 24 hours ahead of freezing large amounts of fresh meat.

- Freeze meats quickly.

- Spread packages out within freezer to allow airflow. Stack later.

- Hold at 0 degrees Fahrenheit for best quality.

Quick Tips

- Thaw frozen meat in refrigerator or slowly in microwave.
- If thawed in microwave, cook meat immediately.
- Cook game meats thoroughly to an internal temperature of 165 degrees Fahrenheit minimum.

When processing a carcass, it is important to remember that meat temperatures must be brought down to 40 degrees Fahrenheit within 16 hours to prevent the growth of spoilage microorganisms that lie deep within the carcass tissues, or in the centers of containers of warm meat. If the meat has not been cooled but is going directly to a freezer, it must reach a temperature of 0 degrees Fahrenheit within 72 hours to prevent the growth of putrefying bacteria.

Rather than freeze meat in large portions that need to be further deconstructed once they are thawed, freeze meat in small, individual sizes that are ready for cooking. Smaller cuts freeze more quickly and evenly than very large pieces or chunks. It is good to minimize the number of times the meat needs to be handled and exposed after it is thawed.

Freezing Ground Meat

Ground meat will maintain better quality frozen rather than canned. Choose fresh, chilled, high-quality meat for grinding.

For large game such as venison, you can add one part high-quality pork fat to three to four parts venison for grinding.

Freezer Storage Chart

Game that's been ground with fat for burger meat doesn't keep as long as plain ground meat, because the fat can turn rancid even in the freezer.

Type of Meat	Wrapping Method	Maximum Storage Time
big-game roasts	standard butcher wrap	10 months
big-game steaks	standard butcher wrap	8 months
big-game ribs	foil wrap	5 months
big-game organs	standard butcher wrap/water pack	4 to 6 months
big-game chunks	freezer bag and paper	6 months
big-game burger	freezer bag and paper	4 months
cut-up small game	standard butcher wrap/water pack	8 months to 1 year
small-game organs	water pack	10 months
whole large birds	foil pack	5 months
whole small birds	standard butcher wrap/water pack	6 months to 1 year
cut-up upland birds	standard butcher wrap/water pack	8 months to 1 year
cut-up waterfowl	standard butcher wrap/water pack	8 months to 1 year
bird giblets	water pack	4 months
game stock	freezer containers	4 months

How to Wrap for the Freezer

1. Begin by placing the meat near the center of the wrap and then bring the edges together at the top.

2. Make a short fold at the top and repeat folds until last fold is tight against the meat.

3. Even out the fold wraps and smooth the ends as you make triangle folds.

4. Fold the ends under the package and seal with freezer tape. Label with date, type of meat and cut, and weight.

Package ground meat for freezing by wrapping it securely in coated or laminated freezer paper or heavy-duty foil.

Wrapping

Rancidity is the bad taste or smell derived from fats or oils that have spoiled. It develops differently in animal carcasses, depending on their fats' ability to absorb oxygen from the air. Rancidity can affect the taste, odor, and palatability of the fat and adjoining tissue. Different animal species produce different fats. Some fat, such as pork fat, is high in unsaturated fatty acids, which have the ability to absorb oxygen, resulting in a shorter storage life. Moose and elk have a higher proportion of saturated fatty acids and are less susceptible to oxygen absorption and generally have a longer storage life.

You can reduce oxidation effects by eliminating the meat's exposure to air. One good way to do this at home is to properly apply a wrapping material that is airtight and moisture proof.

Loss of meat moisture is referred to as shrinkage or dehydration. The loss of moisture from the frozen surface of the meat is called freezer burn. Freezer burn results from surface moisture loss due to using an unsuitable grade of wrapping paper, holes in the paper, or improper wrapping. Severe dehydration results in lower-quality cuts, and fats that have increased exposure to oxygen can turn rancid.

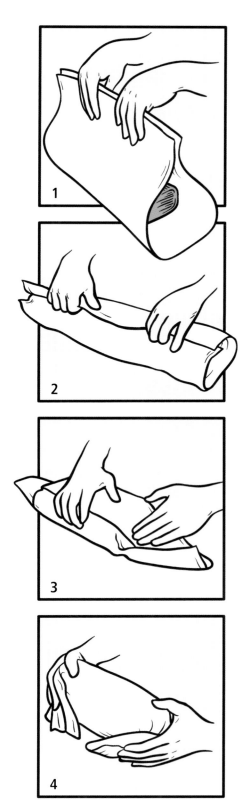

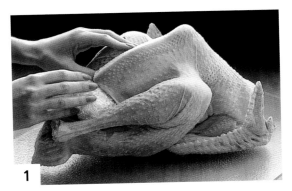

You can wrap a whole large game bird with a few simple steps. First, stuff wadded plastic wrap into the body cavity of a fully dressed bird (this reduces the chance of freezer burn).

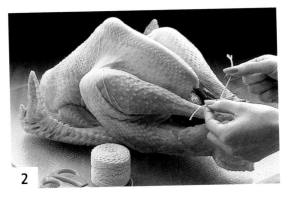

Tie the drumsticks together with kitchen string; they'll stick out less and the wrapping will be easier.

Wrap the bird snugly with heavy-duty aluminum foil (you may need several pieces to cover the entire bird).

Complete the wrapping with a double layer of heavy-duty freezer paper. Seal all the seams with freezer tape, then label and date the package.

To avoid freezer burn and rancidity, use a good grade of meat wrapping paper that is moisture proof. Use proper wrapping and handling procedures that eliminate tears or cuts in the paper. There are many American companies that supply meat wrapping paper, often referred to as butcher paper. When you're finished wrapping, be sure to label and date each package. You can place wrapped meat in a heavy plastic freezer bag for added protection.

Canning

Canning is the second-most commonly used preservation method for long-term storage of meat. Canned meats are generally of two types: sterilized and pasteurized. Sterilized meat products do not need refrigeration and can sit on shelves for extended periods, as long as the container remains intact. Pasteurized products require refrigeration to inhibit spoilage.

When you can meat for home use, use the appropriate procedures to ensure

Pressure cookers create higher cooking temperatures than are possible under normal cooking conditions. Water heated under pressure increases the temperature quickly. Be sure the gauge is accurate, the handles are securely fastened before heating the water, and the petcock functions appropriately to ensure safe use.

Glass jars are used for canning meats and vegetables. Inspect all jars for rim cracks or chips; discard any damaged jars, as they will not create a good, safe seal. Also inspect each rubber ring or metal lid with gaskets you plan on using, discarding any that are defective.

quality and safe storage. Canned meats are preserved by hermetically sealing the container—this prevents air from escaping or entering. By applying heat to the sealed meats, you destroy the microorganisms that are capable of producing spoilage. Using proper sanitation during the breakdown of the carcass will help minimize the number of organisms present at canning time.

Canning involves a time–temperature relationship in destroying most microorganisms. A specific internal temperature must be reached and held for a minimum amount of time to destroy the microorganisms present.

Quick Tips

- Make sure pressure cooker is working properly.
- Test dial gauge.
- Check rubber seals.
- Adjust for altitude.

This method is most often applied to destroy the spores that can lead to botulism. These times and temperatures are at the high end of any other methods. A safe cook, which is considered to be one that destroys the botulism organisms, requires a minimum of 3 minutes at 250 degrees Fahrenheit. Achieving this sterilizing temperature will require the use of a pressure cooker. These typically operate under pressure of 12 to 15 pounds per square inch. Pressure changes the boiling point of water, allowing it to rise above the normal boiling point of 212 degrees Fahrenheit.

There are many advantages to using the sterilization method of canning meat products. The best is a long storage life over a wide temperature range. If the container remains intact and the seal or exterior isn't damaged, canned meats that were done properly may last several years, although some flavor deterioration may occur.

The two most important aspects of canning are providing sufficient heat and

Canning big game in a pressure cooker starts with washing jars, new bands, and lids in hot, soapy water. Rinse them all well, then place jars and bands in hot, clear water. Place lids in a saucepan and cover with hot water; Heat to barely simmering over low heat.

Pack warm smoked chunks into jars, leaving 1 inch of space at the top. Unsmoked meat cubes can also be canned; first cook them to rare, then pack while hot. Add boiling broth, leaving 1 inch space at the top. Wipe the rims with a clean cloth for a better seal.

Place a warm lid and band on the jar. Tighten firmly but lightly. Place sealed jars on the trivet in the pressure cooker. Follow pressure-cooker manufacturer's directions for number of jars and amount of water to add to cooker. Heat until 10 pounds of pressure is reached, then begin timing.

Allow pressure to drop naturally. When pressure drops completely, remove jars with a tong. Place in a draft-free area for 12 hours. Afterwards, check seals for any leaks. Refrigerate jars that have not sealed properly; use within 3 days. Store the remaining jars in a cool, dark place and use within one year.

creating a perfect seal. Only the best and freshest meats should be used because canning only preserves the meat; it does not improve the meat's quality.

Glass jars are typically used in a method called the hot pack. This involves packing the meat into the jars and processing the jars in boiling water or steam. The advantages of

Canning Time Table for Game

Pack	Jar Size	Time (Min.)	Pounds Pressure–Dial Gauge		
			0–2,000 ft.*	2,001– 4,000 ft.	4,001– 6,000 ft.
Without Bone Hot or Raw	Pints	75	11	12	13
	Quarts	90	11	12	13
With Bone Hot or Raw	Pints	65	11	12	13
	Quarts	75	11	12	13

Pack	Jar Size	Time (Min.)	Pounds Pressure–Weighted Gauge	
			0–1,000 ft.	Above 1,000 ft.
Without Bone Hot or Raw	Pints	75	10	15
	Quarts	90	10	15
With Bone Hot or Raw	Pints	75	10	15
	Quarts	90	10	15

*Local altitude

Canning Time Table for Ground or Chopped Meat

Pack	Jar Size	Time (Min.)	Pounds Pressure–Dial Gauge		
			0–2,000 ft.*	2,001– 4,000 ft.	4,001– 6,000 ft.
Raw	Pint	75	11	12	13
	Quart	90	11	12	13

Pack	Jar Size	Time (Min.)	Pounds Pressure–Weighted Gauge	
			0–1,000 ft.	Above 1,000 ft.
Raw	Pint	75	10	15
	Quart	90	10	15

*Local altitude
Source: U.S. Department of Agriculture Extension Service

this method are that the jars are completely sealed and the meat has no further exposure to outside influences or organisms.

Glass canning jars come in several sizes, but are most generally found in pints or quarts. You'll need covers or lids that can be firmly tightened before being placed in water. Rubber rings and metal lids with sealing gaskets attached are two popular options. New rings and seal lids must be used each year; discard used lids or rings.

Many models of pressure cookers are commercially available, such as stovetop and electric models; they are usually made of aluminum or enameled steel. Whichever model you choose, the same principles apply: It should be substantially constructed and should have a pressure indicator, a safety valve, and a petcock or vent.

Begin by thoroughly washing each jar in hot soapy water and rinsing it in clear, hot water. Place the jars on clean towels to air-dry. Inspect the jars and test the cooker before you begin. Examine the jars and lids for nicks or cracks. If they appear intact, fit a new ring to each jar, partly fill with hot water, and adjust the lid and seal. Invert each jar and watch for leakage or small bubbles rising through the water as it cools. An imperfect seal means you should discard the jar or the lid, depending on where the bubbles originate. You can also test the

rubber rings by doubling them over. If any crack, discard them.

Preparing Meat for Canning

Properly handled, high-quality meat, regardless of which animal or bird species it comes from, is an important ingredient in the successfully canned product. Keep the meat clean and cold while you are preparing it for canning. Remove the skin from poultry and waterfowl. Trim fat, bruises, and heavy gristle from the meat. Remove the bones from red meat and larger bones from game birds. Removing the fat not only makes a healthier product, but also helps to ensure a better seal for jar lids. Excess fat can melt out of the meat during pressure cooking, coating the sealing surface of the lid and preventing a complete seal.

Packing Methods

There are two methods for packing meat to be canned: hot pack and raw or cold pack. Both methods can be used for wild game, fowl, and fish.

Hot pack canning refers to partially or wholly precooking the meat to be canned. It requires enough broth in the jar to cover the meat. This will improve heat transfer in the jar and helps ensure adequate heat during pressure processing. The hot pack method is best for most kinds of meat because it consistently yields a safe, high-quality product. Wild game processed using the hot pack method will benefit from a tomato-based broth.

To use the hot pack method, prepare the broth and cook the game meat or fowl to 150 degrees Fahrenheit, then pack the hot meat into clean, hot canning jars and cover with boiling broth, leaving a proper headspace of about 1 to 2 inches at the top of the jar.

The raw or cold pack method is only an option for larger fresh pieces of wild game, fowl, or fatty fish. To use the raw pack method, place the larger pieces of meat loosely into jars, leaving proper headspace. Do not add any liquid as juices will form during processing. Salmon, trout, and other fatty fish are packed raw with no added liquid. Smoked fish can also be packed with no added liquid.

Regardless of the type of pack used, the processing conditions relating to time and pressure must be followed exactly to ensure a safe product.

Check for spoilage

- Inspect filled canning jars before you use them. Spoilage may have occurred if:

  Jars have unsealed or bulging lids.

  Liquid spurts when jar is opened.

  Contents appear discolored or foamy or have an off odor.

- **DO NOT** taste suspect or spoiled food.
- Safely discard or detoxify canned wild game, waterfowl, or fish.
- Handle carefully any jars with spoiled food to avoid illness or death.

To detoxify suspect unsealed jars:

- Place in an 8-quart or larger pan.
- Carefully add water to cover by 2 inches and boil for 30 minutes.
- Cool and discard the jars and their lids in trash and bury food in soil.
- Sanitize countertops and all equipment used with a diluted bleach solution (1 teaspoon bleach per 1 quart water).
- Discard sponges or washcloths used to clean up.

Canning Large Game Animals

Whether you use strips, cubes, or chunks of large game animal meat for canning, always choose high-quality chilled meat portions for use.

- Soak strong-flavored wild meats for 1 hour in brine water containing 1 tablespoon of salt per quart water. Rinse and remove large bones after soaking.
- For hot pack—Precook meat until rare by roasting, stewing, or browning in a small amount of fat. Add 1 teaspoon of salt per quart water (if desired). Fill jars with pieces and add boiling broth, meat drippings, water, or tomato juice, leaving 1 inch of headspace.
- For raw pack—Add 1 teaspoon of salt per quart water (if desired). Fill jars with raw meat pieces, leaving 1 inch of headspace. Do not add liquid.
- Adjust lids and follow recommended canning methods

Canning Ground or Chopped Meat

You can use ground or chopped meat for canning, similar to whole chunks or pieces. Be sure to safely grind or chop wild meat in clean conditions and use high-quality portions. If using venison, add one part high-quality pork fat to three or four parts venison before grinding.

- Use freshly made sausage seasoned with salt and cayenne pepper.
- Shape chopped meat into patties or balls or cut case sausage into 3- to 4-inch links.
- Cook until lightly browned.
- Remove excess fat.
- Fill jars with pieces.
- Add boiling meat broth, tomato juice, or water.
- Leave 1 inch of headspace.
- Add 1 teaspoon salt per quart (if desired).
- Adjust lids and follow recommended canning methods.

Ground meat may be sautéed without shaping it.

Canning Process

Place the jars on the rack inside the cooker. The water level should reach the bottom of the rack, which keeps the glass off the chamber base and allows the water and steam to completely surround the jars. Place the jars so they do not touch one another. The lid or cover should be adjusted carefully and fastened tightly so that no steam can escape through the petcock. The petcock should stay open until steam has poured out steadily for 10 minutes or more. Afterwards, close it to allow the pressure to rise to the level directed in the owner's manual, usually 10 pounds.

To begin the processing, place a small amount of water in the bottom of the cooker. Add the meat-filled jars to the cooker and clamp on the airtight lid. The cooker is then set over heat or heat is applied electrically.

The pressure raises the temperature higher than that used in ordinary cooking, and the food cooks more quickly. A gauge on the lid shows the number of pounds of pressure, indicating the temperature. A safety valve releases pressure after cooking is completed. It will also release excess pressure. The petcock provides an outlet for steam and air.

When the appropriate pressure is reached, you should adjust the heat to keep the same pressure without variation. For meats, process for 3 minutes at 250 degrees Fahrenheit.

When the processing time is completed, the cooker should be taken off the heat and left alone until the pressure goes down to zero. Open the petcock to release the remaining steam. Liquid may be lost from the jars if the pressure varies during processing or if the steam is released too quickly. Jars should not be reopened and refilled under any circumstances unless being immediately used. Do not let the cooker sit unopened for any length of time after the steam is down. This may create a vacuum, which will make it difficult to open the lid. If this happens, reheat the cooker for a few minutes until it is loose.

Take the jars out of the cooker and hand-tighten their lids if necessary. Place the jars on a rack or towel to cool, but keep them away from drafts. Some canners turn the jars upside down as they cool to check for any leaks or bubbles, which indicate a poor seal.

After drying, label the jars with the canning date. After ten days, recheck the jars. Immediately discard any that exhibit cloudiness or signs of spoilage. Do not eat their contents under any circumstances.

Quick Tips

- To reduce gamey flavor, trim fat from meat.
- Add other fat sources to maintain juiciness of meat.
- Use spices or marinades to mask gamey flavors.

Meat Cooking Methods

The cooking method you use depends on the kind and quality of the meat to be cooked. Only tender cuts of meat can be cooked by dry heat. Tougher cuts require moist heat and long, slow cooking. The kind of cooking methods include the following:

Baking—To cook in an oven or oven-type appliance. Covered or uncovered containers may be used.

Barbecuing—To roast slowly on a spit or rack over coals or under a gas broiler flame or electric broiler unit, usually basting with a highly seasoned sauce. The term also is commonly applied to foods cooked in or served with barbeque sauce.

Boiling—To cook in water or mostly water, at boiling temperature (212 degrees Fahrenheit at sea level). Bubbles rise continually and break on the surface.

Braising—To cook by moist heat. Braising is used for the less tender cuts, which require long, slow cooking in the presence of moisture to bring out the full flavor and make them tender. Many cuts, including roasts, can be cooked by braising rather than broiling or pan-broiling. Brown the meat in a small amount of fat, then cover tightly and cook slowly in juices from the meat or in added liquid, such as water, milk, or cream. Add only a small amount of liquid occasionally and do not let boil but keep at a simmering temperature.

Broiling—To cook by direct heat. Broiling may be done over hot coals, or under a flame or electric unit. This method may be used for tender cuts that have adequate amounts of fat. Venison, elk, or moose cuts should not be broiled since they are too low in fat.

Caramelizing—To heat sugar or food containing sugar until it develops a brown color and characteristic flavor.

Creaming—To work a food or combination of foods until soft and creamy, using a spoon, wooden paddle, or other utensil.

Fricasseeing—To braise individual serving pieces of game meat and waterfowl in a little liquid such as water, broth, or sauce.

Frying and sautéing—Some meats may be crumbled and fried in deep fat or oil. Liver and some other meats can be sautéed in a small amount of oil or fat at low temperatures after the first searing.

Marinating—To let foods stand in a liquid (usually a mixture of oil with vinegar or lemon juice) to add flavor or to make them more tender.

Pan-broiling—To pan-broil, place the meat in a sizzling skillet or pan and brown on both sides. Reduce heat, pour off fat as it accumulates, and cook until done while occasionally turning it.

Parboil—To boil until partly cooked.

Pot roasting—To cook large pieces of meat by braising.

Roasting—To roast meat, place it on the rack in a roasting pan, fat side up, and cook in a slow oven, uncovered and without water, until cooked as desired. Large tender cuts of meat are cooked by this method.

Scalding—To heat liquid to just below the boiling point.

Simmering—To cook in liquid just below the boiling point, at temperatures of 185 to 210 degrees Fahrenheit. Bubbles form slowly and break below the surface.

Stewing—To boil or simmer in a small amount of liquid. Cut the meat into cubes and brown on all sides in hot fat, if desired. Cover with boiling water and cook at simmering temperatures in a covered kettle until meat is tender. Less tender cuts containing much connective tissue are best cooked by stewing, which softens both tissue and fiber. The best cuts for stews are those containing both fats and lean meat.

Dutch Ovens

A Dutch oven is a traditional piece of cooking equipment used outdoors. It has a long history of use, and its easy application makes it a favorite of many outdoor hunters.

One advantage is that it can deliver a low, moist heat over long periods of time to allow meat to mellow and develop its own unique taste. Low heat and slow cooking tenderize meat because juices within the cell walls are slowly released during the heating process. Fast cooking purges these juices too quickly.

A second advantage of using a Dutch oven is its versatility. Bread, roasts, and stews can all be cooked in it, making it an excellent camp utensil. Dutch ovens are easy to use and remove much of the uncertainty of cooking small game. Cooking in them does not require you to pay as close attention as with a regular home oven. Many models are available, and you should investigate which one best suits your purposes.

Cooking with Byproducts

As you weigh the potential health concerns against your desire to use internal organs, you should also be aware of some of the health benefits derived from them. Several organs, such as livers, kidneys, and hearts, are high in protein content and highly nutritious. Again, these are generally more perishable than other meat parts and should be frozen or cooked soon after harvest or purchase.

The paragraphs below detail how these byproducts can be cooked and for what purpose.

Liver—After removing all connective tissue surrounding the liver, it can be thinly sliced and cooked in a variety of methods. These include frying, broiling, sautéing, and braising. You can grind or chop liver and use it as an additive to sausages, loaves, spreads, and other dishes.

Heart—The hearts of fowl and small animals, such as squirrels or rabbits, can be cooked with moist heat or ground and used in sausages. The heart is generally less tender than liver, although it has an excellent flavor. Wild game animal hearts should be sliced open for inspection and then may be filled with a dressing, stitched shut with cooking thread, and roasted with moist heat, like a turkey.

Tongue–Tongues from large game animals can make cold sandwich meats after being braised and thinly sliced. You can remove the tough outer membrane of the tongue by blanching, followed by moist heat cooking for an extended period. Once this membrane is trimmed, the rest can be cooled and sliced.

Kidneys—Game kidneys may be broiled and skewered and are more tender than beef kidneys. They can be included in meat casseroles, stews, and other dishes.

Fats—Animal fats have had many uses over the course of human history. They have served as a food energy source, been rubbed into animal hides to make tepee

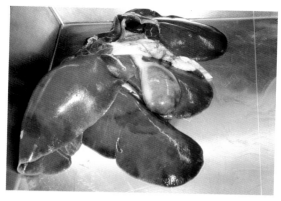

The liver is a brown-colored organ that metabolizes sugars into glucose, providing energy to the body systems. The gallbladder is greenish and is attached near the liver. It must be removed and discarded. The liver should have a bright, healthy look, and be free of abscesses. It can be sliced and fried or used in sausage making.

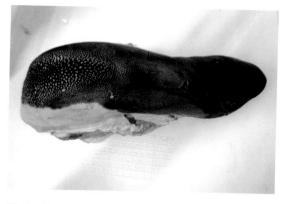

After braising, tongues can be thinly sliced for cold sandwich meats. You can remove the tough outer membrane by blanching (exposing the meat to boiling water for a short period) prior to long-term, moist-heat cooking.

The heart is less tender than the liver, but it has excellent flavor. Small animal hearts can be ground as an additive for sausages. After the heart is removed from the body, you should slice it open and wash out any remaining blood.

Use kidneys in casseroles and stews, or broiled and skewer them. While in the carcass, they are often surrounded by fat, which should be peeled away before use.

leather supple and waterproof, and, in the case of bear grease during the nineteenth century, provided a sheen and unique aroma to human hair. Fats also have been used for making soaps and providing fuel for oil lamps in the days prior to kerosene or gasoline.

Animal and plant fats differ mainly in melting point and saturation. Fats and oils contain both saturated and unsaturated components. Saturated fats are firmer and have a higher melting point than the softer, unsaturated fats.

Cooking and table fats available for use range from liquid oils, derived mainly from plants, to solid fats, which come from animals and other sources.

Lard is the fat most often used in home cooking and is rendered from the clear and edible tissues of pigs. Recent decades have witnessed a decrease in lard production due to health concerns and competition from vegetable fats. However, lard provides a source of energy, and linoleic fatty acid is an essential component of the human diet.

Lard has a melting point that is near body temperature, making it easily digested. This low melting point allows a cook or baker to use it as cooking fat, shortening, a flavor ingredient, and a source of nutrition.

Rendering is the process of extracting fat from tissues by using heat. The raw fat and meat is either cooked or heated to turn the fat into a liquid. The melted fat is then drawn off. This process increases the shelf life of the fat by killing the microorganisms that were present and removing most of the moisture.

You can render pork fat at home by removing the raw fat from the skin to obtain better quality. Begin by chopping the fat into fine pieces. For each pound of fat, add 1/2 cup of water. Place the fat and water in a cooking vessel and heat to boiling, but do not exceed 240 degrees Fahrenheit. Stir as it warms to avoid scorching. As it boils, the steam will remove extraneous odors. Boiling will not occur until the fat liquefies. Allow the fat to cook until the solid material reaches a golden or amber color, then drain into storage containers.

Use several thicknesses of cheesecloth or similar material that can be placed over clean, dry, nonmetallic storage containers suitable for use with hot liquids. Slowly pour the hot fat into the cloths until the containers are fitted to a desired level. Cool the lard rapidly to produce a firm, smooth-textured product. As the lard cools, stir it occasionally when it reaches the creamy stage to keep the oils from separating out and to avoid the development of a grainy texture. Store at temperatures of 40 degrees Fahrenheit or lower. Lard may be frozen but should be packaged in airtight containers and used within six months. This will reduce changes in flavor or aroma due to oxidation.

If you choose to render fat in your home, use caution during the entire process. Avoid spills, because hot grease can cause severe burns to exposed skin. If the fat is spilled on clothing, it will cling to it and can cause deep, severe burns. Never allow children anywhere near your processing area or the containers as they are cooling.

Liver Casserole

1 lb. liver
3/4 c. tomato sauce

Dash salt and pepper
1 tsp. Worcestershire sauce

Wash liver, cut into 1 1/2-inch cubes, and place in casserole dish. Add sauce and seasoning, cover, and bake at 350°F for 1/2 hour. Just before serving, add Worcestershire sauce. Serves 4.

Liver Piquante with Vegetables

2 lbs. liver
1/2 c. butter
1/2 lb. side pork
2 c. boiling water
1 c. sliced carrots

1/2 c. sliced onion
1 tbsp. chopped parsley
1 bay leaf
Small sprig of thyme

Wash liver thoroughly, dry, and rub butter around it. Cut side pork into strips and brown with liver on all sides. Add hot water, vegetables, and seasonings; cover and bake at 350°F until liver is tender, or about 1 1/2 hours. Serve on hot platter surrounded by vegetables. Serves 8.

Sweet-Sour Hearts

1 large game heart	2 tsp. sugar
2 tbsp. flour	1/4 tsp. pepper
2 tbsp. fat	3 c. water
1 tsp. salt	1 small onion, chopped
6 tbsp. vinegar	

Clean heart, remove outside membrane and large veins, and cut into 1/2-inch cubes. Brown flour in fat; add meat and remaining ingredients. Cover and simmer for 1 1/2 hours or until tender. Serve with cooked noodles. Serves 4.

Spanish Kidney

1 large game kidney or 2–3 medium kidneys	6 slices tomatoes
	Bacon

Cut large kidney into six pieces or split open smaller kidneys; remove tubes and fat. Soak in cold water 30 minutes. Arrange tomato slices in greased frying pan; place a piece of kidney on each slice and a piece of bacon on each kidney. Broil under moderate broiler heat 10 to 15 minutes or until kidney is tender. Cover and simmer over direct heat 4 to 5 minutes. Serve with parsley butter. Serves 6.

Virginia Beef Tongue

1 large game tongue
1 c. brown sugar
1 c. stewed cranberries

1/4 c. butter
1 tbsp. whole cloves
1/2 lemon, sliced

Scrub tongue and simmer in water to cover until tender, 3 to 4 hours. Remove skin and trim root end. To 1 cup of liquid in which tongue was cooked, add remaining ingredients. Simmer tongue in mixture 15 minutes. Serves 6.

Tripe Stewed with Tomato Sauce

2 lbs. tripe
1 onion, cut into halves
2 c. tomatoes

1 tbsp. butter
2 tbsp. flour
Salt and pepper

Choose honeycomb portions and thick section of tripe. Wash carefully; cover with hot water, add onion, cover pan, and simmer 35 minutes. Cook tomatoes 10 minutes and strain through sieve. Melt butter, blend in flour, add tomatoes and seasonings, and cook until thickened. Drain tripe well; cut into thin strips and drain again, pressing tripe gently to remove as much water as possible. Add sauce and heat thoroughly. Serves 6.

Creole Tripe—Cook 1 garlic clove, 3 bay leaves, a dash of thyme, and a dash of cayenne with tomatoes.

Chapter 8

CURING, DRYING & SMOKING

The curing or salting of meat is the oldest preservation method used by humans. Salt was used for preserving meat and fish as early as 3000 BC. Through the centuries that followed, civilizations used salt as a way to create a longer "shelf life" for meat products. Salt became such a valuable commodity that it was zealously protected and bartered for, serving as currency in some instances. The purpose of curing, then as now, was to create food that could be safely eaten at a later date.

Native Americans hung strips of meat in the tops of the tepees to keep them out of reach of small animals and dogs. As these strips dried and took on the smoky flavor from the campfire inside their tepee, they became very hard. The dried meat strips were beaten into powder with stones and mixed with dried fruits, vegetables, and berries to make pemmican. This dried meat could be easily transported when their community moved to another area.

Modern-day meat curing and smoking practices are used primarily to create more and varied products, develop unique flavors and colors, extend shelf life, and inhibit the growth of spores that cause botulism, a lethal form of food poisoning. Home curing can be a part of your food preservation plan and can be done safely and effectively.

When curing meat, the use of salt and nitrite is important to prevent botulism food poisoning. By inhibiting the growth of bacteria, these ingredients allow meat products to have a longer shelf life. Cured meats also have a salty flavor that many enjoy. One good example of a smoked meat product is sausage. It is smoked and heated to pasteurize it, extend its shelf life, give it a smoky flavor, and improve its appearance. Smoking and heating also fixes the color and causes protein to move to the surface of the sausage so that it holds its shape when the casing is removed.

Hot smoking is used to cook game; cold smoking is used to flavor game, especially sausages, before cooking.

Curing

The term *curing* is sometimes interpreted to mean both curing and the subsequent smoking of meat. However, curing is not smoking, although these two processes work together. The curing process prevents the meat from spoiling and preserves it for long-term use; smoking adds flavor. Strictly speaking, curing applies only to dry salt curing, brine submersion, or pickling with a vinegar base. However, in a wider sense, curing applies to any saline or alkaline preservation solution with some modifications.

The most commonly used methods of curing include pickle curing, dry curing, dry salt curing, and applying curing solutions by osmosis, stitch pump, spray pump, artery pump, or machine pump.

Salt is the essential ingredient in a successful curing process. It draws moisture from the muscle cells while entering the cells by osmosis. This process distributes the salt through the tissue. It also inhibits the action of certain harmful bacteria and inhibits the function of several types of enzymes. If too little salt is applied to the meat, bacteria that can grow in the presence of some salt will not be fully stopped and spoilage can follow. If too much salt is used, the meat can become hard and dry and taste overly salty.

Generally speaking, several weeks are required for the salts or brine to reach sufficient concentration in the tissues to protect the center of hams, shoulders, and other large chunks of meat. This means you will need a storage space where your meat can be kept away from insects, animals, and children while the curing processes work.

Pickle Curing

A typical curing solution could include water and salt, a mix often referred to as a "plain" or "salt" pickle; water, salt, nitrate, and/or nitrite; or water, salt, nitrate, and/or nitrite to which sugar has been added—often referred to as a "sweet pickle."

Other ingredients could be added to enhance the flavor of the pickle. Use a noncorrosive container to hold the brine

Quick Tips

A basic brine solution generally consists of:

- 1 lb. brown sugar
- 2 lbs. non-iodized salt
- 3 gallons water

and meat during the curing process. Wood, crockery, stainless-steel, or food-grade plastic containers work well.

Place the meat in the container and pour the brine over it until it is covered. If the meat floats, you may have to place a weight over it, such as a heavy nonmetal porcelain plate, to keep it submerged.

Corning

Corned beef is a delicacy enjoyed by many Americans. The corning process can be used for venison, antelope, moose, or bear. This process removes the musky wild flavor and can tenderize the toughest meat portions of a large game carcass.

The term "corn" is derived from Old English and refers to any small hard particles or grains like sand or salt. In a meat-curing context, it refers to granular salts used. The corning process uses a brine—a mixture of water and salts—to pull the wild flavor from the meat and help preserve it for future use.

Corning Process

You will need fifteen days to complete the corning process. During this time you will need to turn the meat pieces in the brine so that all sides receive adequate treatment.

Begin by thoroughly mixing a corning liquid made from the recipe given here and in sufficient quantity to cover all the meat held within the crock or large jar that you use. This is only one recipe that can be used; you may find another one just as effective.

Place the meat into your container and pour enough liquid in until it almost reaches the top lip. All the pieces must be submerged completely. You may have to lay a nonmetallic heavy plate on top to keep the meat fully below the surface of the brine.

On the fifth and tenth days rotate the pieces from top to bottom and stir the brine well. Remove the meat after the fifteenth day and use what you want immediately. The rest should be refrigerated at 38 degrees Fahrenheit. Once the meat is removed from

Corning Liquid

1 1/2 lbs. salt	1 1/2 tsp. black pepper
5 oz. sugar	1 1/2 tsp. ground cloves
1 oz. sodium nitrate	3 bay leaves
1/4 oz. sodium nitrite	6 tsp. mixed pickling spice

Put the ingredients into a large crock or jar and add 3 gallons clean water. Mix thoroughly until salt and sugar are completely dissolved. Place meat in liquid, keeping pieces below surface of brine. Cover the container. Makes 3 gallons.

Quick Tips
Cooking Corned Meat

- Place corned meat in a pan with a cover.
- Add cold water to cover the meat.
- Bring to a boil and remove the scum from the water.
- Reduce heat and simmer for 5 hours or until tender.
- Serve with garnish.

the corning brine, you can cook it, cool it, or freeze it for later use. It can be kept cool for up to 1 week or frozen up to 1 month for later use.

A good corning should produce meat with a grayish pink color that, when cooked, changes to the pink color associated with cured meat products.

Dry Curing

Dry curing involves rubbing the meat with salt or a salt mixture, and then packing the meat in that mixture for a considerable period

Quick Tips
Dry Sugar Cure

- Use the 8-3-2-1 formula for a full concentration:
- 8 lbs. table or curing salt
- 3 lbs. cane sugar
- 2 oz. nitrate (saltpeter)
- 1 oz. sodium or potassium nitrite
- Use 1 ounce of the 8-3-2-1 formula for each pound of meat. Place rubbed meats in boxes under refrigerated (less than 40 degrees Fahrenheit) conditions. Cure 7 days per inch of meat thickness.

of time. Dry curing materials may include salt alone; salt, nitrate, and/or nitrite; or salt, nitrate, and/or nitrite with sugar. Dry sugar cure is one example.

Dry Salt Curing

Dry salt curing is a variation of the dry curing method and involves salt alone or salt plus nitrate. Just before you cover the meat with the dry mix, you can moisten it to enhance penetration of the salt into the muscle.

Pumping or Injection

You can inject pickle ingredients into the meat to cure it from the inside out as well as from the outside in. This protects the meat against spoilage and provides a more even curing. Once the brine solution is applied by any of the following methods, curing should take place in a refrigerated or cool room at temperatures less than 35 degrees Fahrenheit. Ensure even distribution of the cure into the meat by rearranging the meat at least once during the curing process. Don't recycle the brine, because there is the possibility of bacterial growth over time. There are several methods of applying cure solutions to meat and game bird cuts. The most frequently used method is referred to as stitch pumping.

Stitch Pumping

Injecting the pickle ingredients is mostly done by using a thoroughly cleaned stitch pump or ordinary syringe. These have a hollow needle with spaced holes; when the needle is inserted into the meat and the handle is pushed down, brine flows through the holes into the meat.

To use a stitch pump, draw it full of pickle ingredients that have been thoroughly mixed beforehand. For game birds and waterfowl,

How to Apply a Dry Cure

Dry Cure (for 100 pounds of meat):

- 6 lbs. salt
- 3 lbs. sugar
- 3 oz. sodium nitrate or 1 oz. sodium nitrite or commercial cure

Rub mix over entire leg surface as follows: one third of the mix on the first day, one third of the mix on the seventh day, and the final third of the mix on the fourteenth day. Place on flat surface, uncovered, at 38 degrees Fahrenheit for 2 days per pound of leg, or approximately 4 to 6 weeks. Curing action stops when temperature inside the meat dips below 34 degrees Fahrenheit.

When the meat is cured, let the smaller legs soak for 30 to 40 minutes and the larger ones for 60 minutes in lukewarm water. After soaking, scrub with a clean brush to remove grease and salt. The meat is now ready to smoke.

Stitch pumping is the injection of marinade into a game bird to add flavor. With a special meat injector pump (a large syringe), you can make injections in the legs, thighs, and breast. Fill the pump with marinade, then push the tip into the desired area. Gradually depress the plunger while slowly pulling the tip out. Inject once in each leg and twice in each thigh and breast, or follow the instructions on the injector package.

insert the needle all the way into the meat at the legs and shoulders. Push with slow, even pressure. As pickle is forced into the meat, draw the pump toward you to distribute the pickle as evenly as possible. Keep the pump full of pickle to avoid air pockets in the meat.

The meat will bulge a little and a small amount of pickle will run out when the pump is withdrawn. Use three or four pumpfuls of pickle for legs and shoulders that weight 10 to 15 pounds, and five or six pumpfuls for those that weigh 15 to 25 pounds. For smaller legs and shoulders, fewer injections are needed.

After pumping, apply a dry cure mixture. Rub the cure well over all the meat, especially around the bones, hock, and knee joint.

Smoking

The purpose of smoking meats is to give them a unique smoky flavor and an even external color, and to lower the moisture content in the meat, which reduces the opportunity for bacterial growth. For example, country-cured hams and similar cured and smoked meats that don't require refrigeration owe their stability to a combination of low moisture, high concentrations of curing agents, and heavily smoked surfaces. Three factors affect the amount of time a meat product needs to be smoked: the type of meat product, the density of smoke generated within the smoking unit, and the ability of the meat surface to absorb the smoke properties.

Prior to smoking meats, it is critical that the meat's surface is slightly moist, to ensure that the smoke volatiles will adhere properly. Smoke will not adhere to dry surfaces. Dry the surface enough to remove excess moisture, but leave enough moisture to absorb the smoke.

Most smoking is done with dry heat, but water smokers are readily available. A pan of water placed above the heat source produces steam, which helps keep foods moist during smoking.

Options you can use for smoking include natural wood, charcoal, or electric units specially designed for smoking meats. The products you use for creating the smoke will have a significant effect on the meat.

Natural wood smoke is generally produced from hardwood sawdust, wood chips, or logs. Hickory wood is the most popular, although other hardwoods are also used, such as oak, maple, ash, mesquite, apple, cherry, and other fruit woods. Avoid using pine and other coniferous trees because of their high tar content, which can produce a bitter flavor.

Natural wood smoke contains three major components: solids, such as ash and tar; air and combustion gases and acids; and carbonyls, phenolics, and polycyclic hydrocarbons. The ash, tar, and gases do not contribute very much to the flavor, aroma, or preservative properties of smoked products. The phenolics have been identified as the primary source for aroma and flavor and preservative properties, and the carbonyls are the source of the amber-brown color generated from the smoking process.

The length of time that the smoke fills the chamber will largely determine the amount of smoke deposited on the surface of the meat. Variations in smoke density will also affect how much the smoke components adhere to the meat.

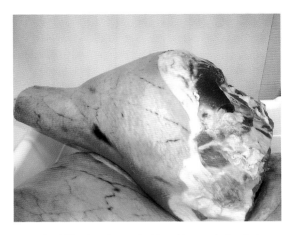

Hams should be rinsed or soaked in cold water before being cured and smoked. This removes excess salt on the outside and eliminates the formation of salt streaks on the meat when exposed to the heat of the smokehouse.

Heat will dry the surface of meat, which will then inhibit the amount of smoke it will absorb. An even temperature should thus be maintained during the smoke cycle.

After the smoke cycle is completed, you can gradually increase the temperature inside the chamber to cook the meat. Avoid a rapid increase in temperature, as this will dry and overcook the surface before the desired internal temperature is reached. Increasing the temperature in increments will conduct the heat through the meat to minimize the difference between the surface and internal temperatures. A long, slow cook of the meat will produce maximum tenderness.

If possible, try to cook pieces that have a similar or uniform size, as this will allow you to cook them at a specific temperature for an equal time and achieve a uniform result. Unevenly matched pieces may be overdone and too dry or undercooked, depending on temperature and time. You may be able to circumvent these problems by using individual temperature probes to determine when target internal temperatures have been reached and the cooking cycle should be stopped. However, this may not be practical, so several cooking sessions may be needed. As a rule, high smokehouse temperatures (125 degrees Fahrenheit and above) with a light smoke will speed up the drying, and lower temperatures (80 to 110 degrees Fahrenheit) with a dense smoke will intensify the smoky flavor in meat.

The type of cured and smoked meat product you want to produce will determine the level of smokehouse temperature. To have a fully cooked product, you need to bring the internal temperature of the meat to at least 148 degrees Fahrenheit. If you will store the meat at room temperature, you should keep the smokehouse temperature at 170 degrees Fahrenheit until the internal temperature of the meat reaches 148 degrees Fahrenheit. You can then lower the smokehouse temperature to 125 degrees Fahrenheit and maintain that until the desired color is reached.

Quick Tips for Smoking

- Soak wood chips in water for at least an hour before using them to promote smoke rather than flame. You can use small chips or sawdust over small electric hot plates and spray them with a mister bottle to dampen them.
- Temperature control is important in smoking, especially when making foods like salami, which will receive no further cooking.
- Monitor the smoker temperature constantly with an instant-read or oven thermometer.

Remove the meat after it has been cured and wash it to remove salt and fat streaks from the surface. Cooked meat products should be cooled quickly to 40 degrees Fahrenheit or less. At this point, it is important to maintain sanitary conditions and avoid contact with uncooked meat or surfaces that have come in contact with uncooked meat. This will minimize recontamination of the cooked products with organisms that may create spoilage.

Smokehouses and Equipment

A smokehouse is a simple version of a heat-processing unit used by today's meat industry. The size may be vastly different, but the principles are the same: it is an enclosed area where the temperature and smoke level may be controlled with acceptable accuracy. If you decide to build a smokehouse, it does not need to be an elaborate structure to do an effective job. However, it must be adequately built and allow for the monitoring of temperature and smoke level so that the meat is properly cooked—this will minimize health risks.

The purpose of a smokehouse is to enclose heat and smoke, and reduce, but not entirely eliminate, airflow. Depending on how much smoking you want to accomplish, you may construct your own smokehouse or purchase a commercial unit. Because smokehouses are generally located outdoors, you should check if any local ordinances or fire codes apply before you begin construction.

Many types of smokehouses can be used successfully to smoke meats, fowl, and fish. Smokehouses can include such simple equipment as a charcoal grill for very small amounts of meat, or, in more extensive units of frame or concrete construction, metal barrels and water and electric smokers. The

A basic plan for a barrel for a metal drum smoker.

more elaborate structures will cost more to build. By understanding your end goals, you can make a reasonable assessment of which type will work best for you. Depending on where you live, you may be able to get your smoke work done with a local meat shop. The paragraphs below detail the different types of smokehouses to consider.

Charcoal grill: One of the least expensive ways to smoke small amounts of meats and sausages is on your covered charcoal grill. This will require an oven thermometer to monitor the temperature. Fill the bottom of your grill with briquettes and burn them until gray ash appears. Separate the coals onto two sides of the grill and place a pan of water between them. Place the grate over the top and place your sausages above the water. As the sausages heat and cook, the fat will drip into the heated water and create steam that will help destroy harmful bacteria. Keep the vents open on the cover. For hot smoking, you will need to maintain an air temperature between 225

A barrel or wood smoker is easy to construct and useful for smoking small amounts of meat, fowl, and fish. Use metal racks to place or suspend your sausages. Wood is held in one part, and the smoke transfers to the large chamber. Set a container of water inside the large chamber to slow the drying process.

and 300 degrees Fahrenheit throughout the process.

Vertical water and electric smokers: A vertical water smoker is built with a bottom fire pan that holds charcoal briquettes and generally has two cooking racks near the top. The water pan positioned above the coals supplies moisture and helps regulate the internal temperature. An electric smoker is similarly constructed, except the smoke is controlled by premoistened wood chips rather than charcoal. This provides a more constant temperature and may require less attention during smoking. The sizes of electric smokers vary, with some accommodating up to 40 pounds of sausage at one time.

Barrel smoker: A clean, uncontaminated 50-gallon metal barrel, with both ends removed, can be used as a smoker for small quantities of meat, fowl, and fish. Set the open-ended barrel on the upper end of a shallow, sloping, covered trench or 10- to 12-foot stovepipe. Dig a pit at the lower end for the fire. Smoke rises naturally, so having the fire lower than the barrel will aid its movement toward the meats. Mound the dirt around the edges of the barrel and the fire pit to eliminate leaks. You can control the heat by covering it with a piece of sheet metal.

Use metal or wood tubes as racks to suspend your sausages in the barrel. At the beginning of the smoking, you want a rapid flow of air past the meat to drive off excess moisture. Less rapid air movement near the end of the smoking period prevents excessive shrinkage of the meat. Use moist wood chips, sawdust, or charcoal for starting your fire. You want a lot of smoke but very little flame. Once your fire is going, you can add green sawdust or green hardwood to cool the fire and make more smoke. *Never use gasoline or other accelerants to start your fire.* Besides their explosive potential, which can cause serious injury, the fumes and residues will contaminate your sausage.

Metal strips can be attached to the cover to help hold it in place, trapping the smoke

A charcoal kettle grill is one of the cheapest methods of smoking small amounts of meats and sausages. You will need an oven thermometer to monitor the temperature and air vents to adjust the heat.

You can use vertical water smokers when smoking small amounts of meat and sausages. They may have either a gas or electric heat source and an extra grate below the food for holding a pan of water. The steam keeps the food moist.

Insulated variable-temperature smokers offer excellent temperature control and are a growing favorite among many cooks. These tend to be the most expensive smokers available, but are very easy to use.

All smokers require wood to produce smoke. Various woods such as hickory, cherry, alder, apple, and mesquite are the most popular. Essential materials for wood smoking include wood chips, tree trimmings, or smoking sawdust. A digital thermometer (2) monitors the internal temperature of summer sausage or large cuts of meat without opening the smoker, which causes heat loss. An instant-read thermometer (3) monitors smoker temperature through the smoker vent hole or a hole specially designed for a thermometer.

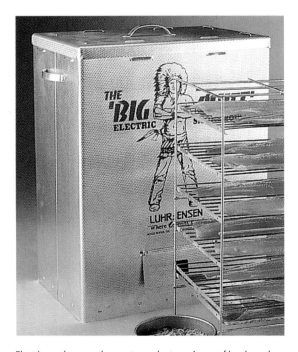

Electric smokers are the most popular type. A pan of hardwood chips rests on a burner at the bottom, while the food sits on removable wire racks. These smokers are convenient and available in several sizes, but they don't work well in cold weather.

near the meat. You can monitor the inside temperature by suspending a thermometer from one of the meat racks.

Frame or concrete smokehouse: You can build a smokehouse out of wood or concrete blocks. These more elaborate structures accommodate larger quantities of meats at one time and last for many years. They have the advantage of making temperature control easier and reducing fire hazards. Their tight construction and well-fitted ventilators can control airflow past the meat. A larger building will provide space for several tiers of racks, which lets you adjust the hangers to the size of the pieces of meat being smoked. Meats can be crowded into a smokehouse, so long as no piece of meat touches another or the wall.

Any building you construct should have four features: a source of smoke, a place to hold the smoke, a method to hold the meat in the smoke, and a draft regulator near the top or bottom. A smokehouse is a very slow oven in which the temperature does not exceed 200 degrees Fahrenheit. Even though you will use and maintain low temperatures, build your smokehouse in a safe location away from other buildings, particularly your home, and away from all combustible materials. Check with local ordinances and fire codes before you begin any construction.

The size of your smokehouse can be calculated based on the amounts and weights of meat used. These requirements vary with the weight of the cuts. To estimate the capacity of your smokehouse, use an accepted measure of 12 inches in width, front and back, and 2 feet in height for each row. Construction plans for smokehouses are generally available from university extension offices or commercial supply companies.

Smokehouses are excellent for processing meats, but they do not make a good storage area for smoke-finished meats. After your smoking processing is complete, flies will eventually get in either on a piece of meat or when the door is open. Smokehouses can be used for storage, however, if each piece of meat is properly wrapped, bagged, and hung separately, provided everything is insect-proof.

To make jerky, slice meat evenly, about 1/8 inch thick. Meat sliced with the grain produces chewy jerky, while meat sliced against the grain makes a tenderer jerky. Meat is easier to slice if it is partially frozen.

Combine marinade ingredients in a large nonmetallic mixing bowl. Stir to dissolve salt and add meat strips. Cover with plastic wrap and refrigerate 24 hours, stirring occasionally. In a large mixing bowl, cover wood chips with water and soak for 1 hour. Place an oven thermometer in the smoker and heat to 120 degrees Fahrenheit.

Other Considerations

You may become enthused or enchanted by your smoking ability and the flavors you create. However, do not replace your normal cooking procedures and dietary needs with this practice. Eating too much smoked meat may cause some health concerns. The problems generally are found in the smoke, which contains coal tars that are considered carcinogenic. You may want to use your smoked meats as special treats rather than as daily meals.

Spray smoker racks with nonstick vegetable cooking spray. Drain wood chips and meat strips, discarding water and marinade. Pat strips lightly with paper towels and arrange them at least 1/4 inch apart on racks. Place racks in smoker.

Open damper in the smoker. Place a handful of wood chips inside and close damper, cracking slightly when the wood chips begin to smoke. Smoke meat strips for 3 to 6 hours, or until dry but not brittle, adding wood chips if necessary. Cool completely. Store jerky, loosely wrapped, in refrigerator for no more than 1 week, or wrap tightly and freeze up to 2 months.

Cured, Dried, and Smoked Products

Many different wild game meat cuts can be smoked and cured to produce a variety of flavors and textures. These include the following:

Bacon—Wild pork bellies can be trimmed into a rectangular shape and smoked and cured before being sliced into strips. Although it has been smoked and heated, bacon must be cooked before it is consumed. Cooking methods include frying, grilling, broiling, or cooking in the microwave.

Dried beef—The round and larger muscles of the shoulders may be used to make dried beef. Dried beef has a lower moisture content than many other beef products. It is smoked to varying degrees but is fully cooked and ready to eat after curing.

Jerky—These are dried meat strips that may be produced using a combination of curing, smoking, and drying. Take lean beef and cut it into strips about 1 inch wide and 1/8 inch or less thick, of varying lengths. Marinating the strips overnight in a refrigerator will allow the marinade's flavor to penetrate the meat. A salt–nitrite cure mix can be added to other flavorings and spice when making jerky. Cured strips should be rinsed of excess ingredients and placed on a screen in a smokehouse to be smoked, cooked, and dried. The drying and cooking should be done slowly. Dried jerky does not need refrigeration if it is packaged to prevent it from absorbing moisture and contamination from its surroundings during storage. Jerky processing techniques may also be used for wild game and lamb.

Waterfowl and Game Birds—You can cure and smoke whole birds by controlling the smoke intensity and duration, both of which will affect the final smoke flavor. Hollow birds will cook more rapidly than solid hams or other cuts. Ducks and geese have larger amounts of carcass fat than other birds. You should trim as much fat as possible to reduce the amount of grease that will drip away. Fat from these birds has a low melting point, and it may streak the smoked surface during the cooking phase.

Wild Pork Hams—Hams are a popular smoked meat product that may be boneless or bone-in. Because they're a larger size than other meat cuts, hams will take longer to cook, cure, and smoke.

Smoking pork raises certain considerations. If you are smoking pork and want to eat it without further cooking, you must smoke it to an internal temperature of 137 degrees Fahrenheit to make sure you kill any trichinae, which are the cause of trichinosis. Use a meat thermometer to check the temperature. The meat in the smokehouse is approximately 10 to 15 degrees lower than the smokehouse air temperature. Raise the smokehouse temperature to 155 degrees Fahrenheit, just to be safe.

Current USDA Recommendations

Concern about improper drying methods used in homes for making jerky has prompted the United States Department of Agriculture (USDA)'s current recommendations. They strongly advise that for making jerky safely, meat should be heated to 160 degrees Fahrenheit before the dehydrating process. This step assures that any bacteria present will be destroyed by wet heat. Be aware that many dehydrator instructions do not include this step, and a dehydrator may not reach temperatures high enough to heat meat to 160 degrees Fahrenheit.

Before you put meat in a dehydrator, you must first cook the meat by baking or simmering. Using the dehydrator alone will inactivate microorganisms but not kill them. The right conditions of heat and moisture may cause the microorganisms to reactivate without you being aware of a potentially dangerous situation.

After heating the meat to 160 degrees Fahrenheit, maintain a constant dehydrator temperature of 130 to 140 degrees Fahrenheit during the drying process. This is important because the process must be fast enough to dry food before it spoils, and it must remove enough water to prevent microorganisms from growing.

Three Marinade Recipes for Wild Game

LEMON–GARLIC MARINADE

1/2 c. lemon juice
1/2 c. olive or vegetable oil
2 tsp. dried oregano leaves

1 tsp. favorite yellow mustard
3 cloves minced garlic
1/8 tsp. pepper

Combine ingredients in small saucepan and heat until bubbly, constantly stirring. Cool to room temperature before using.

ASIAN MARINADE

1/4 c. sliced green onions
3 tbsp. soy sauce
2 tbsp. honey

1 tbsp. sesame oil
1 tbsp. molasses

Combine ingredients and stir well. Heat until warm but not bubbly. Let cool to room temperature before use.

GREEK MARINADE

1/2 c. olive oil
1/2 c. sweet vermouth
1 tbsp. lemon juice

3/4 tsp. dried tarragon leaves
1 thinly sliced small red onion
1/8 tsp. black pepper

Combine ingredients in small saucepan and heat until bubbly, constantly stirring. Cool to room temperature before using.

How to Make Jerky

Drying or "jerkying" meat has been done for generations. There are many recipes available. Below is one method; look for others that may interest you. The following can be used with a small metal smoker.

- Slice meat evenly, about 1/8-inch thick. Slice across the grain for more tender jerky. Meat is easier to slice if it's partially frozen.

- Combine marinade ingredients in a nonmetallic mixing bowl. Stir to dissolve salt. Add meat strips. Cover with plastic wrap. Refrigerate 24 hours, stirring occasionally.

- In a large mixing bowl, cover wood chips with water. Soak for 1 hour. Place an oven thermometer in the smoker and heat to 120°F.

- Spray smoker racks with nonstick vegetable cooking spray. Set aside.

- Drain wood chips.

- Drain and discard marinade from the meat strips. Pat strips lightly with a paper towel.

- Arrange meat strips at least 1/4 inch apart on prepared racks. Place racks in smoker.

- Open damper. Place handful of wood chips in the smoker. Close damper, cracking slightly when wood chips begin to smoke.

- Smoke meat strips for 3 to 6 hours, or until dry but not brittle, adding wood chips as necessary.

- Cool completely. Store jerky, loosely wrapped, in refrigerator for no longer than 1 week, or wrap tightly and freeze up to 2 months.

Hot Pickle Cure Jerky

To make a hot pickle cure jerky, use fresh lean deer, moose, elk, or other large wild game meat that is free of fat and connective tissue. If you use five pounds of fresh meat, you'll end up with about 2 pounds of dried or smoked meat.

- Set out 3 tablespoons salt, 2 tablespoons sugar, and 2 teaspoons black pepper, and mix thoroughly. Slice 5 pounds of meat into ¼-inch thick strips and spread out on clean surface. Sprinkle ingredients over one side of strips and turn over and sprinkle other side. Put strips in a pan or dish and let stand in refrigerator for 24 hours.

- Work spices into both sides of meat using a meat mallet. For added flavor, dip meat for 1 to 2 seconds into a liquid smoke solution of 5 parts water to 1 part liquid smoke.

- Dissolve ¾ cup salt, ½ cup sugar, and 2 tablespoons ground black pepper in 1 gallon water to make a brine. Stir until salt and sugar completely dissolve.

- Place brine over heat and bring to a low to medium boil. Immerse meat strips (a few at a time) into boiling brine for about 1 to 2 minutes or until they turn gray. Remove strips from brine using a clean tongs or another utensil that has not touched raw meat.

- Spread seasoned meat on a clean rack in the top half of a kitchen oven or on a clean dehydrator rack. If oven is used, open door slightly (to the first stop) and heat to 120°F to 150°F for 9 to 24 hours. Periodically monitor oven for safety. Remove meat before it get too hard or brittle: properly dried jerky should bend in half, not break into pieces.

- Use clean jars or plastic bags to store jerky. To freeze, wrap in freezer paper. Properly prepared jerky will last a long time if kept dry, but the quality deteriorates after a few months.

Deer/Elk/Moose/Beef Jerky

Use any high-quality large game meat. Debone the hind legs and divide the meat into three portions: top, bottom, and tip. Pump these pieces with a brine mixture of 2 pounds commercial salt cure per 1 gallon water. For easier slicing, you may wish to freeze the brined meat before making the jerky.

- If you've frozen the meat, take it out and allow it to partially thaw. Remove as much fat as possible to prevent off flavors. Slice partially thawed meat into long, ¼-inch thick strips.

- Mix 2-3 cups of marinade to be used and place it in a large saucepan.

- Place saucepan over medium heat and bring to a full rolling boil. Place unmarinated meat strips directly into boiling marinade, making sure they are completely covered by liquid. Reheat to a full boil for 1 to 2 minutes or until gray.

- Remove pan from heat. Remove strips from hot marinade with clean tongs that have not touched any raw meat. Spread strips separately on drying rack; don't allow them to overlap. Repeat steps until all meat has been precooked. Add more marinade to pan as needed.

- In oven, smoker, or dehydrator, dry strips at 140°F 150°F. Remove strips to cool and test for doneness. Strips should bend but not break. Do not leave any moist or underdone spots. Return to heat if any are found.

- Refrigerate overnight in plastic bags and check again for doneness. Dry further if necessary.

- Always put unmarinated strips directly into the boiling marinade. Do not soak meat strips in marinade before cooking, as marinade could become a source of bacteria.

Bacon

Bacon is a meat product typically associated with pork. It is taken from the belly section of the carcass and cured. In large game animals the belly contains mostly fat, but has a thin layer of muscle running through it. It is possible to make "bacon" from some large game animals by trimming the belly or abdominal wall and treating it in a manner similar to pork. The quantity and thickness will likely not equal that of a pig, however. The meatiest part of the belly is located back near the loin. The forepart can be used but will have to be stripped off the ribs to get the most meat.

Begin by trimming the belly into desired shapes, usually squares or rectangles. These allow you to slice uniform pieces once it has been cured and smoked.

To cure bacon, salt may be used alone or with sugar. Sugar and nitrite can also be used; this is often referred to as a sugar cure, which uses dry ingredients, liquid ingredients, or combinations of both.

If you don't have a refrigerated curing room or equipment for brine curing, a dry sugar cure is your safest choice. A recipe for curing ingredients can include:

> **8 lbs. salt**
> **3 lbs. sugar (cane)**
> **3 oz. sodium nitrate**
> **1/2 oz. sodium nitrite**

Mix ingredients well. Bacon should be rubbed thoroughly once along with a light sprinkling over the flesh side after rubbing. Place the rubbed meat on a wood surface to dry and cure. Avoid using cardboard or galvanized containers or surfaces. The curing time should approximate 7 days per inch of thickness. For example, if bacon is 2 inches thick, it should be cured for 14 days. Dry curing should be done in a cool place to reduce the risk of spoilage.

Bacon may only have a 1- to 2-month freezer life because of the salt content. Use within that time frame. Any uncured portion can be frozen until cured.

Ham

Hams come from the uppermost rear leg portion of the pig. There are two hams, one from each side. For hams, the curing process can include three separate rubs at 3- to 5-day intervals. If a ham is about 5 inches thick through the thickest part, it should be cured for about 35 days. It is all right to leave the ham in cure longer, because the saltiness does not increase.

Dried Beef

Dried beef most commonly refers to a meat product derived from domesticated animals. It can also be used in reference to game animal meat that is derived from the top and bottom rounds found in the hindquarters of venison, elk, moose, or antelope. The muscles comprising this portion of the skeleton are highly exercised as the rear legs propel the animal through its habitat. This means they have a good deal of connective tissue and require methods to tenderize them for a more satisfying meal.

Dried beef is similar to corned beef, except that corned beef is usually made from the brisket, while dried beef is made from the rear quarters. Dried beef is also usually hung to dry for 24 hours before given a light or heavy smoke in a smokehouse.

Dried beef may be prepared using a straight dry cure by rubbing 1 to 1 1/2 ounces of the dry cure on each pound of meat, or as a wet cure using a pump method.

SMOKING METHOD

20 lbs. meat, free of fat
25 gallons clean, fresh water
1 1/2 c. commercial cure

3 c. salt
3 c. sugar

Mix ingredients thoroughly with water into a brine. Chill brine and meat to 38°F. Using pump, insert brine into meat evenly to avoid air pockets, up to 8 percent of meat weight (20 pounds of meat x .08 = 1.6 pounds of brine).

Completely submerge meat in remaining brine for 10 days, rotating occasionally. Remove and soak in cool, clean, fresh water for 3 hours, changing water every hour. Remove and allow to drain. Hang in smokehouse preheated to 100°F for 12 hours to dry. Raise temperature to 115°F and hold for 24 hours, then raise to 125°F with smoke. After 12 hours reduce temperature to 115°F and shut off smoke. Allow to cool to room temperature and slice.

Preparing to Smoke Bacon or Ham

After the curing process has been completed, rinse the pork bellies or hams with clean fresh water and tamp dry thoroughly with towels. The meat will not take smoke if the surfaces are wet. A wet surface will lend a dull color and off taste to the finished product. Once dry, the portions are ready for smoking.

Chapter 9

SAUSAGES

Wild game meat can make excellent sausage when properly processed. Sausage is one of the oldest known forms of processed food. Ancient Babylonians produced and consumed sausages 3,500 years ago. Homer's *Odyssey*, written in the eighth century B.C., referred to sausage.

In the Middle Ages, many different kinds of sausages were produced in Europe. In the cooler climates of Germany, Austria, and Denmark, where preservation was less of a problem, people made fresh and cooked sausages. In warmer climates, such as in Italy, Spain, and southern France, dry and semidry sausages were popular, and remain so today.

Many sausages consist of the less valuable parts of animal carcasses, such as meat trimmings and fats that have accumulated during carcass fabrication. Fats add juiciness and flavor to sausages but little nutritional value to the final product.

As European sausage makers discovered various spices, they became skilled at creating new and distinctive products bearing their influences. Some of these included types that are still well known today, such as bologna from Bologna, Italy, and braunschweiger from Brunswick (Braunschweig), Germany.

Sausage making did not develop in the United States on an industrial scale until after the Civil War, although early Native Americans produced a type of sausage called pemmican. This was made by combining meat with dried berries and pressing it into a cake or a skin that was smoked or sundried.

After the end of the Civil War there was an influx of European immigrants, and among them were many people with sausage-making skills. As German, Polish, Italian, Danish, and other groups settled throughout the United States, they brought their recipes with them, extending their influence and tastes wherever they went.

Today's sausage industry is diverse in size and type of production. Most major sausage-processing plants in the United States are highly mechanized and automated to handle large volumes of products with speed and efficiency. However, home sausage making has been slowly developing its own niche.

This chapter will provide information about basic types of sausages that can be produced at home and their characteristics; the safety and sanitation issues involved; spices, additives, and casings used; and the fillings used in the process.

Homemade sausages are popular among hunters, who prefer to use all parts of the wild game they bring home. Home sausage making typically has been associated with rural areas, but urban residents with enough expertise can also make delicious and distinctive sausages.

The USDA classifies all the varieties of sausage produced in this country as one of two types: uncooked, which includes fresh bulk sausage, patties, links, and some smoked sausages; and ready-to-eat, such as dry, semidry, and cooked sausages.

Like other fresh meat, fresh sausages are highly perishable and must be refrigerated or frozen until they're cooked. Fresh sausages must be cooked prior to consumption to avoid health risks. Ready-to-eat sausages have been processed and preserved with salt and spices and may have been dried or smoked. These types of sausages, such as jerky or sticks, can be eaten out of hand or cooked and heated, like hot dogs.

Fresh Sausages

Fresh sausages are made from uncooked and uncured cuts of meat. These sausages include those seasoned and stuffed into casings, or those in bulk form that will be pressed into patties. However, they are not cured or smoked. Fresh sausages should be eaten within three days of processing, and they should be thoroughly cooked before being served. The following is a sample of different sausages available from domestically raised animals. Wild game that is fresh, high quality, and carefully prepared can be substituted for traditional domestic meats to create unique sausages that still follow the basic recipes.

Bockwurst—A German-style sausage made from ground veal or veal and pork combined. It is typically flavored with onions, parsley, white pepper, paprika, or cloves, and often sold fresh. Cooked bockwurst has an longer shelf life and is usually cooked by simmering, although it can be grilled.

Bratwurst—A German-style sausage made from pork, beef, and veal. It looks like a big hot dog and is flavored with allspice, caraway, and marjoram, although recipes can vary between regions and countries. It can be produced fresh or cooked.

Chorizo—Originating in Spain, this term encompasses several types of pork sausage, which can be fresh or cured. Fresh chorizo is similar to Sicilian sausage but is much spicier. Cured or dried chorizo can resemble pepperoni in size and shape but has a sharper taste and smell. Different countries have different recipes for making chorizo, and some have a sweet or spicy flavor.

Country-style or breakfast sausage—One of the most common kinds of sausage found in the United States. It is known by several names, can be made into patties or small links, and is flavored with sage, savory, and thyme.

Pork sausage—A fresh, uncooked sausage made entirely from pork and seasoned with salt, pepper, and sage. It is often sold in bulk, in a chub or link form, or as patties.

Kielbasa—Similar to Italian sausage in that its name is more of a generic term than a reference to a specific sausage. In the United States, it refers to a Polish or Polish-style sausage. It is typically made from coarsely ground lean pork and is sometimes combined with beef, veal, or both. Commercial kielbasa is usually an uncooked, smoked sausage with a medium red color.

Italian sausage—A fresh sausage that must be fully cooked before eating and can have either a hot or sweet taste. It is traditionally a pure pork sausage with pepper, fennel, and other for flavoring.

Liverwurst—A popular German-style sausage. It is made from finely ground pork and pork liver to which wild game meat may be added. It can be stuffed into a nonedible

Grind wild game meat and combine it with spices to make a variety of different sausages.

casing and must be thoroughly cooked before being served. Spices such as ground black pepper, marjoram, allspice, thyme, ground mustard seed, and nutmeg are used to provide distinctive flavors. The term is sometimes interchanged with braunschweiger because of the similarities between the two in production, taste, and texture.

Thuringer sausage—A lightly smoked, German-style sausage similar to summer sausage. It is often semidry and is more perishable than other cured sausages, even though, technically, it is cured. Some are not fermented and sold fresh. It is mostly made from pork, but beef and sometimes veal can be used. Flavorings used to make Thuringer sausage are similar to those used in fresh pork breakfast sausages, but without the sage.

Cooked and Smoked Sausages

Cooked sausages are usually made from fresh meats that are cured during processing, fully cooked, and/or smoked. Cooked sausages should be refrigerated until eaten. They will generally keep 3 days after being opened. Because they are fully cooked, they are ready to eat once opened, although you may prefer to serve them warm or hot. Examples include the following. (Wild game meat, properly processed, may be substituted.)

Frankfurters—Also known as the common hot dog, these are touted as the most consumed sausage in the world. Processed hot dogs contain mostly water and fat and have a soft, even texture and flavor. Homemade frankfurters can be made with a blend of beef, pork, and/or poultry meat. In the United States, if fillers are used, such as cereal or soy, the name must be changed to "links" or their addition must be identified on the label.

Bologna—A generic term for a fully cooked, mildly seasoned sausage made from low-value pieces of beef, pork, or both. It can be eaten cold or reheated. Bologna is usually produced in large-diameter rings or chubs, which give it several distinctive styles and shapes although they are constitutionally much the same as hot dogs. Beef bologna is an all-beef version that has a redder color because it does not have a mixed meat composition. It can also be made from pork, turkey, or chicken.

Vienna sausage—Sometimes called garlic sausage, it is made in the general shape of a hot dog, although it can be longer and somewhat thinner. It is a sausage with a creamy meat texture and is made primarily from pork and beef, although chicken and turkey can be used. Veal is sometimes added to create a milder flavor. The predominant flavors include onions, mace, and coriander. Sometimes pistachio nuts are added for seasoning.

Beerwurst or bierwurst—A large sausage, usually 2 to 3 inches in diameter or larger, of a dark red color. It is stuffed into veined natural casings or vein-decorated artificial casings. It is made from coarse-ground beef and pork and spiced with garlic, black peppercorns, paprika, and mustard seeds. Contrary to its name, it does not contain any beer. It is usually sold as sandwich meat.

New England sausage—Also known as Berliner, this sausage is made from coarse-ground pork with pieces of ham or chopped beef interspersed throughout. Generally, it is stuffed into large casings, similar to beerwurst.

Braunschweiger—A creamy-textured, German-style liver sausage of pure pork origins. It has a mild flavor that includes onions, mustard seed, and marjoram. It is nearly always smoked and generally served cold as a spread for toast or used as a filling for sandwiches.

Mettwurst: A strongly flavored German-style sausage made from raw minced pork and preserved by smoking and curing. It contains ginger, celery seed, and allspice. Although it is smoked, it needs to be cooked thoroughly before being served. Mettwurst can have either a soft or hard texture, depending on the length of smoking time used.

Dry and Semidry Sausages

Dry and semidry sausages are made from fresh meats that are ground, seasoned, and cured during processing. They are stuffed into either natural or synthetic casings, fermented, often smoked, and carefully air-dried. True dry sausages are generally not cooked and may require long drying periods of between 21 to 90 days, depending on their diameter.

The distinctive flavor of these sausages is due to the lactic acid produced by fermentation. This fermentation occurs after the meat is stuffed into casing and the bacteria metabolize the sugars, producing acids and other compounds as byproducts and the resulting tangy flavor.

Semidry sausages, such as summer sausage, are often fermented and cooked in a smokehouse. Both dry and semidry sausages are ready to eat and do not require heating before serving, although a cool temperature or refrigeration is recommended for storage. Dry and semidry sausages include summer sausage, pepperoni, salami, and Landjäger, among others. These are detailed in the paragraphs below.

Summer sausage—A general term for any sausage that can be kept without refrigeration. It is typically a fermented sausage with a low pH to slow bacterial growth and provide a longer shelf life. It is usually made from a mixture of beef or beef and pork. Venison can also be used to make summer sausage. It resembles some of the drier salamis but is milder and sweeter in flavor. Summer sausage can be either dried or smoked, and although curing agents can vary considerably, some sort of curing salt is almost always used.

Pepperoni—A hotly spiced Italian-style sausage made from coarse-ground, fermented pork with ground red pepper as the main flavoring. It is a dry sausage and increases in flavor as it progresses through the drying process.

Salami—Not necessarily a specific sausage; most often refers to those products that have similar characteristics; is made from beef, pork, or both. Salamis can be found in many sizes and shapes, and they may be dry and quite hard. Most are made with garlic, salt, various herbs and spices, and some minced fat. Salamis are made by allowing the raw meat mixture to ferment for 24 hours before it is stuffed into either a natural or synthetic casing and then hung to dry. Most are treated with an edible mold culture that is spread over the outside, which prevents spoilage during curing. Pepperoni is one type of salami; others include Genoa, kosher, Milano, Sicilian, Novara, and Sorrento.

Landjäger—A traditional Swiss-German dried sausage that is a popular snack food. Its taste is similar to dried salami, and it can be boiled and served with vegetables. It is made from equal portions of beef and pork (substitute venison, moose, or elk for beef), with fat or lard, sugar, and spices added. The meat is pressed into small casings for making links, usually 6 to 8 inches long. They are then pressed into a mold before drying. This gives the strips their characteristic rectangular shape. After drying, they can keep without refrigeration if needed.

Game Meat Sausage

Most sausages contain pork or beef, separately or in combination, but game meat can be substituted to create unique and original flavors. Most any meat from wild animals can be used, but, like meat from domesticated animals, it is important to handle the meat properly after the animal is killed. The same awareness of temperatures is required: dressing the animal as soon as possible while keeping the meat under 40 degrees Fahrenheit will help limit bacteria growth, reducing the chance of a food-borne illness.

Game meat does not need aging if the meat is to be used for sausage, because it will be tenderized and broken down through the grinding process. For big-game sausages, use trimmed meat from any part of the animal. Using the less tender cuts and trim pieces increases the volume available. Game bird sausages work well with a combination of breast and thigh meat.

Game meat contains a distinct flavor that comes from the fat and not necessarily the meat itself. Removing all external fat prior to grinding will allow you to process game meat in the same way as beef or pork. However, game meat is leaner and contains less fat in the muscle. This will make a dry and unpalatable sausage unless you add unsalted pork fat when grinding. The pork shoulder butt is often used as a fat for game sausages. Generally, you will need to mix in a fat content of 15 to 20 percent to have a desirable flavor and texture. If you purchase pork fat from a butcher or local market, be sure to specify hard pork back fat. Lard should not be used; it is too soft and will produce a greasy sausage.

Blending different meat and fat percentages will affect your final product. Experiment to discover which mixtures you like best.

Recommendations for Game Meat

There are several recommendations for making sausage from game meat. These include:

- Wash your hands with soap and water before working with meats, after changing tasks, and when finished.
- Start with clean equipment and sanitize surfaces with a solution of 1 tablespoon chlorine bleach per gallon of water.
- Select only fresh, high-quality meat and other ingredients (spice, cure, and so on).
- Remove or excise all bruised, damaged, or tainted muscle found around bullet or arrow wounds and do not use for sausage.
- If using frozen meat, thaw in a refrigerator or cooler.
- Select the proper lean-to-fat ratio to ensure good texture and binding properties.
- Use cure ingredients (sodium nitrite) purchased from a reputable source. Sodium nitrite will give sausage its characteristic pink color, improve flavor, and inhibit growth of *Clostridium botulinum*, which can cause botulism poisoning.
- Keep the temperature of the meat as cold as possible (less than 40 degrees Fahrenheit) during grinding and mixing.
- Mix the dry ingredients in water to dissolve the curing ingredients and allow for even distribution throughout the product during regrind.
- If you have the grinding equipment, coarse-grind the meat, add the rest of the ingredients, and regrind.
- If stuffing sausage, choose only high-quality hog casings that have been salted.
- Soak casings in clean water 30 minutes before use and rinse them in cold water to remove excess salt.
- Clean grinding and stuffing equipment thoroughly and sanitize surfaces with a

solution of 1 tablespoon chlorine bleach per gallon of water when done.

- Use meat thermometers to ensure cooked sausage products have reached proper internal temperatures of 160 degrees Fahrenheit.

Selecting Ingredients, Additives, and Spices

Your sausages will be a combination of raw meat and other ingredients, such as additives and spices. The quality of all the ingredients, and the way they interact with each other, will determine the taste and texture of your sausages.

By understanding the properties of each ingredient you add to your sausage, you'll be able to create products that satisfy your tastes and meet your requirements, whether it is to limit the preservatives you eat or to avoid high-fat products routinely found at retail markets.

Keep one simple rule in mind when creating your sausages, regardless of what kind they are: your finished product is only as good as the ingredients it contains. The meat you start with should be fresh, have a proper lean-to-fat ratio, and exhibit good binding qualities. Clean meat that has been cut in sanitary conditions is a necessity. The meat should not have been contaminated with bacteria or other microorganisms at any stage of processing or cutting.

Most of the ingredients you'll use are readily available at local supermarkets or meat markets, or from other specialized commercial businesses. Licensed retail outlets that specialize in such products are another source. Internet businesses that sell ingredients for meat processing can provide them for sausage making. If you're buying ingredients from businesses outside your area, be sure to check their licenses and ask about their sources.

Always check labels to be sure you know what you're adding to your meat.

The main ingredient for your sausage is likely to be meat derived from your wild game harvest of venison, elk, moose, squirrel, rabbit, or birds; or domestic pork, beef, and veal, either separately or in combination. Other ingredients may include hearts and livers. If you use wild game for processing, be certain the meat appears healthy and disease free.

Several nonmeat ingredients are used to provide flavor, inhibit bacterial growth, and increase the amount of sausage produced. These may include water, salt, sugar, nonfat dry milk, soy products, binders and extenders, and spices.

Binders and Extenders

Commercially produced sausage often contains ingredients referred to as binders and extenders. Some of these products are used for both purposes. Binders are used to help the meat particles adhere to each other or to prevent them from separating during the production process. Extenders are used to increase the moisture content and texture of the product, as well as stretch the amount of product derived from a certain volume of meat.

Extenders often include nonfat dry milk and similar dried milk-based products, including dried whey. Binders can include many derivatives of milk plus cereal flours, wheat gluten, and soy flours.

Other common components of sausage production are:

Water and ice—Sometimes used to add moisture and keep the sausage cold during processing. Cold temperatures delay bacteria growth and add to the final product's quality. Water also helps dissolve salts for better distribution within the meat.

Salt—Serves three functions in the meat: preservation, flavor enhancement, and the drawing out of protein to help bind the mixture. Sodium nitrate and nitrite are used for curing meat, as they inhibit the growth of a number of pathogens and bacteria that cause spoilage, including those that cause botulism. Nitrate and nitrite are the most regulated and controversial of all the sausage ingredients. It is strongly recommended that a commercial premixed cure be used when nitrate and/or nitrite is called for in the mixture.

Sugar—Used for flavor and to counter the bitter taste of salt. It helps reduce the pH in meat because of the fermentation of the lactic acid.

Ascorbates and erythorbate—Vitamin C derivatives that speed the curing reaction. They can be used interchangeably in cured sausages to which nitrite has been added.

Spices, Seasonings, and Flavorings

Many different spices, seasonings, and flavorings are used in sausage production to increase taste. For home sausage making, they are generally added by personal preference and taste or to follow general guidelines for a particular recipe. By combining different levels of various spices, you can create unique and distinctive sausages.

Spices vary greatly in composition and may be added as whole seeds, coarsely ground, or in powdered form. Some of the spices used most often include:

Allspice—A reddish-brown pimento berry sold whole or ground. Pungent, clove-like odor and taste.

Basil—Marketed as small bits of green leaves, whole or ground. Aromatic, mildly pungent odor used in dry sausage.

Bay leaves—Elliptical leaves marketed whole or ground. Fragrant, sweetly aromatic with a slightly bitter taste. Used in pickling spice for corning.

Caraway seed—Curved, tapered brown seeds sold whole. Slightly sharp taste.

Cardamom seed—Small reddish-brown seeds sold whole or ground. Pleasant, fragrant odor.

Cloves—Reddish brown, sold whole or ground. Strong, pungent, sweet odor and taste. Whole cloves can be inserted into meats during cooking.

Coriander seed—Yellowish brown, nearly globular seeds sold whole or ground. Lemon-like taste.

Cumin seed: Yellowish brown oval seeds sold whole or ground. Strong, bitter taste; used in chorizo and other Mexican and Italian sausages; used in making curry powder.

Dill seed—Light brown oval seeds sold whole or ground. Warm, clean, aromatic odor.

Garlic, dried—Sold powdered, granulated, ground, minced, chopped, and sliced. White color; strong, characteristic odor with pungent taste.

Ginger—Irregularly shaped pieces, brownish to buff-colored; sold whole, ground, or cracked. Pungent, spicy-sweet odor; clean, hot taste.

Mace—Flat, brittle pieces of lacy yellow to brownish-orange material sold whole or ground. Somewhat stronger than nutmeg in odor and flavor.

Marjoram—Sold as small pieces of grayish-green leaves either whole or ground. Warm, aromatic, slightly bitter flavor.

Mustard—Tiny, smooth, yellowish or reddish brown seeds sold whole or ground.

Nutmeg—Large, brown, ovular seeds sold whole or ground. Sweet taste and odor.

Onion, dried—Similar to garlic.

Oregano—Sold as small pieces of green leaves, whole or ground. Strong, pleasant odor and taste.

Paprika—Powder ranging in color from bright red to brick red. Slightly sweet odor and taste. Used in cooked and smoked sausage products.

Pepper—Black, red, white in color and sold whole or ground. Penetrating odor and taste, ranging from mild to intensely pungent. Black pepper is the most used of all spices.

Rosemary—Needle-like green leaves available whole or ground. Fresh, aromatic odor, somewhat like sage in taste. Used in stews.

Saffron—Orange and yellowish in color, sold whole or ground. Strong odor and bitter taste. Most expensive of all spices and used primarily for color in a few sausages.

Sage—Grayish-green leaves sold whole, ground, or cut. Highly aromatic with strong, slightly bitter taste.

Savory—Sold as dried bits of greenish-brown leaves. Fragrant, aromatic odor.

Thyme—Gray to greenish-brown leaves, whole or ground. Fragrant odor with pungent taste.

Whether they are added by volume or weight, herbs and spices are a very small percentage of any sausage but have an enormous influence on the character and flavor of the end product. In either case, the best herbs and spices are those that are homegrown and recently harvested or purchased fresh. Try to buy new products rather than older ones because they'll have more potency. Store herbs and spices in a cool, dry area away from heat and light. Freshly dried herbs and spices rarely retain their optimum flavors longer than six months.

Salt and Pepper

Salt and pepper add flavor and aroma to sausages. Many different types of salt are available, but those without additives like iodine provide maximum flavor. Pepper can be purchased as whole peppercorn and ground when needed. Recipes may make distinctions between three forms of pepper: fine grind, medium grind, and coarse grind. Finely ground pepper is a fine powder with no large pieces in it. Medium grind refers to flakes that will pass through a typical shaker. Coarse grind has small bits; it can be ground in either a pepper grinder with a coarse setting or with a mortar and pestle.

Sodium Nitrite and Potassium Nitrate

Nitrates and nitrites are chemical compounds containing nitrogen and oxygen that are commonly used in curing meat. For thousands of years, salt was used to preserve food and meat products, but today sodium nitrate, potassium nitrate, and sodium nitrite are the most common preservatives used in processed meats. They are typically added in the first step of the curing process to inhibit bacterial growth; they do this by removing the moisture bacteria could live on and by killing bacteria through dehydration. Sodium nitrate is particularly effective in food preservation and is widely used because it contributes to a longer aging process.

Many recipes that have been handed down through the years call for saltpeter, or potassium nitrate. Most sausage supply companies no longer sell saltpeter, but you may find other commercial products that will achieve similar results, such as Morton Salt's Tender Quick® mix. It is a fast cure containing 0.5 percent sodium nitrate and 0.5 percent sodium nitrite and is used in some recipes at the ratio of 1 teaspoon per pound of meat or .17 ounces (7 grams).

When sodium nitrate and potassium nitrate are added, they alter meat products in three ways: produce a lasting red or pink color; leave a salty flavor; and subtly alter the meat's texture.

When nitrates or nitrites are combined with fresh meat, a series of reactions occur and nitrite is converted to nitric oxide. Nitric oxide combines with myoglobin, the pigment responsible for the natural red color in uncured meat. Together, they form nitric oxide myoglobin, which is a deep red color. This will change to a bright pink normally associated with cured and smoked meat when heated during the smoking process.

As nitrite compounds convert to nitrous oxygen gas, it kills bacteria such as those causing botulism. Just as nitrous oxide gas reacts with hemoglobin in meat, it can react with human blood hemoglobin with toxic effect if the concentrations are too high. Nitrous oxide converts human hemoglobin into methemoglobin, which does not carry oxygen in red blood cells as well as normal hemoglobin does. With less oxygen available for body tissues to function, a condition called cyanosis can occur. The symptoms include a discoloration of the lips and skin, which typically develop a purple or bluish color.

Some people have sensitivities to nitrates and nitrites—they get migraine headaches or allergic reactions when consuming these substances. In addition, protein amines can combine with nitrates to produce nitrosamines, which may be carcinogenic. This may be influenced by the amine concentration, length of storage, amount of nitrite added during processing, storage temperatures, and cooking methods or the degree of doneness after cooking.

A fatal dose of potassium nitrate for an adult is 30 to 35 grams ingested in a single dose. Sodium nitrite is lethal at about 22 milligrams per kilogram of adult body weight, or about the same amount as potassium nitrate. To reach a lethal toxicity level, an adult weighing 150 pounds would have to consume about 20 pounds of brine-cured meat containing 200 parts per million (ppm) nitrite in one meal. Unless that person's diet consists entirely of cured meats, it would take extraordinary stamina to eat enough to reach a lethal level. Even if a person could eat the amount of cured meat containing those levels at one sitting, it is likely the salt level, not the nitrite, would be the toxic factor.

Interestingly, a person with a normal American diet consumes more nitrates from leafy vegetables such as celery, spinach, radishes, cabbage, beets, and lettuce than from cured meats with nitrates and nitrites, because these plants readily absorb nitrogen fertilizers used in food production from the soil in which they are grown.

Considering all this, a 200 ppm level has been set to preserve the antimicrobial power of these compounds while preventing the development of high nitrosamine, or carcinogenic, concentrations. The USDA limits nitrate and nitrite levels in commercial meat products to 200 ppm. This is the grams of nitrate or nitrite times one million divided by the grams of cured meat that it treats. For example, 200 ppm of nitrate for 50 grams of cured meat is equal to 0.01 grams of nitrate (0.01 x 1 million ÷ 50 = 200).

It is difficult to remove nitrates or nitrites from the meat-curing process without increasing the risk of harmful bacteria, particularly botulism, and a thorough discussion of alternatives is beyond the scope of this book. Some sources recommend cooking the product at a high temperature for a short amount of time (since slow cooking at a low temperature can encourage bacterial growth) and then keeping it refrigerated until you eat it. If you decide that you want to avoid nitrates and nitrites when making your own cured meat products, be sure to research your options thoroughly.

Casings

It isn't necessary to stuff fresh sausage meat into a casing. It can be left in bulk form or made into patties. But if it's ground into bulk form, it will have to be used within one or two days to retain its freshness and quality. Most sausages are made by inserting the ground ingredients into some forming material that gives them shape and size and holds the meat together for cooking and smoking, or both. This material is called a casing.

There are two types of casings used in sausage making: natural and

Natural casings are made from animal intestines, particularly sheep, pork, and beef. Before using intestines for casings, make sure they're thoroughly cleaned and washed. Intestinal membranes are strong, flexible, and resilient, but they tend to lack the uniformity of manufactured casings.

Thin, light-colored casings manufactured from beef collagen are often used for fresh sausages. Certain types don't work for smoking because they can dissolve during the cooking phase and the sausage will fall out.

Artificial or manufactured casings come in several sizes, thicknesses, and colors for different types of sausages. Most manufactured casings must be soaked in clean water before use to make them pliable.

1

You can prepare your own natural casings. First, carefully spread out a hank of salted casings on a clean work surface. Gently remove as many lengths as you need out of the bundle of hanks. Resalt and freeze the remainder for future use.

2

Open one end of the casing and slip the end over a faucet. Hold your hand over the casing to keep it from slipping off. Run a steady, medium stream of cold water through the casing until it is completely filled and the water runs through. Continue flushing for a few minutes, then rinse the outside of the casing.

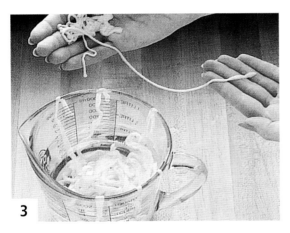

3

Place the rinsed casing in a large measuring cup filled with cold water after draining out all the water and air. Let one end of the casing hang over the edge of the cup. Rinse remaining casings, adding them to the measuring cup.

4

Slip one end of a rinsed, wet casing over the sausage-stuffing horn. Push until the end of the casing is at the back end of the horn; continue pushing until the entire length is gathered onto the horn. Pull the casing forward so 1 inch hangs over the open end of the horn.

manufactured. Although their purposes are the same, their origin is very different. The sausage you make will determine the casing you select.

Natural sausage casings are usually used for fresh sausages, since they are tender and edible. They are made from parts of the alimentary canal of various animals that can include the intestinal tracts from pigs, cows, or sheep. One advantage to using them is that they are made up largely of collagen, a fibrous protein, whose unique characteristic is variable permeability. This allows smoke and heat to penetrate during

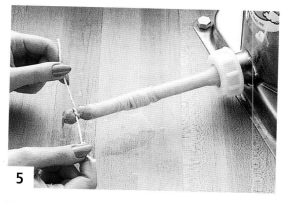

5

Turn the crank of the sausage stuffer until some of the sausage mixture comes out of the horn. Tie off the end of the casing with kitchen string, pinching off a small bit of meat (the pinching helps eliminate air at the end of the link). Continue cranking until sausage is desired length. Use your hand to guide the casing away from the horn.

6

If making links, twist the first one several times, then crank until a second link is formed. Fill until casing is almost firm so it does not break. Continue twisting and filling until you come to the end of the casing. Tie off the last link with string.

the curing process without contributing undesirable flavors to the meat.

Natural casings can be purchased from companies that offer sausage-making products or they can come from an animal that you are butchering. Packinghouses that save casings will flush them with water and pack them in salt before selling them to casing processors. The casing processor does

the final cleaning, scraping, sorting, grading, and salting before you purchase them.

Manufactured and Artificial Casings

Manufactured casings are a good alternative to natural ones. They are made from edible or inedible materials. Fibrous casings, which are made from a special paper pulp mixed with cellulose, must be peeled away before eating but provide the most strength of any casing available. Other common types of manufactured casings include collagen, cellulose, and plastic.

Collagen casings are made from the gelatinous substances found in animal connective tissue, bones, and cartilage and mechanically formed into casings. Because of their lower structural strength, these casings generally are made into small-diameter products and are ideal for breakfast links or fresh, smoked, and dried sausages. Unlike large cellulose and fibrous casings, collagen casings should not be soaked in water before use; they are easier to work with when dry.

Cellulose casings are made from cotton linters, the fuzz from cottonseeds, which are dissolved and reformed into casings. Cellulose casings are crimped into short strands, and an 8-inch length may stuff as much as 100 feet of sausage. Small cellulose casings work well for skinless wieners and other small-diameter skinless products.

Artificial casings are frequently made from plastic and are inedible. They can be used for sausages cooked in water or steam, such as bologna.

You can purchase manufactured or artificial casings from meatpacking companies, sausage supply businesses, local butcher shops, or ethnic markets. They can be purchased in various sizes, including 22mm and

1

You can also use synthetic casings. First, soak them in a mixture of 3 tablespoons white vinegar to 2 quarts lukewarm water for 30 minutes, or as directed by the manufacturer. The vinegar helps the casing peel smoothly from the finished product and helps prevent mold growth.

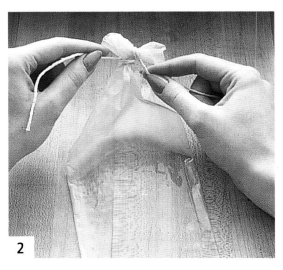

2

Wrap the middle of a 20-inch piece of kitchen string tightly around one end of the casing several times, then fan it like butterfly wings. Wrap one end of the string tightly around one wing several times. Repeat with the other side.

3

Stuff casing with sausage mixture by hand or with a stuffing horn. Pack the casing tightly and be sure to squeeze out air pockets. Tie off with a butterfly knot and make a loop in the string for hanging the sausage for smoking.

32mm collagen casings, which are edible; and 3 1/2-inch synthetic-fibrous casings, which are peeled and discarded before the sausage is eaten.

Essential Equipment

You only need a few pieces of equipment to make sausage in your home. The three most important pieces of equipment you will need are a meat grinder, a sausage stuffer, and a thermometer. Other pieces that you may find useful include a mixing tub, a scale, and a smoker if you want to do your own meat smoking and preservation. Sausage-making equipment is usually available from meat equipment supply companies.

Meat grinders

A meat grinder is used to reduce the size of meat pieces into a pliable mixture. They can be electric or hand-operated. Some food

Meat grinders reduce large pieces into a soft, pliable mass into which spices, fats, or other additives can more easily be mixed. Grinders can be hand- or electric-driven and come in many different designs and shapes.

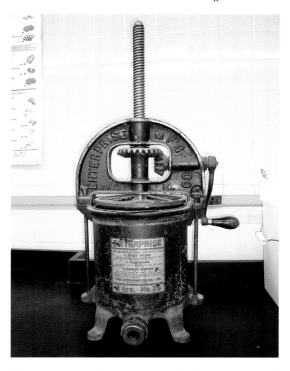

Old-style sausage stuffers were made of cast iron and operated by a hand crank that pressed the plate, forcing the meat through the funnel opening at the bottom and into the casing.

processors can do a good job of chopping meat, and some heavy-duty mixers may have a grinding attachment that will work.

Hand grinders have been used for generations and usually have several different-sized grinding plates or chopping disks, ranging from fine, with holes 1/8 inch in diameter, to coarse, with holes 3/8 inch in diameter. All hand grinders will have a screw augur that is attached to the outside handle. A disk cap screws over the top of the grinding plate to hold it in place while the meat is forced through the holes by the auger. It is a simple process once you have it set up. Hand grinders typically have a tightening screw at their base so that they

can be mounted to a table or sturdy support frame.

If you are making small amounts of sausage, a hand grinder should be sufficient. Some large grinders make use of a small motor with a belt attached. This is a fast, efficient way to grind a very large amount of meat in a very short amount of time. Food processors can be useful in producing finely ground or emulsified sausages, such as frankfurters, bologna, and some loaf products.

Sausage Stuffers
You should consider buying a sausage stuffer if you plan on making your own sausages. There are several types available, including hand,

A modern sausage stuffer relies on the same principle as the old style, but is made of aluminum or stainless steel. It is lighter in weight than its predecessor and has multiple funnels, or horns, for different-sized casings. Be sure to thoroughly wash, sanitize, and rinse the stuffer and funnels or horns prior to and following each use and between sausage-making sessions.

push, crank, and hydraulic (operated by air or water). They can be made of plastic, stainless steel, or cast iron. Many small meat grinders are capable of supporting a small stuffing horn.

The piston-type stuffer is one of the most common for home use. It is operated by air or water pressure and will press the sausage quickly into the casing, producing fewer air pockets than hand-operated, screw-style stuffers.

A push stuffer is quick to reload but has a small capacity. With this type of stuffer, you manually push down on a handle to force the meat into the casing. A crank stuffer has more capacity than a push stuffer and takes less effort to press the sausage into the

casing because of the pressure created by your combined arm and screw action.

Sausage Funnels or Horns

The sausage funnel or horn constricts the movement of the sausage from the meat tub into the casing. As the casing fills, it pushes itself away from the funnel as it elongates. The size of the funnel is directly related to the size of the casing. Funnels are straight tubes, not tapered, and may range from 4 to 6 inches in length. To decrease the possibility of tearing the casing, coat the funnel with water or grease to help slip the casing over it.

Scales

For weighing meats and other ingredients, a reliable scale is essential. A scale that measures both in pounds and ounces should be sufficient for most of your needs. For recipes or curing chemicals where weights are measured in grams or ounces, a smaller scale may be necessary. If curing ingredients are being used, particularly sodium nitrite, it is very important to use a scale that can measure to the nearest tenth of a gram.

Measuring Cups and Spoons

Measuring cups and spoons, ranging from 1/4 teaspoon up to 1 tablespoon and 1/4 cup to 1 cup for liquids or dry ingredients, will be useful for many sausage recipes.

Thermometers

Thermometers are essential to monitor and maintain appropriate temperatures during the processing and cooking of sausages. Several types are available, including instant-read and oven thermometers.

Regardless of the type of thermometer used, make certain the calibration is correct

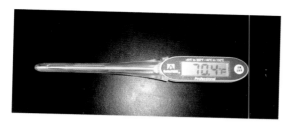

Digital thermometers are very popular for home cooking. However, because they are less resistant to high external temperatures, they should not be used inside ovens.

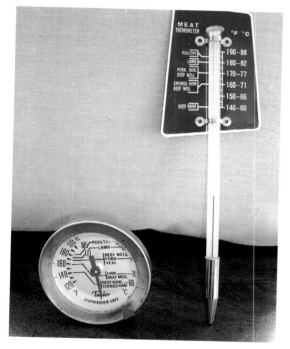

Instant-read thermometers have stems that are inserted into large pieces of meat, such as hams or roasts, to monitor internal temperatures. They are essential for accurate cooking and smoking.

to achieve accurate cooking temperatures. You should calibrate thermometers before first use and whenever they are dropped. They are sensitive and can lose calibration from extensive use or when going from one temperature extreme to another. Inaccurate thermometers will give incorrect cooking temperatures and can be responsible for undercooked or overcooked foods. Undercooked foods can pose health risks.

Two different methods can be used to calibrate thermometers: using ice water and using boiling water. In the ice water method, use the following steps:

- Fill a 2-quart measure with crushed ice and water and stir well.
- Let sit 4 to 5 minutes to provide an environment of 32 degrees Fahrenheit.
- Completely submerge the sensing area of the stem or probe but keep it from touching the sides or bottom of the container.
- Hold for 30 seconds or until dial stops moving.
- If the thermometer is not within plus or minus 2 degrees of 32 degrees Fahrenheit, adjust accordingly. The ice water method permits calibration within 0.1 degree Fahrenheit. Some digital stemmed thermometers have a reset button, which can be pushed.
- Repeat the process with each thermometer.

For the boiling point method, follow these steps:

- Fill a container with distilled water and bring to a rolling boil.
- Insert thermometer to completely submerge stem or probe sensing area without touching the sides or bottom.
- Hold for 30 seconds or until dial stops moving.
- If thermometer is not within plus or minus 2 degrees of 212 degrees Fahrenheit, adjust until it does. The boiling point method permits calibration to within 1.0 degree Fahrenheit. Some digital stemmed thermometers have a reset button that can be pushed.
- Repeat process with each thermometer.

Once all your sausages are finished, place them on racks for smoking. Regardless of the number of sausages, their size, or the type of smoker you're using, keep the individual pieces spaced so that they do not touch one another or any part of the smoking unit.

The boiling point of water is about 1 degree Fahrenheit lower for every 550 feet above sea level. If you are in high-altitude areas, adjust the temperature by calibration. For example, if you are at 550 feet above sea level, the boiling point of water would be 211 degrees Fahrenheit.

Any food thermometer that cannot be calibrated can still be used by checking it for accuracy using either method. You can take into consideration any inaccuracies and make adjustments by adding or subtracting the differences, or the thermometer can be replaced, which will provide greater assurance of accurate cooking temperatures.

Sanitation and the Three Cs

Strict sanitation is critically important in sausage making—it must be maintained to prevent bacterial contamination and food-borne illnesses. It is essential to handle raw meat in a safe manner that reduces the risk of bacterial growth. No meat product is completely sterile, but using proper procedures will minimize your risks. The most basic sanitation procedure involves using and maintaining clean surfaces before and after processing sausages. It is easy to remember the three Cs of sanitation: keep it clean, cold, and covered.

Keep It Clean

Wash all surfaces that you use with a diluted chlorine bleach solution of ten parts water and one part bleach, as well as antibacterial soap. Nothing will replace vigorous scrubbing of the surface area with these products. This removes any grease or unwanted contaminants from the preparation area. Keep the area free of materials that do not relate to meat preparation or that will be used later but may accidentally come in contact with the meat. Utensils and your hands should be thoroughly washed before beginning. Be sure to remove any rings, jewelry, or other metal objects from your hands, ears, or other exposed body parts.

Keep It Cold

Bacteria grow best in temperatures between 40 degrees Fahrenheit and 140 degrees Fahrenheit. If you are cooking or cooling meat for cooked sausages, be sure your product passes through this range quickly, because meat can be kept safe when it is cold or hot, but not in between. Whether being cooked or cooled, the meat you process should pass through this temperature range within 4 hours, but preferably less. (This includes any butchering time.) Cooling the fresh carcass is essential to a good meat product and is discussed elsewhere in this book.

During processing, cooked sausages should have an internal temperature of 160 degrees Fahrenheit, as this effectively kills pathogenic bacteria. Poultry meat should be cooked to 180 degrees Fahrenheit because of a more alkaline final pH. Ground meats are more likely to become contaminated than whole pieces because they have increased surface-area exposure and go through more processing steps.

After cooking, cool the sausages quickly. This will prevent bacteria from attaching themselves and having an opportunity to grow while you're handling them.

The shelf life of any sausage is limited. To minimize bacterial growth, refrigerate or freeze your sausage. Fresh or uncooked sausage can be kept safely refrigerated for several days; cooked sausages should

Cooked summer sausage should first be put through a fermentation cycle at 95 to 100 degrees Fahrenheit if a lactic acid starter culture is used. The temperature should slowly be raised until an internal temperature of 158 degrees Fahrenheit is reached during the next 3 to 4 hours to finish cooking. Smoking takes place during cooking; the amount can vary depending on your preference. Once the cooking is done, cool the sausage to complete the process.

be used within one week, unless frozen. Always remember that sausages are highly perishable products that don't get better with age. Never eat or serve sausage that has developed a slimy texture or an off smell. There is a good biological reason that your nose is placed near your mouth—if it doesn't smell right, it is better to discard it than to risk eating it.

Keep It Covered

Meats, carcasses, and wholesale or retail cuts should be covered when you're not working on them. Your processing equipment should be properly stored in between uses. In any area where butchering is done, maintain screens, barriers, or traps to keep out vermin and reduce access for flies and insects.

Venison Summer Sausage

15 lbs. venison
10 lbs. pork trimmings
2/3 c. salt
1 1/2 tablespoon commercial cure
2 1/2 tbsp. mustard seed

1/2 c. black pepper
1/2 c. sugar
1 tbsp. marjoram
3 tbsp. garlic powder

Mix salt and cure with coarse-ground meat. Pack in a shallow pan and refrigerate at 38°F for 3 to 5 days. Add remainder of spices and mix thoroughly. Regrind and stuff in fibrous casings about 3 inches wide and 6 inches long. Smoke to 140°F for 2 hours, then raise temperature to 160°F for 2 hours. Finish at 170°F until internal temperature reaches 155°F. Makes about 25 one-pound sausages.

Wild Game Polish Sausage

40 lbs. pork trimmings
3 lbs. venison/moose/elk
    trimmings
1 1/3 c. salt
1 qt. water
3 tbsp. commercial cure

1/2 c. black pepper
4 tbsp. mustard seed
4 tsp. marjoram
3 cloves garlic or 3/4 tsp. garlic
    powder

Coarse-grind meat trimmings. Add salt, water, cure, and spices. Mix thoroughly. Regrind through 1/4-inch plate and stuff into pork casings about 3 inches wide and 6 inches long. Smoke at 120°F for 1 hour, then 150°F for one more hour, then 170°F for 2 hours or until an internal temperature of 141°F is reached. Cook just before serving for best taste. Makes about 40–50 1-pound sausages.

Moose/Elk Salami

8 lbs. elk or moose meat, crumbled
2 lbs. pork fat, cut into 1-inch pieces
2 c. water
2 c. soy protein concentrate
1/4 c. plus 2 tbsp. canning/pickle salt
2 tbsp. powdered dextrose

2 tbsp. ground nutmeg
1 tbsp. white pepper
2 large cloves garlic, minced
2 level tsp. commercial cure
Synthetic casings, 3 1/2x12 inches

Combine meat and pork fat in nonmetallic mixing bowl. Thoroughly mix other ingredients; add meat and pork. Mix again until evenly distributed. Cover and refrigerate 24 hours.

Stuff 3-inch casings with mixture and tie ends to make sausages 6 inches long. Smoke to 130°F for 30 minutes or until surface of casings are dry. Raise temperature to 150°F and smoke for 1 hour. Increase temperature to 165°F and smoke for 5 to 6 hours or until internal temperature of largest sausage reaches 152°F.

Remove sausages and flush outside with clean water until internal temperature is 120°F. Store sausages in refrigerator up to 1 week, or freeze up to 2 months. Makes about 10–12 one-pound sausages.

Venison/Moose/Elk Chili

1/2 lb. ground venison/moose/elk
   meat, crumbled
1 lb. venison/moose/elk stew
   meat, cut into 3/4-inch cubes,
   well-trimmed
1 tbsp. vegetable oil
2 cans (16 oz.) dark red kidney
   beans, undrained
1 can (28 oz.) whole tomatoes,
   undrained, cut up

1 1/2 c. chopped green pepper
1 c. chopped onion
1 can (6 oz.) tomato paste
5 cloves garlic, minced
1 tbsp. chili powder
1 tsp. sugar
1/2 tsp. pepper
1/2 tsp. salt

Heat oil over medium heat in stockpot. Add ground meat and cubes. Cook for 8 to 10 minutes, or until meat is no longer pink, stirring occasionally. Drain liquid off. Stir in remaining ingredients, bring to a boil, then reduce heat to low. Simmer, partially covered, for 4 to 5 hours, or until meat is very tender. Stir occasionally. If desired, serve with shredded cheese, sour cream, or sliced green onions. Serves 6 to 8.

Sweet Italian Game Sausage

75 lbs. moose/elk/venison/
antelope meat
15 lbs. ground pork
3 qts. water
3 c. salt
1 c. sugar
6 tbsp. commercial cure
7 tbsp. plus 3 tsp. fennel seed

3 oz. paprika
1/3 c. black pepper
1/3 c. cayenne pepper
1/3 c. garlic powder
2 tbsp. oregano
1 tbsp. sweet basil
Natural 3-inch hog casings

Combine wild game meat with pork in large mixing tub. Combine remaining ingredients in mixing bowl, except casings. Sprinkle seasoning mixture evenly over meat and thoroughly mix by hand until evenly distributed. Use sausage stuffer with 3/4-inch horn and press into casings. Twist off in 6-inch links. Wrap tightly and freeze sausage for later use. Sausages can be pan-fried with sliced onion and green pepper, if desired. Makes about 90 1-pound sausages.

Potato Sausage

1 lb. trimmed deer, antelope, elk
    or moose
1 lb. boneless fatty pork shoulder
    or pork butt
1 qt. water
2 lbs. peeled red potatoes
1 medium onion, coarsely chopped

1 egg, beaten
1 tbsp. salt
1/2 tsp. ground allspice
1/4 tsp. dried ground sage leaves
1/4 tsp. dried basil leaves
1/4 tsp. sugar

In 2-quart saucepan, heat water to boiling. Add potatoes. Return to boiling. Reduce heat and cover. Simmer until potatoes are fork-tender, 25 to 35 minutes. Drain. Cool potatoes and cut into 3/4-inch cubes.

Cut deer and pork into 3/4-inch cubes. In large mixing bowl, combine deer, pork, potato cubes, onion, and egg. In small bowl, mix remaining ingredients. Sprinkle over meat and potato mixture; mix well. Cover bowl tightly with plastic wrap. Refrigerate at least 1 hour to blend flavors.

Chop or grind meat and potato mixture to medium consistency. Shape into thin patties. Fry in nonstick skillet over medium-low heat in a small amount of vegetable oil until browned and cooked through, turning once.

Fry this sausage in patties for breakfast, brunch, or dinner, or use it to make a meatloaf. Makes about 16 four-ounce patties.

GLOSSARY

—◆—

Aging—the time process used to mature or ripen meat enzymes in order to increase flavor and tenderize meat.

Aitchbone—the rump bone.

Anterior to—toward the front of the carcass, or forward of.

Antioxidant—a substance that slows down the oxidation of oils and fats and helps check deterioration.

Backstrap—an inedible, yellowish connective tissue composed of elastin running from the neck through the rib region of beef, veal, and lambs, and also at the base of the ribs.

Blade meat—the lean meat overlying the ribeye and rib portion of the primal cut.

Bone-in cuts—meat cuts that contain parts of bone.

Bruising—an injury that does not break the skin but causes discoloration in the muscle.

Butterfly—to split steaks, chops, cutlets, and roasts in half, leaving halves hinged on one side.

Carcass weight—the weight of the carcass after all butchering procedures have been completed.

Collagen—a fibrous protein found in connective tissue, bone, and cartilage.

Creatine phosphates—amino acid molecules that are an important energy store in skeletal muscles and the brain.

Cubed—refers to the process of tenderization using a machine with two sets of sharp, pointed disks, which score or cut muscle fibers without tearing.

Cure—any process that preserves meat or fish by salting or smoking, which may be aided with preservative substances.

Cutting yield—the proportion of the weight that is a salable product after trimming and subdivision.

Dorsal to—toward the back of the carcass, upper or top line.

Dressing percentage—the proportion of the live weight that remains in the carcass of an animal, sometimes referred to as yield. It is calculated as carcass weight ÷ live weight x 100 = dressing percent.

Elastin—a yellow, fibrous protein that is the basic constituent of elastic connective tissue, as in a lung or artery.

Epimysium—the sheath of connective tissue surrounding a muscle.

Fabrication—the deconstruction of the whole carcass into smaller, more easily used cuts.

Fillet—to slice meat from bones or other cuts. Also refers to boneless slices of meat that form portion cuts.

Forequarter—the anterior portion of a carcass side such as the front shoulder.

Freezer burn—discoloration of freezer-stored meat due to loss of moisture and oxidation.

Fright or flight response—a behavioral reaction by animals to a stressful or threatening situation that increases heart, lung, and muscle activity.

Gambrel—a frame shaped like a horse's hind leg, used by butchers for hanging carcasses.

Glycogen—a polysaccharide produced and stored in animal tissue (especially in the liver and muscle), and changed into glucose as the body needs it.

Grade—a designation that indicates quality or yield of meat based on standards set by the United States Department of Agriculture (USDA).

Herbivore—an animal that feeds mainly on grass and plants.

Hindquarter—the posterior portion of the carcass side.

Intoxication—when microbes produce a toxin that is subsequently eaten and sickness results in humans.

Lactic acid—an organic acid produced by the fermentation of lactose by certain microorganisms.

Marbling—streaks and flecks of fat located within the muscle or between muscle groups.

Muscle pH—the acidity or alkaline level in the muscle. It generally declines after harvest, and the rate of decline is an important factor affecting meat quality.

Oleic acids—an oily, unsaturated fatty acid present in most animal and vegetable fats and oils.

Omega-3—a family of unsaturated fatty acids that appear to have health benefits for humans.

Omega-6—a family of unsaturated fatty acids that may increase the probability of a number of diseases and depression in humans.

Omnivore—a person or animal that eats food from plant and animal sources.

Palmitic acids—a colorless, crystalline, saturated fatty acid found in animal fats and oils.

Perimysium—connective tissue covering and binding together bundles of muscle fibers.

Petcock—a small faucet or valve for draining or releasing gas or air, or draining.

Posterior to—toward the rear of the carcass, behind.

Primal cuts—basic major cuts into which whole carcasses and sides are first separated.

Render—to melt down fat.

Rigor mortis—the progressive stiffening of muscles that occurs several hours after death as a result of the coagulation of muscle proteins.

Salt pork—pork cured in salt, especially fatty pork from the back, side, or belly of a pig, often used as a cooking aid.

Shrinkage—the weight loss that may occur throughout the processing sequence. May be due to moisture or tissue loss in both fresh and processed products.

Side—one matched forequarter and hindquarter, or half of a meat animal carcass.

Silverskin—the thin, white, opaque layer of connective tissue found on certain cuts of meats, usually inedible.

Subprimal cuts—the subdivisions of the wholesale or primal cuts that are made to make handling easier and reduce the variability within a single cut.

Yield—the portion of the original weight that remains following any processing or handling procedure in the meat-selling sequence. It is usually quoted in percentages and may be cited as shrinkage.

METRIC EQUIVALENTS AND CONVERSION

Conversions between U.S. and metric measurements will be somewhat inexact. It's important to convert the measurements for all of the ingredients in a recipe to maintain the same proportions as the original.

General Formula for Metric Conversion

Ounces to grams	multiply ounces by 28.35
Grams to ounces	multiply grams by 0.035
Pounds to grams	multiply pounds by 453.5
Pounds to kilograms	multiply pounds by 0.45
Cups to liters	multiply cups by 0.24
Fahrenheit to Celsius	subtract 32 from Fahrenheit temperature, multiply by 5, then divide by 9
Celsius to Fahrenheit	multiply Celsius temperature by 9, divide by 5, then add 32

Approximate Metric Equivalents by Volume

U.S.	Metric
1 teaspoon	5 milliliters
1 tablespoon	15 milliliters
1/4 cup	60 milliliters
1/2 cup	120 milliliters
1 cup	230 milliliters
1 1/2 cups	360 milliliters
2 cups	460 milliliters
4 cups (1 quart)	0.95 liters
1.06 quarts	1 liter
4 quarts (1 gallon)	3.8 liters

INDEX

ACKNOWLEDGMENTS

I wish to thank my wife, Mary, for her constant support. Her comments and suggestions helped improve this book from beginning to end.

Our son, Marcus, took a number of the photos that appear, making this his fifth book with photographs for Voyageur Press. Our daughter, Julia, loves our woodlands as much as any in our family and, together, we all have spent many wonderful hours in them listening to and watching the wildlife.

I want to thank my friend, Jim Ruen, for his lighthearted touch. His answers to my myriad of questions always came with an undertone of playfulness and humor, undoubtedly developed through his extensive writings for farm magazines and his blog.

Jerry and Ruth Apps have been friends and mentors for over a decade and have always encouraged my efforts.

A special thank you to my editor, Elizabeth Noll, who worked diligently to bring my manuscript to publication and helped to strengthen its content with her comments and questions. Her critique and assistance with this book has helped to achieve its purpose.

About the Author

Philip Hasheider is a fifth-generation farmer who raises pasture-grazed beef with his wife and two children in southcentral Wisconsin. *The Hunter's Guide to Butchering, Smoking & Curing Wild Game & Fish* is his sixth book for Voyageur Press. He is also the author of *The Family Cow Handbook*, *How to Raise Cattle*, *How to Raise Pigs*, *How to Raise Sheep*, and *The Complete Book of Butchering, Smoking, Curing, and Sausage Making*, all available at www.qbookshop.com.